JARED DETTER

Breaking Into Real Estate Investing

SKELLIG PRESS

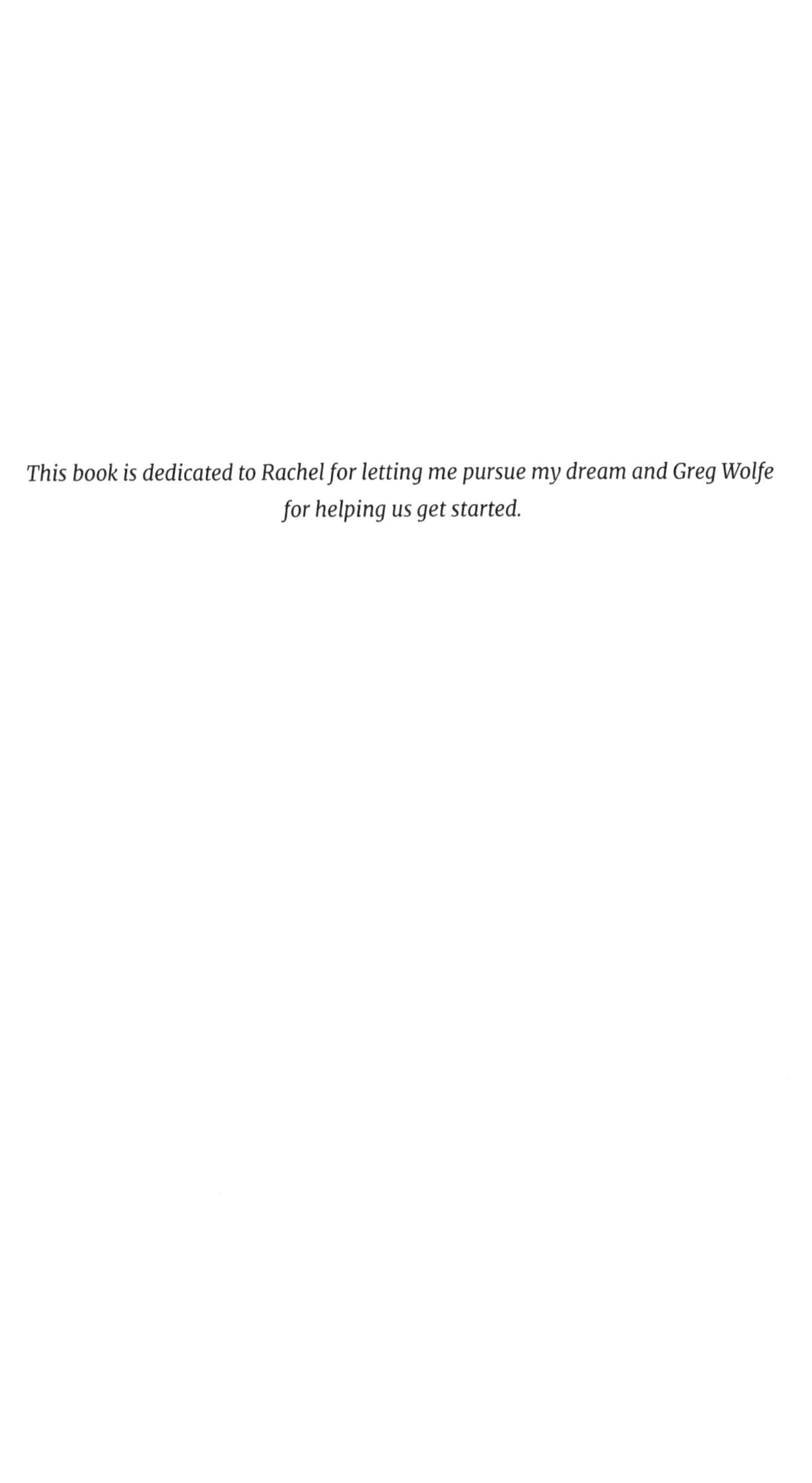

This book is dedicated to Rachel for letting me pursue my dream and Greg Wolfe for helping us get started.

Contents

Acknowledgments

There are many people to thank, not only in the process of making this book a reality, but I'd like to start off with the people who are helping to make the dream happen. The following people are members of our team, each having an important expertise that we need to succeed: **Greg Wolfe**, our realtor, for being an encourager and helping us get the ball rolling. **Jamie Taylor**, our commercial banker at Unified Bank, for supporting our growth and making the mortgage process easy. Believe it or not, it was an offhand comment you sent in an email that gave me the idea to write this book. **Tom Adams**, our contractor, for always doing such a great job on our renovation projects and being there when we need you. **Bryan Komazec**, owner of Mr. B's Plumbing, for doing a great job with our plumbing work and being a valuable consultant on our projects. **Emanuel Burgos**, our flooring guy, who's always ready to do a new project, and nobody does it faster - or better. **Mike Raff**, our electrician, for making sure none of our properties burn down. **Jamie Taylor** (not the same one as above), our basement waterproofer, for being an expert at all-things basement, like keeping our basements dry, reinforcing walls, and putting in egress windows. **Eric Reiss**, our insurance guy from Assured Partners, who makes sure that our properties have the right coverage for our needs. **Jim Ralston**, our neighbor and friend, who taught me the ropes on my first flip, renovated our basement, and is always willing to help in a pinch with handyman tasks. **Summer Jones**, our cleaner, who keeps our mid-term rentals looking good and who has a big heart for those who have been displaced by fire. **Chris Myers**, our HVAC guy and owner of Myers Unlimited, who is always responsive and does quality work every time. **Matt Lee**, our drain guy, for tackling every clog we've thrown at you. **Larry Staskey**, our landscaper, who turned around the look of our mid-term rental in just a few days. **Larell Dunson**, our appliance repair guy, who is both a consultant to us and an expert in this area. **Mindy Harsh**, at Harsh's Cleaning Services, from prompt responses and getting carpet and upholstery clean for us. Finally, **Campbell's Landscaping**, our lawn treaters, who keep the weeds at bay in our mid-term rentals. Many of these people will make appearances in this book without their names being used, but they are named here in appreciation for the work they've done.

There are more people I'd like to thank that go beyond the scope of the team we've put together. These folks were willing to talk with me about their rental experiences, to help me wrap my mind around the business, give me information and perspective, as well as encouraging me. **Laban Marsh, Kevin Long, Aaron Lundberg,** and **Sheena Roth** all allowed me to pick their brains before I even got started. These conversations helped lay the groundwork that prepared me to eventually take action. I'd also like to thank **Ryan Mancuso** and **Chris Larson**, both Realtors in Prescott, AZ, who were willing to share their knowledge with me. A special thanks to **Brian DuMont**, who is light years ahead of where I'll ever be with investing. You've been a great encourager, and I'm grateful that you pushed me to think bigger than my initial plan. I would be remiss if I didn't mention **Kris** and **Hannah Moll**. I can't really thank you for having a house fire, but what your family went through gave us the idea and the purpose behind our mid-term rentals. I'd like to thank my dad, **Al Detter**, for reading my book in draft form and giving me valuable feedback. I appreciate it more than you know. I'd also like to thank my good friend **Ryan Burks**, who read it from a real estate outsider's perspective to make sure I was explaining things clearly.

Finally, I'd like to thank my wife, **Rachel**. Without you, this whole dream falls apart. This would never work without you. You're a great sounding board and interior decorator. You're a great property manager. You really care about the people who rent from us - you have such a big heart. You've done most of the work of building our team and keeping them happy. And most importantly, you let me get started. You're more important to me than this investing adventure, so thanks for tolerating the headaches and allowing me to pursue my dream. And thank you for having me read my book out loud to you. I appreciate your suggestions, and it's a helpful exercise to hear it read aloud. My hope is that we'll have built something great to hand off to our boys, **Luke, Justus, and Micah**.

Disclaimer

The information in this book is based on my personal experience as a real estate investor. It is provided for educational and informational purposes only. Although I discuss topics involving legal structures, contracts, taxes, lending, and accounting, nothing in this book should be interpreted as legal, tax, financial, or accounting advice. Laws and regulations vary by jurisdiction and change over time, and the strategies described here may not be appropriate for your specific circumstances.

You are solely responsible for your own decisions. Before taking any action that could affect your legal rights, tax obligations, financial position, or business operations, you should consult a qualified attorney, certified public accountant, or other licensed professional. The author and publisher make no representations or warranties regarding the accuracy, applicability, or completeness of the information contained herein and expressly disclaim any liability for any loss or damages arising from the use of this material.

Introduction

Before 2021, I felt like I was on the outside looking in. I had wanted to get into real estate for years, and it felt like it would never happen. But then it did. And it changed my life. This book is about that story and what you might be able to learn from it. My hope is that this book will inspire people who are also on the outside looking in – or perhaps have one foot in the door and aren't quite sure how to get the other one in.

But before we get too far into the details, let me tell you why I'm writing this book:

- If I felt like I didn't know how to break through into investing, I'm sure there are others who feel that way too. You don't have to stay there.

- Much of the information I came across was for people who were already investing and wanted to get better at it – like how to buy your first vacation rental or how to create advanced systems for your real estate empire. I didn't need that type of advice. I just needed to know how to get started.

- Many authors writing these books have been investing for years. They run real estate syndicates that have thousands of doors. They mentor and coach others who also aspire to the great wealth they have. They own properties in dozens of locations. I've read their books, and I've heard them on podcasts, and they weren't talking to me. In fact, I think many have forgotten what life is like when you haven't yet purchased your first rental. The advice they give is for someone other than me - who could only window-shop for properties.

- Mentors are hard to find. While these authors and podcasts can be helpful, in truth they're very inaccessible. You can't call them up and ask for advice. They're so successful that they don't have time for someone like me. And to be able to access the super-successful, you have to pay a price. I met people who coach real estate investors at the cost of $10,000 or more. That's not for people like us, if you're reading this book. Although a book can't be a mentor, perhaps it can answer some important questions you have.

- Details are hard to find. Even if I do find someone locally to talk to about real estate, I find the conversations to be of limited help, because people tend to talk in generalities. I don't need generalities; I need specifics. That's how I operate, and if I can't truly understand what they did, it's not very helpful. This is true for books and podcasts as well. The podcast host might ask a question like, "How did you redo the electricity in the house?" The answer is often something like, "Well, it's easy. All you have to do is fish some wire up from the basement, run it from the outlets in a circuit in the living room, then connect it to the breaker box." If you're not an electrician, that may not sound simple at all, and you may have no idea how to do what they described – it's just too general. The same applies for much investment advice – it doesn't have enough detail to understand what they did, so it's not very useful. I want to provide as many details as possible in this book to help overcome this tendency.

- It's all so confusing. There are many ways to get into real estate. You can buy single-family homes. You can buy multi-family properties (both residential and commercial). You can invest in debt notes. You can arbitrage properties. You can flip properties. You can fund properties by giving money and be a silent partner in the deal (or be a hard-money lender). You can house-hack properties. You can wholesale properties. You can buy properties, and you can build your own. You can do long-term rentals, mid-term rentals, and short-term rentals. It's almost dizzying how many things you can get yourself into from a real estate perspective, and it's hard to know the pros and cons of each to determine what might work for you and what won't.

- Many sources of information have the wrong focus for many would-be property investors. They focus on tactics to be successful in investing. While that's helpful for many, what is not talked about enough is what you need to do before you even purchase your first property. It's about laying a healthy foundation for real estate investing, and I want to spend some time on that very important topic in this book.

- I want to let people know that it can be done. Real estate investing isn't just for the rich. While real estate investment is one of the commonalities that rich people have, they're not the only ones who should be able to enjoy the benefits that real estate investing provides. I want to give people optimism that they can succeed with it as well.

My desire is that these reasons above give you some clarity why I want to write a book like this – for people who are interested in real estate but can't quite see the way to start, for people who perhaps have one property but have tied up all their money in it and don't see how they could possibly get their next one. I want to provide hope and clarity for anyone who picks up this book.

While you'll learn more about me in the next chapter, I'll make this clear here: I'm not a mega-investor.I don't own hundreds of doors. I haven't been doing this for twenty years.My real estate investing business is relatively humble (currently five single-family homes, a duplex, and a triplex), with 10 doors total. I've been doing it for three years, and I have a mixture of long-term and mid-term rentals. I've flipped two houses. I don't know everything there is to know, and I'm still learning as I go along.However, my experience is still fresh in my mind. I still remember what it felt like four years ago in 2021. I still remember the fear that things weren't going to go the way I was hoping, and things would get all messed up. I know the levers I've been pulling to build success. I'm not far off from where you are, and I hope that very fact is what makes this book a better 'mentor' than the super investors out there. I haven't forgotten the things that you'll want to know to break through, because I'm still living it.

I can't imagine this book would have as helpful for the advanced investor as the beginner. It might hold some interest for seasoned investors, but I think it can provide immense value for my target audience – those who really want to get in and don't know how and those who have just started and aren't sure how to pick up momentum. If that's you, I sincerely hope you find value between the covers of what you're holding.

1

Our Story

Although this chapter is titled 'Our Story', I'll start off with mine, then join it up with my wife's when she comes along. I was born in Erie, PA in a VERY middle-class family. My dad was famously frugal. We rarely went out to eat unless it was partially funded by coupons. I mostly wore hand-me-downs, and my mom patched the knees of my pants when they got holes in them. I didn't know what back-to-school clothes shopping was. In fact, I don't think I knew a brand name soda until almost middle school. We just called it by its color, like 'black pop', 'orange pop', etc., because we always got the generic. We didn't live in the lap of luxury, but my parents knew how to save, and as I grew up, we were able to move more firmly into the middle of middle-class.

We lived in a regular suburban neighborhood, and our house was upgraded over time through the combined efforts of my dad and my maternal grand-father. When I was young, they replaced a screened-in porch with a full-fledged family room. They built a shed out back that still stands decades later. They built a playhouse for us kids (that got torn down after we got older). In essence, my dad and grandfather were both handy. I didn't inherit this from either of them. To be fair, I was really young when these things got built, but I don't think I would have shown a natural interest in them anyway. I was better with thinking than I was with my hands.

When I was in middle school, my maternal grandfather moved from Illinois to a 62-acre plot about 30 minutes from us. I came to really enjoy this property (unless it was wintertime, and the outdoors held no attraction when it threatened to freeze me to death). Imagine being 14 years old, and you have the run of 62 acres.You can explore the woods, try to spot wild animals, climb down the small ravine that the creek ran through, and almost break both your shins in a zip-lining mishap (true story). There was a two-story barn on the property that offered a lot of exploration opportunities as well.

As the years flew by, the property became too much for my grandfather to manage. Then my parents took it over and found that renting a property in rural PA with busy lives was more than they wanted to manage. They ended up selling it. Although this event happened after I had grown up and had been out of the house for a number of years, the loss of the property impacted me. I began to fear that I wouldn't be able to provide that type of opportunity for my kids, when I had them. That's when I began to think about the idea of owning property in the future.

I went off to college in Canton, OH and met my wife, Rachel. Virtually her whole dad's side of the family lived there, and she was surrounded by lots of aunts, uncles, cousins, grandparents, etc. She probably would have stayed there, too, if she hadn't met me. I majored in psychology, and when I graduated, we got married and headed off to Indiana, PA, where I studied to get my doctoral degree in Clinical Psychology. This is where I got my first exposure to real estate. We rented a small apartment my first year in grad school, and we paid a whopping $380 per month. A month before our lease was up, we were notified that the rent was increasing to $405 per month, and we didn't like the idea of getting no return on our rent investment. So, at 23 years old, I became a homeowner. We paid $53,500 for a 2-bed, 1-bath, roughly 1000 square foot house built in 1914. It served us well, and we sold it by owner three years later for $68,500. We had made $15,000 on the sale at a time when we barely made enough to cover expenses, and I started to really like this home ownership thing.

Throughout my life, I had no problem working hard. I delivered a weekly newsprint advertising circular (called Greensheets) starting at 10 years old. I think I was technically supposed to be 12 to do it, but my older brother, Jason, was 12 and got a route, so they decided to allow me to have one as well. So, rain or snow, I delivered these for several hours each Saturday. I literally mean rain or snow. My mom had to come find me in a blizzard one time. She wasn't aware of how bad the weather had gotten while I was out. I came home another time with the fingers of my gloves frozen over, as I kept breathing on my fingers to warm them up. Little did I know that just made things worse. No wonder I hate cold weather.

When Jason turned 13, he got a newspaper route, and I took over his Greensheet route. When I turned 13, I got my own newspaper route. When I turned 15, I got a work permit and started working at a restaurant. I worked this job year-round until I graduated high school. My parents taught me to tithe 10% of what I made and to save at least half. They put $25 a month away for me while I was growing up, which I combined with what I had made, and I used that to pay for college (with the help of academic and athletic scholarships). I worked between semesters in college and all summer long to add to my savings, because I wanted to have as little college debt as possible (as I was responsible for paying my way).

When I was in graduate school, I worked two part-time jobs and went to school full-time. Rachel went to school part-time and worked part-time. We made just over $20,000 a year when I was in graduate school, and we barely covered costs. We began tracking every cent we spent and created a strict budget to make sure we were being responsible with our money. In the end, all the hard work and skimping paid off. With some other good financial decisions and the sale of our house, I graduated with my doctoral degree in psychology with no school debt.

I joined the Air Force to complete the year-long internship that was required for me to graduate with my doctoral degree. This was in San Antonio, TX. Since I was only there a year, we rented, and we had a great time exploring San Antonio – it's a beautiful city. While we explored, I noticed that there were lots of what looked like the old newspaper dispensers that you would put a quarter into, open the door, and take a paper – except these didn't require a quarter to open the door, and they didn't hold newspapers. They held magazines, some of them advertising places to rent, some of them advertising homes for sale, and some advertising land. I rarely passed these up without taking some of the ones that advertised homes and land. I was astounded at all the properties for sale and the abundance of land that one could buy in Texas. This brings me back to my grandfather's old property. I missed those 62 acres, and I developed a strong desire to have something like that for myself someday. This is the first time in my life that I began to really dream about real estate. I would rip pages out of the magazines and keep them to remind me of the types of land I would love to own one day.

But I wasn't anywhere near being able to own anything yet, because the Air Force moved me to the Central Coast of California (where our first two boys were born). Although I was making enough money as a psychologist in the Air Force to be able to rent a nice home, we had almost no savings. When our time was up on the Central Coast, we had to move, despite loving it there. We then headed back to San Antonio, and I got a job as a psychologist with the San Antonio Police Department. This is where we bought our second house. This was in 2009, and we were fortunate that the real estate market was still in the depths of being depressed from the Great Recession (although San Antonio wasn't nearly as bad as many places were). We bought a house for around $233,000. Although we had always been frugal in our married life with money, it was in San Antonio that I came across Dave Ramsey's Total Money Makeover, and that changed the way we managed our finances. We paid down vehicles and a loan from my parents much faster than we originally planned. We built up our savings and worked to strengthen our financial position.

When we sold our house in 2012 to move to Gainesville in Northern Virginia, we sold our house for about $235,000. It wasn't much of a gain, but we had some equity in it that we could roll over into our next one. I had changed careers from doing therapy work to becoming an organizational consultant. Although I would be getting paid better in my new career, moving to the greater Washington, DC area came with a certain amount of sticker shock. To keep housing costs down, we had to move further west than was ideal, but we still had to pay $453,000 for our home. The good news is that with our savings and the equity from our last house, we were able to put 10% down. While here, we worked really hard to follow Dave Ramsey's plan and built up a sizable amount of savings. We were able to sell this house in 2016 for $485,000.

Our next move was back to the Central Coast of California, where Rachel and I had always wanted to get back to. So, we headed west with our three boys (our last one being born in Virginia), and we bought a house in Santa Maria for $482,000. With our savings and equity from the sale of our house, we were able to put 20% down.Although my desire to own property never went away, it was dormant in Northern Virginia, because Rachel and I didn't love the area and knew we didn't want to stay. But we loved Santa Maria from when we lived there during my time in the Air Force. I knew I couldn't afford rentals at that price point, but rural land was available at a relatively reasonable price, and I still wanted to buy a large property somewhere. The place where I did the most looking was outside Yosemite National Park, which is one of my favorite places on earth. I even met with a Realtor to look at some land on several of my trips, as I was hoping to eventually develop it into a vacation property. The numbers just never worked out, and that was just as well, because we moved to Canton, OH in 2020.

I had been doing counseling work in California, and I wanted to get back into consulting. An opportunity presented itself, and we decided to take the chance of moving our family across the country to Ohio for a less-than concrete consulting prospect. You may remember that I hate cold weather. I hadn't forgotten this fact, but I told Rachel that if moving to Ohio allowed me to get into real estate investing, then it would be worth it.So, we sold our house in California for $576,000 and moved to Canton. As it turns out, the pandemic killed the consulting opportunity, as the leads dried up. I had to lean back into my psychology experience, and I opened a part-time practice in Canton. I also did some counseling on an online therapy platform and some Social Security disability evaluations for folks with a mental health component to their disability. But that all took time to set up. I literally made $0 in our first three months after our move. The pandemic created a big delay in getting my psychology license in Ohio, which delayed my empaneling with insurance companies (which allows me to bill them for the counseling I did), and people weren't paying with cash for therapy during the early pandemic-related economic turmoil.In addition, it took a while for me to get set up and build a clientele on the online platform, and the disability evaluations came along in 2021, so it wasn't initially available to me as a way to make money.

What allowed us to survive is that we didn't have a mortgage. We paid for our $250,500 house in Canton in cash, leveraging our savings and the significant equity we had built from rolling over equity from previous houses and the large market increase in Santa Maria. Even though we didn't have a mortgage, I still needed to make money (as Rachel was a stay-at-home mom for her entire time as a parent), and making nothing for three months wasn't going to cut it. I finally decided to do something about it, and I became the most educated Door Dasher in Canton (I had my Master's in Psychology, my Doctoral degree in Psychology, and I had gone back to school to get my MBA when I was in California). I had to swallow my pride and do something to make money. I just couldn't go another month with zero income. Fortunately, my Door Dashing days were limited, as I got empaneled with insurance, picked up work on the online therapy platform, and began to do the disability evaluations. I also started work with two small consulting clients. But it still wasn't enough – it was all piecemeal work and didn't bring in anything significant. I decided I had to do something else to make ends meet. As they say, desperate times call for desperate measures.

When Rachel was in middle school, she met someone named Greg Wolfe, who experienced some family issues that led him to stay with Rachel's mom for a while on several occasions. At the time, Rachel found Greg extremely irritating, but fortunately that changed over time as they grew up. Through my relationship with Rachel, I got to know Greg as well. As time passed, we got to know each other better and became friends. Greg (a flight attendant at the time) flew into DC and came to visit us when we were living in Northern Virginia. He was shocked at what he saw. We lived in a 5-bed, 4.5-bath house that was 4150 square feet, including the walk-out basement. Greg was shocked, because we lived in a big, beautiful house in an expensive part of the country, and we were doing so on only one salary. Greg and his wife made a lot more than we did and lived in a much cheaper part of the country (Canton, OH) and couldn't afford what we had. This triggered something in Greg, and he and his wife drastically changed their tactics to pay down a massive amount of debt in a relatively short period of time. This allowed Greg to pursue a dream of his, which was investing in real estate.

Fast forward to the desperate times I mentioned above. When we moved back to Canton, Greg had made great strides in his real estate investing, which was starting to generate significant income for him. I spent a lot of time talking to Greg about his journey and trying to learn as much about it as possible. When I visited my family in Erie, I would contact friends who invested in real estate and take them to lunch to pick their brains. I was looking to learn from anyone I could, but I absolutely felt like I was on the outside looking in. We had moved to Ohio to pursue my consulting career, be closer to family, and financially thrive in an area with a much lower cost of living, only to find myself without regular employment, not doing much consulting, and feeling further away from my financial goals than I ever had before. The real estate desire was growing, but it felt like the dream was receding.

To help me out, Greg suggested that I come with him to the county sheriff's auction, where properties that had been repossessed from tax delinquency were sold. I began to research the houses that were coming up for auction, talked to Rachel about it (who was NOT excited about the possibility), and I went with Greg to the auction. I ended up buying the property I had my eye on for $33,000 (with help from my parents, who invested with us). If this didn't stress Rachel out enough, the property was in rough shape when we finally got the keys and could get inside it. Even my parents (who had trusted me to do the purchase) were scared by what they saw. Fortunately, I'm not afraid of hard work, and I had a vision for what it could become. We hired our neighbor to be the brains of the rehab (did I mention I'm not very handy?), and I spent about 2.5 days per week out there with him (with my psychology work on the other days) to fix the property up. It took longer than we planned and was more expensive than we anticipated (which further stressed Rachel out), and it took longer to sell than we thought, once it was done (which further stressed Rachel out). However, once the dust settled after closing, we walked away with a $23,000 profit (not counting my parents' cut), which was no small amount, given our financial situation. I had done my first flip, and it was a success!

I finally found a consulting job with a great organization out of State College, PA, which I started in January 2022 as a remote employee. It paid me a good salary and provided steady income. I was now in a position where we could afford to buy property and hold on to it.I continued my conversations with Greg, and he encouraged us to consider buying our first rental. Given Rachel's stress levels with the flip, she was very reluctant to jump in, but she was willing to open a Home Equity Line of Credit (HELOC) on our home, just in case we wanted to take the leap. If you're not familiar with a HELOC, it's essentially like a credit card that draws from the available value of your house. Since we paid cash for our home, they gave us access to about 75% of the equity. You don't pay anything unless you use the money, so it allowed us to be in a flexible position.

I happened to be at lunch with Greg one day (talking about real estate), and I said that since Rachel won't let me use the HELOC on a rental, if he ever wanted to borrow some money to make a purchase, we could potentially make it available to him. Greg took us up on the offer, and I became a hard-money lender for the first (and only) time to date. He bought a home at auction, paid cash for it (from our HELOC), fixed it up, and did what's called a cash-out refinance. That means he takes a mortgage out on the property for 80% of the appraised value (after renovations) and that mortgaged amount becomes available to him as cash. It appraised for high enough that he paid us back in a lump sum (plus a fixed fee for borrowing), paid himself back for the renovation costs, and had something like $15,000 left over. He also got a renter in for $1500 per month, which was his highest grossing single-family rental.

You better believe I was all over Rachel for the success Greg was having with the property he bought with our money. It was helpful for her to see first-hand how the rental process worked, and she finally agreed to commit to looking for our first one. We got close a time or two, and we were actually under contract with a multi-unit property, but it fell through when we decided to back out after some shady behavior from the seller. We sat tight and continued to look for a few more months. We finally came across a single-family home (which is where Rachel felt most comfortable starting), and we decided to put in an offer. We had enough money in our HELOC to pay cash, and we decided to do this to give us a leg up on our competition. It was August of 2022, and the sellers accepted our offer! We finally had a rental property. This house was very important in helping to shape our 'Buy Box' (more on that in chapter 9). There was some work to do before we got tenants in it, but not much. We found tenants very quickly, and we were off to the races.

I'll talk more about 'finding your why' in chapter 3, but my 'why' was very much about recapturing more time with my family. I didn't want to work until I was 65 or 70. I wanted to be able to retire early to spend time with my kids and grandkids, wherever they might be. And that would require more properties. To keep from freaking Rachel out with my big plans, I initially pitched to her that we might be able to buy a property once every three years and slowly work to accumulate properties and cash flow. Then I sat down to do the math one day and realized that this plan was way too conservative to get me where I wanted to go. I began to talk to Rachel about speeding up the plan, and for some reason she played along. We bought our second single-family home in January of 2023.

Now, within three years of our starting, we flipped another house and are currently up to 10 rental units. We have five single-family homes, a duplex, and a triplex. Eight of those units are long-term rentals, and two of them are mid-term rentals. We own more than $1.5 million in property and will gross approximately $190,000 in 2026 with good occupancy rates. It's amazing how I went from the outside looking in, wondering when and if I would ever break through and in perhaps the scariest financial situation of my life four years ago to being where we are today. By the way, Rachel is the one who does most of the looking for our properties these days. Greg warned her that it was addictive, and she didn't believe him. I have been blessed on this journey, and I have learned more than I ever thought I would.

I've found it odd to spell out our story, because I wasn't sure how much others would care. Then I remind myself that when I was first getting started, I was most interested in hearing peoples' stories. I wanted to know how they turned a dream into success. I wanted to hear something in their story that was like mine that would give me hope. And maybe you've found something in our story that gives you hope. My desire is also that you can pick out some lessons from my story. Here are a few that want you to take away:

- **Hard work pays off.** I wasn't afraid to work hard, which allowed me to persist even during challenging times.

- **Learn as much as you can.** I talked to a bunch of people about real estate. Although I didn't specifically mention this above, I read a lot of books and listened to a lot of podcasts. I tend to be a sponge when it comes to learning, and I learned so much so quickly about real estate that I soon became more knowledgeable than people who had been doing it a lot longer than I had.

- **You can't do it yourself.** Our success didn't happen in a vacuum. We had the support of my parents for that first flip. We learned a lot from Greg (who is also our Realtor), and our business wouldn't be nearly as successful as it is without Rachel.

- **Financial responsibility is table stakes for success.** Over the course of our marriage, Rachel and I have always been better at paying down debt than building wealth. While this was frustrating for me at times, as it took longer than I wanted to hit savings goals, it taught us to be frugal and be focused on financial health.

- **Real estate begets real estate.** Although it wasn't until recently that we've been able to start building wealth through real estate investing, real estate has been making us money for years. The reason why I listed the purchase and sale prices of the homes we've owned is to show something important. Much of our success has come from investing in good primary homes. We have totaled $143,000 in market appreciation that we've realized from the sale of our homes over the years. We couldn't have been as successful as we have been without this.

· **You don't have to come from wealth or be handy to be successful in real estate.** While being handy can be helpful, I think it can also limit you. People who Do-It-Yourself (DIY) everything can't grow very much, and that's a hard shift for people to make. I never had to make the shift away from DIY. We just had to partner with good contractors. Similarly, coming from wealth can help you a lot in real estate, but I never would have learned the life lessons I did without having to find ways to make it work.

· **Have a healthy relationship with debt.** We worked very hard to limit (and eventually get rid of) personal debt. We think Dave Ramsey is on to something there. However, business debt is what allowed us to grow quickly. It's important not to be flippant with debt, but debt that your salary is paying off is different than debt your tenants are paying off.

· **Keep at it, even if it seems like it will never happen.** I was 26 when I picked up real estate magazines in San Antonio and began to dream about owning property. For years, I didn't have the earning power or savings to consider investing. Then when my earning power increased, I lived in areas that were just too expensive to make anything happen. We bought our first rental property just two months shy of my 44th birthday. That's almost 18 years from the start of the dream to making it happen. Don't give up. Being patient and building a strong foundation is much better than rushing into poor choices.

2

Is It For You?

Now, enough about me. Let's talk about you. If you're in my intended audience, then you're probably where I was four years ago – wanting to get in and wondering if it will ever happen. Or you're sitting on your first property and aren't sure what your next move is (or if there's even going to be a next move). Before you get too far on your journey, it's extremely important to know if investing in real estate is something you're going to love (that's me) or something you're going to dislike (there's a lot of those folks out there, too). This is an extremely important question to answer before you dedicate too much time and lots of financial resources.

Rachel and I have talked to plenty of people who used to be in real estate, only to run into an unpleasant renter who significantly damaged a property, and that was enough to have them sell and leave real estate. I've known people who get several properties in, only to feel like it's too much work or they've bought the wrong types of property. They lose motivation and get out of it. But before we see if real estate is for you, here are some reasons why it might not be for everyone. This won't be a comprehensive list, but it should give you some food for thought.

- **People who are already at their stress limits.** Real estate will introduce stress into your life and at times you can't predict. There's nothing that will kill your desire to stay in real estate like the little things pushing you over the edge of frustration all the time. This will rob your joy and keep you from feeling like you're operating effectively in any area of your life. You must have some time and stress margin to be effective in real estate. We'll get into ways to reduce the time investment and stress levels as an investor, but you need to have some margin to start with.

- **Short-term thinkers.** There is a lot of research out there about the difference in success between short-term thinkers and long-term thinkers. It essentially boils down to this: Short-term thinkers give up long-term gain for what they want now – and what they're giving up is almost always much bigger that what they're getting 'right now'. Long-term thinkers give up what they want in the moment for the much greater benefit of long-term gain. My oldest son, Luke, asked me a year or so ago, "Dad, are you making much money from rentals?" My answer was honest, "No, not right now." He followed up with another question, "Then why are you doing it?" I replied quickly and with complete clarity, "I'm not doing this for my 45-year-old self. I'm doing this for my 55-year-old self." If you're a short-term thinker, you'll keep chasing the immediate hits that will completely undermine your long-term success, and that is no way to be successful in real estate.

- **Those who are undisciplined.** Real estate isn't always easy. It requires patience. It requires persistence. It requires follow-through and organization. If you pay late fee penalties on your personal utilities, because you forget to pay them on time, you probably don't want to invest in real estate. If you have a habit of agreeing to do something, then having a hard time closing that task out, you probably don't want to invest in real estate. If you look at the information banks require for a mortgage, and you can't remember where to find most of those things, you probably don't want to invest in real estate. There are a lot of moving pieces, and you can end up with a lot of trouble if you aren't able to stay on top of things.

- **Those who are impatient.** I totally get being impatient. I had to wait almost 18 years before I could start realizing my dream. There were times when I was impatient to pay down more debt. I was impatient to build up our savings faster. Now I'm impatient to pay down real estate debt and build up more significant cash flow. However, impatience is not a good investment strategy. If you jump into a bad investment just because you can't wait for a good one, then you'll find trouble following you in your properties. If you jump into investment before nailing down your personal finances, you might find that investing pulls you under. Good things come to those who wait.

- **Those who give up quickly.** There is a Bible verse (John 16:33) that says in part, "in this world you will have trouble." This is a good mantra for real estate – in real estate you will have trouble. We've had two basements taking on water at the same time. We've had to evict a tenant and lost thousands on the deal. We had another tenant we forced to leave because of lease violations, only to skip town owing us several thousand dollars. Don't let these things scare you off. There are lots of good things coming if you're willing to persist.

- **Those who have no financial margin.** There needs to be a foundation of healthy personal finances to make real estate investments work for you. If you don't have some wiggle room, you might be one leaky roof away from insolvency.You most definitely don't want to be in this position.

- **Those who don't want to be inconvenienced.** You'll get calls at two in the afternoon. You'll get calls at eight in the evening. You might even get a call at two in the morning (although we haven't dealt much with that, as our tenants are usually sleeping, too). We've gotten a call to balance a wobbly fan. We've gotten a call to fix a leak under a sink that just required tightening of a coupling. We've gotten a call to fix a slow shower drain that's filled with hair from the tenants (it's as gross as it sounds). Again, there are ways to manage your properties to reduce these inconveniences, but you'll probably have to deal with them for a while, as most people self-manage properties initially (which I think is a good idea).

· **Those who don't like dealing with people (or expect people to care for properties like you do).** You're going to be dealing with people – all sorts of people. So, if you don't like interacting with them, then real estate might not be where you want to spend your time. Rachel loves the people part of real estate, except for when they don't care for properties like we would. This is something she's been working on for a while (and isn't quite there yet). One of her biggest sources of frustration (and real estate-based anxiety) is putting a property that we own and have made nice into someone else's hands. If the thought of that is too much to deal with, you probably don't want to get into real estate (or at least some forms of it).

· **If you're a 'Taker'.** We all take things from the environment around us, but good citizens give back as well. If you take peoples' rent and don't want to take the time to create a good place for them to live, then stay away.If you want your contractors to do a great job while you want to go cheap on paying them, don't get into the game.If you swoop in on deals you hear others talking about, just so you can build your portfolio, we don't want you in our real estate community. You'll burn all your bridges and end up struggling mightily in the long run. While we all get into real estate to benefit ourselves financially, we have an ethical responsibility to those around us in the real estate community to give back.

Now that I've covered who real estate is not for, we can draw some conclusions about who is likely to really enjoy their time investing. I'm going to avoid just listing the opposite of what I said above, because I'm sure you're smart enough to figure that out. Here are a few things that I believe would contribute to you loving this as much as I do.

- **You like to problem-solve.** If you talk to enough investors, you'll realize that there's no one way of doing things. That makes things more challenging, because it's not a plug-and-play business. You must be able to understand problems and find creative ways to accomplish your goals. As soon as you think you've got a property under contract, the seller decides to go with someone else (this happened to us with a duplex). You think you've got a lead on a tenant, and they ghost you. You really want a property, but you have to get creative around how to fund it. There's always a problem to solve, always a pivot to make.

- **You're a dreamer.** Have you ever driven by a billboard that shows how much the Powerball lottery jackpot is and dreamed about what you'd do differently in your life if you won? That's the kind of dreamer I mean. Sure, you could buy one or two properties and just stay there, but people invest to generate wealth – to have your money make money. But money shouldn't be the end goal (more on that in chapter 3). What purpose does the money serve? The more you dream about that, the more you'll enjoy real estate.

- **You like processes.** Real estate isn't something to be done willy-nilly. The more properties you have, the more your processes need to be tight and consistent. There is flexibility in how process-oriented you are, but with so many moving pieces, processes keep you sane and consistent. Part of the problem-solving I mentioned above is creating processes to control the headaches you come across. The better your processes, the more you'll enjoy real estate.

- **Facelifting a property excites you.** One of the most fun parts for me with real estate investing is to go into a property and make it better. It's exciting to take an average, run-of-the-mill property and turn it into something tenants are excited about when they view it. This lets your creative juices flow and allows you to start thinking about design and how to improve properties. Although it costs money and creates more complications, improving a property is a great investment and extremely satisfying.

- **You're a goal-setter.** I'm an organizational consultant, and goal setting is tough at times. If I do $500,000 in billable work in a year, I might set a goal for $600,000 the next year. That's great, but what does it mean to me? It means I'm busier, and my company makes more money. I will have job security, and perhaps some of that extra revenue will trickle its way down into a bonus. That's not a critique of my employer (it's the best one I've worked for), but it's the nature of the job. But the goal of retiring by 55? Wow, is that motivating! What do I need to make that happen? How many more properties do I need? What is my revenue goal? How can I pay the properties down faster? There are so many goals to set, and all of them line up to reinforce the big goal of financial freedom. The goals create alignment in your actions and motivation. If you're not a goal setter, it will be harder for you to know what you're aiming at, which makes the whole thing much less motivating.

- **You have a learning orientation.** This is extremely important. I'm a learner by nature. It's in my DNA. I've probably listened to nearly 500 hours of real estate podcasts and read numerous books. I talk to people about real estate whenever I can, looking for that next nugget of knowledge. We couldn't have been nearly as successful as we have without learning. It's helped us navigate tough decisions and find optimal solutions to real problems. I don't know everything there is to know about real estate, but I'll never stop learning. I study my market. I study markets I'd love to own property in someday. I listen to podcasts on the tax code of real estate. I want to learn everything I can, because what I don't know could sink my real estate ship someday. And I'm going to do everything I can to keep that from happening.

- **You have good support structures in place.** I mentioned this above briefly. You can't do this alone. I'm not sure I'd have the time with a full-time job to manage my properties effectively. That's where Rachel comes in. If I didn't have a Rachel, then I'd need to find a partner on the property management side. You need people looking out for you and mentoring you. You may need financial backers at some point. You need to find a community to encourage you in the discouraging moments and rooting you on when you succeed. You need people to hold you accountable. There's a CEO and mega real estate investor in Raleigh, NC who I've gotten to know, and I text him every time I close on a property, because he's genuinely excited to see my progress. Find your people; it makes the whole journey better.

- **You can see beyond what's right in front of you.** Let's be honest, we've all seen those people who are looking for a new primary home, and they pass on a property because they don't like the paint color on the wall. Paint is just about the easiest thing to fix about the appearance of a house, but they can't see past it. If this is you, then you'll struggle in real estate. But if you can walk into a property and see in your head what it can become, if you can overlook the 'ick' and see the beauty, then you've positioned yourself to find some great deals on the market. You'll have a big leg up on your competition.

- **You are willing to fail.** This is a big one. We all make mistakes. Of course, we try to avoid them, but sometimes we don't know what we don't know. It's not failing that's the problem, it's not learning from the mistakes. I've heard it said, "if you don't fail, you can't succeed." I believe this is true. If you're doing real estate right, then you'll make mistakes. If you don't make mistakes, then you're probably not doing much real estate. Don't let fear hold you back, but make sure you're not being irresponsible with your choices.

My hope is that as you read these two lists, you were doing a bit of self-assessment. If you're saying to yourself that you tick off too many in the first list and not enough in the second one, don't lose heart. You can grow into a person who aligns more with the latter list. Work on yourself and come back to these characteristics later to see if you're moving in the right direction. I believe you can get there if you want to.

3

Finding Your 'Why'

This may be my favorite chapter in the book. It's so exciting for me to think about my 'why' (see last chapter about being a dreamer). I think one of the reasons why Rachel and I were able to grow much faster than initially anticipated is that I was becoming crystal clear on my 'why' and realized that I needed to move faster to get there. It's also important to note that your 'why' may not be static over time. It might change, as ours has slightly. It may change again down the road, and that's okay. Your 'why' is what keeps you motivated and focused, and this may need adjustment from time to time. So, let's jump into my 'why' – it may get you thinking more clearly about yours.

Why #1 – Financial (and time-based) Freedom

I have been very intentional as a parent to invest in my kids. I want to be there for every sporting event and major moment in their lives. I have spent countless hours over the years creating quality time moments with each of them. Eighteen years seems like a long time, but I know that it goes by so quickly. I want my whole body of work as a parent to indelibly etch my dedication to my children on their hearts. For much of my career, this wasn't an issue. When I was in the Air Force and the San Antonio Police Department, I came home to my family every night. I had evenings and weekends free to build depth into my relationships with my children. I did some traveling when I was a consultant in Northern Virginia, but my boys were still little, being nine, seven, and less than a year when we moved back to California in 2016. Although I was getting my MBA while on the West Coast, I was still home with my family. All that changed when I got my current consulting job.

Now don't hear that I'm complaining. I chose the consulting career field. The company I work for has been amazing. But I do a lot more traveling than I used to. In fact, as I write this chapter, I'm on a work trip in Pennsylvania that required me to leave my home around 4:30pm on Sunday, as the multi-day workshop I was leading started at 8:30am on Monday. I hate losing weekend time with my family. I'm also in the midst of an 11-week stretch, where I'll be traveling during eight of those weeks. Not all stretches of time are like that, but I find that it's wearing on me. I was gone on my oldest son's birthday two years in a row. Don't think he didn't notice that. I missed my second son setting his middle school record in the 800-meter run. My youngest son has told me that he doesn't like my work trips and wants me to quit my job and just do real estate. I was gone for my wife's birthday several years back, and she has to operate like a single mom with three boys while I'm gone. I recently drove back eight hours after a workshop that wrapped up at 4pm, just so I wouldn't be gone another day from my family. My absence impacts everyone.

A life change is happening in real time that drives this 'why' home even more for me. My oldest son, Luke, just graduated high school and will be going off to college in Phoenix, AZ. I have invested so much time in him that I know I'm going to struggle mightily while he's gone. And this eight weeks of travel in an 11-week span is happening during my final summer with him before he leaves for college. That has been very hard for me. I also saw a statistic on Facebook that by the time your kids turn 18, you've spent 90% of your time with them. That hit me like a gut punch. My second son, Justus, will be leaving for college in two years, and now that I've been sensitized to how short the time is with him, I'm going to struggle on every trip that I take. My youngest son, Micah, will graduate from high school when I'm 55.

So, my 'why' is I want financial and time-based freedom, so I can spend an outsized amount of time with my children when they're gone and out of the house. I don't want to have to settle for a one-week trip each year to see my boys and hope they've got the means to come visit us for Christmas. I want to keep investing in them and their spouses (when they get them) and their kids (when they come along). It's hard for me to emphasize enough how much this drives me. I don't want to have to visit my kids around my work schedule and pinch my pennies to afford the trip. I want to be retired (or semi-retired) by the time I'm 55. We'll be empty nesters then, and I want the freedom to flip the script on that 90% stat.

Why #2 – Financial security for Rachel

Rachel has always wanted to be a stay-at-home mom. In fact, when she was younger and asked what she wanted in a husband someday, she said she wanted to marry a rich man, so she could stay at home and raise kids. She got to stay-at-home; I'm still working on the rich part. When we got married, I had completed my Bachelor's degree. She had started college but hadn't finished before we moved when I started graduate school. We both knew that my education was going to pay the bills, so that's what we focused on, although she did enroll in a new school and completed her Associate's degree. After I joined the Air Force, she got pregnant, and it never really made sense for her to go back to school. She also didn't have significant job experience. She had worked in a day care, worked some retail, worked as a waitress for a while, and served in an admin position in a dental office, but she really hadn't developed a lot of marketable job skills.

It didn't really matter that much as long as I was making enough to pay the bills. But what would happen if I died? In what kind of position would that leave her? We did buy $1.5 million worth of life insurance for me, but that wouldn't be enough to take care of her forever. I didn't want her to have to work low paying jobs for the rest of her life to make sure she was getting by. I owed her more than that for making herself economically vulnerable to raise our kids.

This is where real estate came in. If I died today, my life insurance would more than cover the debt we have on our properties.It would leave her several hundred thousand dollars in the bank, and she would be making six figures each year in profit from our real estate business. It's a wonderful thing to know she's being taken care of financially, even if I'm not here anymore as the primary wage earner. But death isn't the only thing that could cause Rachel financial problems. What if I didn't die but was disabled in some accident. There's no life insurance money coming now. I could potentially collect disability, but it likely wouldn't be enough. She'd have to work, even with kids still at home. And if I was disabled, I may need her to care for me too. Again, real estate to the rescue. Instead of reinvesting our cash flow to pay off debt, we could draw the cash flow as income and be able to make ends meet. And drawing cash flow isn't like drawing from your retirement account. Your retirement funds may eventually dwindle down to $0, but the rent keeps rolling in.

Why #3 – Leaving a Legacy for Our Boys

Proverbs 13:22 says, in part, "A good man leaves an inheritance to his children's children…" This verse focuses on three things: a long-term financial vision, good stewardship of your resources, and having generational impact. That's exactly what I want. I've heard it said that good leadership is planting a tree under whose branches you may never rest. That's what I want to do for my family. I'll get more into this in chapter 15, but our properties are all in our Limited Liability Company (LLC – this is a business entity type, and the one we've chosen for our real estate), and our boys will inherit it someday. If the LLC has been liquidated by that time, they'll inherit those proceeds instead. I want to plant the seeds of generational wealth that will allow my family to prosper. I don't want my grandchildren to be spoiled brats who never had to work for wealth.No, that's the opposite of what I want. I'm working hard to instill responsibility and stewardship in my children, so they can enjoy the fruits of our labor now. My paternal grandfather worked hard to set my dad up to be more successful than he was. My parents have worked hard to set me up for more success than they had. And I'm working hard to do the same. I'm determined not to let the pattern stop with me.

To be clear, these aren't my only 'why's, but they are my big ones. Here are a few others that drive my real estate investing (in no particular order):

- **Rediscover my relationship with Rachel** – Not that we've gotten lost along the way, but our phase of life will be changing, and I want to make sure that I have the time to invest in that most important relationship as we move toward an empty nest.

- **Travel** – I love to see new places and visit old friends. I believe that real estate is my ticket to see the world.

- **Health** – I believe that all the work travel I do drains me. I feel like I have less energy, and I'm having to be more intentional to fit in exercise. Honestly, I'm in the worst shape of my life, and I want to turn that around. That's tough to prioritize like I want to with my current situation.

- **Stress** – Although I'm pretty good at what I do as a consultant, I still feel a lot of pressure to perform for the organizations who pay good money to bring me in to work with them. I've noticed that the pressure I feel seems to be increasing as of late, and I don't like that constant feeling. I feel like I've been in the 'rat race' for a long time professionally, and I'm not motivated to stay in it any longer than I have to.

- **Autonomy** – Part of the pressure I feel consulting is that I'm judged by my clients in part by how well they follow through on what we've set up. This is outside of my control, and I don't like being judged by someone else's follow-through. Not true with the autonomy of real estate. I'm responsible for my own success or failure. Rachel and I can do as little or as much as our finances and creativity will allow, and we've got our hands on the steering wheel.I'm really enjoying that.

- **Generosity** – I've been given a lot in my life, much of which I didn't deserve. Thus, I believe in giving back. We believe in being generous to our tenants and generous with the money we make from real estate. There is so much research out there that links generosity to gratefulness and overall emotional well-being. We never want to focus so much on making money that we lose focus on generosity.

I mentioned above that your 'why' may change over time. We've experienced this a bit since we've started to invest. The major thing that has changed is that we want to be a blessing to the people in our properties. When I say it's changed, I don't mean to say that we didn't want to be a blessing to begin with. We added this 'why' when my sister-in-law and her family suffered from a devastating house fire. It kept them from their home for the better part of a year, introduced an immense amount of stress, and served as a massive and traumatic disruption in their lives. They were fortunate, in that her mother had just purchased a new house and hadn't yet sold the old one, so she and her family were able to move into the house she grew up in while their house was being rebuilt. Not everyone is so fortunate at a time like this. Many move into a hotel at first, then desperately look for a longer-term solution, sometimes even accepting a cramped apartment for anywhere between six months to a year until their house is rebuilt.

We realized we were poised to meet a need here. We bought a 2-bed, 1-bath house adjacent to our home, we fixed it up, and we completely furnished it, expressly for the purpose of housing people who had been displaced. We didn't have to wait for long. A single mother and her son, who was a senior in high school, lost their house in a fire. They stayed at this house for about 10 months. When she came to see the property for the first time, she got out of her car and started crying. She was so grateful that a fully furnished home was available for her, which was a huge thing she didn't have to worry about now. A month before she left, we were notified that another student at the local high school had been displaced by a house fire. We put them temporarily into a newly opened unfurnished unit in our triplex for a month (the insurance company paid for rented furniture). That month was a big blessing, because there were four people being displaced this time. Rachel, in a herculean feat, project managed a basement remodel that added a bedroom and a full bathroom to accommodate the family in a mere 3.5 weeks. The family then moved into our property and are just now moving out into their beautiful new home. We have become very focused on providing properties that both our long-term and mid-term renters feel grateful to inhabit. It makes the journey so much more meaningful.

This brings me to my last point in this chapter. It should never be about the money. If your 'why' is money or getting rich, you need to come up with a better one. This may seem counterintuitive, because of course we get into real estate for the financial benefit. But it's not our primary motivator. Money is a means to an end, not the end in itself. I've seen landlords who are primarily motivated by money, and they become slum lords. They defer maintenance to make as much money as possible, and their properties get run down. Good tenants don't want run-down properties, so the landlords get worse tenants. Worse tenants don't take good care of the properties, which creates more deferred maintenance issues. Eventually, worse tenants become bad tenants, who don't pay. The eviction process is expensive and takes a long time, and they may do more damage to the property. The end result is that the property becomes just too expensive to fix up, and they're not making money on it anymore, so they have to sell – at a discount for what the property would have been worth had they just taken care of it.

Not all money-hungry investors are that bad. But I've seen landlords blame tenants for problems that clearly pre-existed them, just to try to make them pay to fix the problem or use their deposit money for it. You get high tenant turnover that way and a bad reputation as a landlord. Another problem with money-focused investors is that they run their properties like a publicly traded company. They think too short-term to maximize the long-term value of their properties and cash flow. These folks may quibble with their contractors, manufacturing reasons to complain, to increase their negotiation leverage. If that's your style, you'll eventually find that your contractors always seem to be busy when you need work done. When you put second priorities first, it works against your success. Rachel and my mantra is – "People over profits." We care about profits, but we can't be successful without taking care of the people involved – the profits will follow. To state it one more time: money is never a good 'why'. If you don't get into real estate for the love of real estate (and what it can provide), it's not for you. Real estate investing is NOT a get rich quick scheme.

4

What Are My Options? Part 1: Deeded Real Estate

My sincere hope is that you have found something of value in the first three chapters. However, I suspect this chapter is something that a lot of outside-looking-in, would-be investors have been waiting for. Here, I'm looking to educate about many of the different ways to get into real estate – and there are much more than I first realized. When I was wrapping up my bachelor's degree in psychology and considering where I wanted to take my career, I was under the impression that I had two pathways – either teach and do research or do therapy. A career in research didn't seem fun to me, so I decided to focus on therapy. Once I had been in the field for a while, I discovered that there were many more career paths than just the two that I knew about. If I had to do it all over again, I might have chosen Industrial/Organizational Psychology (to get into consulting faster) or Sport Psychology, which is where I probably would have gone. I don't want you to have the same experience I did, finding out later than you should have that there are so many more options than you realized. I won't claim that I have found every possible type of real estate investment, but this should be a reasonably comprehensive list to get you thinking through where your best entry is.

House Flipping

Because I'm not very handy, I never would have expected that my first move in real estate investing would have been a flip. However, it made tactical sense at the time. You may remember that I was in a difficult position jobwise, and I needed to make some money – and it worked. Flipping has become very popular thanks to shows on HGTV. It has entered popular culture as something that many people now aspire to do. Because this is so well known, I don't need to go into much of an explanation of what this entails, but it's worth discussing the pros and cons to see if this is for you.

Pros

This can be a very gratifying way to invest in real estate. You take a real clunker and turn it into something beautiful. It's an amazing creative expression, and it's awesome to show people the before and after pictures. In addition, this can make you a lot of money. If you have a good pipeline of properties coming to you and you create a good system for flipping efficiently, you can make a good living. If you flip three houses per year and profit $35,000 from each one, you've just made $105,000 before taxes. That's a great 'salary'. Some people I know who have strong contractor teams can tackle more than one house at a time. They might flip six or eight houses per year. How does $250,000 per year in profit sound? Depending on where you live, you can make $200,000 on one flip, if you manage it the right way. That's why the flips on TV in LA are more interesting than those in Toledo, OH. High dollar flips look great, but keep in mind that isn't where you'll start. This is where advanced flippers end up.

Cons

There are a lot of unknowns with flips. Many run into unexpected issues that cost a lot more money and take a lot more time to fix than initially anticipated. It's extremely common for projects to get behind schedule and over budget. In addition, you have to really be on top of your project management. Your final cost is largely a product of each decision you make along the way, and if you consistently make more expensive decisions, it may take six months to flip a house and net $10,000, because you didn't give yourself much margin. You need good systems and consistent monitoring of your spending and contractors. In addition, part of good project management is scheduling your project to reduce downtime. It's no fun realizing you should have ordered those doors two weeks ago. Now you're just sitting for two weeks until they come in, which creates wasted time.

If you're a DIYer, make sure you know what you're doing. Research local regulations. Make sure you're renovating to code. Don't do plumbing or electricity unless you're an expert. There's nothing worse on your property than a fire or water event. It's frustrating to buy a property and have to undo bad work (we've been there). DIYing not done right can backfire in a big way. I remember when Rachel and I were looking to buy our first house when I was in graduate school, we looked at a house a guy flipped, and it wasn't pretty. Each room was painted a different color. Each room had a different texture on the wall (probably because he wasn't good at drywall). He was killing carpenter ants on the kitchen counter as he showed us the house, and you could see a lot of daylight coming through under the exterior doors. It makes me shudder to think about it.

If you're not doing it yourself, then you're relying on contractors. That can be good if they know what they're doing, but not all contractors are created equal. Even those who are licensed contractors can do sketchy work, although they tend to be more reliable in that department. However, you need them to show up on time and show up consistently. This can be a battle, and if you can't get your people to show up, then you're stuck (we've been there too). A less common risk is that an economic downturn can leave you stuck with a property. If property values drop or if buyers get nervous, it may take a lot longer to sell, and you may have to drop your price. And if the margins are too thin to begin with, you may decide that selling isn't an option without generating a loss. Now you're facing becoming a landlord by necessity. It's not fun to be stuck like that, and it may take several years for property values to come back up to where selling makes sense.

Let's say that you find a way to avoid the risks and end up being very successful. What cons might you run into then? There are two primary ones I can think of. First, if you make a $50,000 profit on each flip, it's not all profit. You still have to pay capital gains taxes. Unless the tax code changes after this writing, if you flip as your full-time business, the money you make will be taxed as ordinary income, plus you may have to pay a 15% self-employment tax (Social Security/Medicare). If you occasionally flip, it's still taxed as ordinary income, unless you've held the property for at least 12 months. Selling after 12 months means you'll pay the long-term capital gains tax rate, which is lower than being taxed as ordinary income – but most people don't plan on holding a flip property for at least 12 months. You can get around these taxes if you do a live-in flip and have lived in it as your primary residence for at least two of the past five years. This allows up to $250,000 of capital gains to be tax free. However, most people don't flip houses they live in. There is the option of what's called a 1031 exchange to postpone paying taxes on your profits. This is a very complicated process, and it doesn't keep you from eventually paying taxes on profits, it just allows you to temporarily roll those profits into your next purchase. As I said, this is a very complicated process, and it's easy to do incorrectly, which would force you to pay the taxes anyway. Many just pay the capital gains to avoid the headache of a 1031 exchange. The second con of being a successful flipper is that you've just exchanged one job for another. It's full-time work doing a flip, and after doing two of them, I know this is not going to be my primary path in real estate. I'm not ruling out another one down the road, but I want financial freedom AND time freedom. I don't want to switch out one full time job for another one.

Buying Single-Family Homes

This is the other one that is most thought of when people consider getting into real estate. And that makes sense, because many people live in rental homes, and it's the most accessible for an entry point, as most people can't afford to buy multi-unit or apartment buildings right off the bat.

Pros

There is a lot of flexibility in what you do with a single-family home. You can do long-term rentals, mid-term rentals, and short-term rentals (more on these in later chapters). You are also putting yourself into a position to drive wealth in more than one way, because you're not only generating monthly revenue from rents, but the value of the home is likely climbing over time. I'll discuss these and other ways that owning property drives wealth in chapter 6. Another pro is that you have a lot of control over how successful you want to be. You can upgrade aspects of the property so you can charge more rent. You can raise rent over the years to keep up with inflation (or outpace it, if the market allows). You get to pick who your tenants are. If you have a great renter in place, it's almost like 'set it and forget it'. You can go a long time without needing to do much with the property. It's a good feeling knowing that you're providing quality housing to people who need it.

This is often a good way to get started in real estate. If your credit is good and you have sound personal finances, most people can get to the point where they can buy a home to rent. Depending on how you finance it, you might be able to put as little as 3% down in special circumstances. The most you'd likely have to put down is 20%. This is why single-family homes are not beyond most investors' ability to purchase. Compared to other types of real estate investing, single-family homes often show the most consistent appreciation per unit. Lastly, there are typically lower maintenance costs for single-family homes than with multi-family homes, and they're relatively easy to manage (the tenant often takes care of mowing the lawn and snow removal, for example).

Cons

While you can pick your tenants, you can't always pick how they behave. They might not treat the property like you would treat it, and they may flat out cause a lot of damage. They might stop paying, which could trigger a costly eviction process.You might get contacted at inconvenient times to address the dumbest stuff. You might have two basements taking on water at the same time, and you have to drop what you're doing to problem-solve. There may be things that go wrong that are expensive to fix, like the furnace or air conditioning going out. You might buy a house that has unknown problems that can be costly. While getting inspections helps to minimize this risk, it doesn't guarantee that you won't end up with a money pit.

You typically don't have great cash flow (profit) from single-family homes unless you're paying cash.Some people will buy a house if they can cash flow $100 per door (rental unit). That's too low for me. I like at least $300 monthly if I'm going to buy a house to give me some cushion, but if I own 10 doors, and I'm getting $100 per month in cash flow, I'm only profiting $12,000 per year. I don't know about you, but with the cost of purchasing 10 rental units, I'd like to be profiting more than $12,000 per year. Just to use round numbers, if you were looking to replace a $120,000 salary, you'd need 100 rental units to generate $120,000 at a run rate of $100 per month per unit of cash flow. Let's say you pay cash and can generate $900 per month in cash flow per unit. Now, you're generating $108,000 per year with 10 rental units. Sounds great right? But who has the money to pay cash for 10 rental units? I sure don't. In other words, you can reach your financial goals with single family homes, but you're definitely playing the long game that way.

Also, vacancy per property is all or nothing. If the property is sitting vacant, it's making you zero dollars. That's not true with multi-family, in which case one unit being vacant can be compensated for somewhat by occupancy in the other units. It's harder to manage 10 rental homes spread out geographically than 10 units in an apartment building. Lastly, people tend to be more emotional about the property they're living in. People are more transient in apartments and other multi-unit properties. They don't see them as much as their permanent home.It's a bit different with single-family homes. They may live there for years, and since it feels like home, they may not plan on moving. As such, things like rent hikes, and the potential sale of the property can hit the tenant more emotionally, which may lead to them behaving poorly.

Buying Multi-Family Properties

Before we get into the pros and cons, it's important to note that there are two types of multi-family properties. The first is called Residential. This is for any building that has four or fewer rental units. I mentioned above that Rachel and I have a duplex (two rental units) and a triplex (three rental units). So, we have five doors across two buildings. If I had five doors in one building, it wouldn't be considered Residential anymore. It would be considered Commercial. Don't let this confuse you. Just because it's called Commercial, it doesn't mean people aren't living in it, it's just different than commercial real estate where you own an office building, for example (we'll talk about that type of commercial real estate later in this chapter). The real difference, from a practical perspective, between Residential multi-family and Commercial multi-family properties is how they're financed. You have to get a commercial loan on Commercial properties (which requires a different process, different mortgage underwriting, and different interest rates on the loan – I'll also talk more about this in chapter 12). Again, most people don't start off buying Commercial multi-family, because it's an expensive entry point, so don't worry about the differences too much right now.

Pros

First and foremost, these properties will make you more money – and it's not just because you're making the same per-door profit as a single-family but with more doors. Here's why multi-family is more profitable. Where I live, you might be able to buy a 2-bed/1-bath single-family home for $150,000. You might be able to buy a 4-bed/2-bath duplex for $240,000. That's $120,000 per unit with the duplex, instead of $150,000 with the single-family house. So, the per-unit cost is lower. Sure, the rent might be slightly lower than with a single-family, but not that much. Also, the fixed costs are proportionately lower with multi-family. Here's how it might break down:

Comparison of Cash Flow Between a Duplex and Single-Family House

	Price	Down-payment	Interest Rate	Loan Term	Taxes & Insurance	PITI*	Monthly Rent	Cash Flow
Single-Family	$150,000	20% ($30,000)	6.5%	30 years	$4500/yr	$1133	$1300	$167
Duplex	$240,000	20% ($48,000)	6.5%	30 years	$7200/yr	$1814	$2400	$586

PITI is principal, interest, taxes, and insurance – your monthly payment (fixed costs)

Let's say that you buy a single-family house for $150,000 and put 20% down. Let's assume the interest rate is fixed at 6.5% over 30 years and you pay $3000 per year in property taxes and $1500 per year in insurance. Your PITI is about $1133 per month. Let's also say that you get $1300 for rent. That's $167 per month cash flow (for the time being, let's ignore that you haven't factored in maintenance, capital expenditures [CapEx], and vacancy). That's not great. Let's run the numbers with a 4/2 duplex. The assumptions are $240,000 with 20% down, same interest rate and term length, $4800 for taxes, and $2400 for insurance (these last two I figured by taking the single-family tax and insurance cost and multiplying by 1.6x, which is the same ratio as $240,000 to $150,000). The PITI in this case is roughly $1814 per month. Let's say you can charge $1200 rent on each side for the duplex. We are now looking at $586 in cash flow ($2400 in revenue minus $1814). That's not double the cash flow for buying two units in the same building, it's 3.5x the cash flow. And it doesn't work that way with buying two single-family houses, as you'll just get $167x2. This is why more experienced landlords tend to be more interested in multi-family properties. As for other pros, maintenance can be more efficient, in that if you have roof damage in a storm, you only have to replace one roof. Similar to what was mentioned above as a risk to single-family homes, the pro to multi-family is that it's not an all-or-nothing vacancy situation. Lastly, while multi-family properties are more expensive, you get a per-door purchase cost efficiency.

Cons

One of the primary cons of multi-family is with the tenants. First, they tend to be more transient. They don't see the apartment building they're living in as their long-term home. More turnover means more vacancy and more fix-up costs when they leave. In addition, the tenants tend to be of lower quality. This means that they likely have lower credit scores and more financial uncertainty (raising the risk of non-payment-based issues). Lastly, because there are more tenants in close proximity, it's more likely that you're going to run into tenant drama issues. Outside of the tenant issues, you'll often have twice the costs to outfit it or repair things. For example, you'll have two furnace/AC units to deal with in a duplex, two fridges, two ovens, etc. You're more likely to be paying for lawn care (or doing it yourself), because it's not obvious which tenant should do it, and they may not have any lawn care equipment. As discussed above, multi-unit buildings are more expensive, so there's a higher barrier to entry financially. It *may* be harder to sell once you're done with it. Several years ago, a duplex didn't move nearly as fast as a single-family home in my area. That's not true anymore. Residential multi-family properties are going pretty fast now, but it may go back to selling more slowly at some point. If you have a Commercial multi-unit property, the cost of the property will reduce the number of potential buyers. Multi-unit properties tend not to appreciate as consistently on a per-unit basis, as well.Lastly, it can be harder to finance Commercial multi-units, because the loan process and underwriting is different than with Residential properties.

House Hacking

This is a really fascinating type of investing, and is getting very popular, particularly with younger folks. This is a permutation of buying residential multi-family, except you live on one side and rent out the other. While it's not for everyone, it's become an increasingly trendy way to take your first step in real estate.

Pros

The reason why this is such a popular way to break into real estate is that you need somewhere to live, and you have someone else helping to pay for it. If you go back to the example above, you can pay $1133 in PITI if you buy yourself a single-family home to live in, and that whole amount is being funded by your day job. If you buy that duplex and pay $1814, while collecting $1200 from the other side, only $614 is coming from your paycheck. That's $519 per month that you're saving (over $6000 per year). That sounds great to me. In addition, since you're living in it, you can get owner-occupied financing, which can lead to a smaller down payment and perhaps a lower interest rate. But the goodness doesn't end there. What some people are doing is living in the duplex for a year, then buying another one. This is really a brilliant play. Owner-occupied financing requires that you live in it for at least a year to start.If you meet that requirement, then move into a duplex, you get to keep the owner-occupied financing on the first duplex, and you get to put owner-occupied financing on the new duplex. In addition, you rent out the other half of the duplex that you just vacated. After a year, you move out again into a new duplex and rinse and repeat.Some people are growing a strong portfolio relatively quickly with very favorable financing terms, all while living for free (or close to it). It's not hard to see why this has become popular. Lastly, this is a great way to ease yourself into property management. Your tenant is right next door, which makes problem-solving issues more convenient. It's also easier to keep an eye on your investment if you're living in it.

Cons

I said above that this isn't for everyone. There's no way this would work for me. After being married for 24 years and having accumulated stuff over that time (to include three boys-worth of stuff), we would never be able to fit into one half of a duplex. Plus, we've lived in a single-family home for so long that we wouldn't enjoy the smaller space with someone sharing a wall with us. And remember the tenant drama that you might have with multi-family properties? Make sure you choose your tenant well, because they are right next to you. Oh, and remember how convenient it is to fix issues with someone next door? It also makes it easier for them to track you down to report issues. While you run into the same cons with duplexes you're living in as the ones you aren't (like double the HVACs that could go out, double the fridges, etc.), there really aren't very many cons unique to this investment type – another reason why it's so popular.

Some people count it as a con that you're getting lower revenue ($1200 as opposed to $2400 if you rented both sides), but that's not sound thinking. Let's say you live in apartment that costs $1100 per month, and you're paying $1814 for the duplex that you have two tenants in. That's $2914 in PITI against $2400 in revenue. That means it costs you $514 more than what you're bringing in to live in an apartment and rent out the duplex. You're paying $614 extra by living in the duplex you own. So, it does actually cost you $100 more per month to house hack. However, you're paying taxes on $1200 of revenue per month while house hacking, and you're paying taxes on $2400 of revenue while renting both sides of the duplex. That often evens out the numbers. Additionally, you're not getting the owner-occupied finance terms, etc.

ADUs, Renting by the Room, and Garage Rentals

This is called 'using what you already have'. As such, this doesn't require you to buy any new property, although there may be expenses associated with it. The first I have listed above is an ADU, which is called an Accessory Dwelling Unit. This essentially is adding a 'room' on your property. Sometimes this is under your roof, sometimes it isn't. It may be adding an in-law suite with a separate entrance. It may be converting your garage into an apartment.It may be plopping a tiny home onto your land. As always, check zoning laws first, building codes/regulations, and HOA (Home Owners Association) rules (if you have one). If you're going to do this right, these need to be self-contained, meaning they have a bedroom, bathroom, living area, and kitchen or kitchenette. All this can be in the form of a studio room.

ADU Pros

The nice thing about ADUs is that they're right on the same property, making maintenance and management much easier. You have great visibility into how the unit is being treated. Sometimes you even get to know the tenant really well, which can turn into a friendship. The big pro, obviously, is that you're making money on what you already have. When you develop it, you can do what you want with it, allowing your creativity to work its way into the project. You can make it as nice as you want. Although we haven't talked yet about local laws restricting short-term rentals, laws often don't stop you from doing short-term rentals if you live on the property where you're doing the renting, so this gives lots of flexibility with how to lease the property.

These are also easier to fund. You can pay cash, you can fund it through your Home Equity Line of Credit (HELOC), and you can take out a Home Equity Loan. As an aside, if you're not sure about the difference between a HELOC and a Home Equity Loan, you don't pay anything on the HELOC unless you withdraw money. And you can withdraw money whenever you want, in whatever size increments, as long as the balance doesn't exceed the limit of the HELOC. It's much like a credit card that way. A Home Equity Loan is different, in that the bank gives you a loan – a lump sum all at once. You're paying interest on the amount whether you do anything with it or not, and you can't make another draw from it. You just get that lump sum. The main point here, however, is that you often won't have to go through the whole process of getting a mortgage, which is complex, expensive, and time consuming. Lastly, these often improve the value of your property.

ADU Cons

First, you can't do this if you don't own the property. So, this is only an option for property owners. Next, you can get yourself into a lot of trouble if you end up inadvertently violating zoning laws, building codes, or your HOA (you definitely don't want to mess with your HOA!). You really need to have your homework done. Another con is what you run into anytime you do construction. It can go over budget, run behind schedule, and your contractors (assuming they show up), might not be doing a good job.Construction projects can be stressful headaches. A more minor con is how accessible you'll be for the tenants if there are issues. More significant is if you find a tenant who is a problem – you're living with them on your property for better or for worse.

* * *

Next one is renting by the room. This is kind of like having an ADU, but they're not living in their own separate space. They're sharing your kitchen and living areas with you. I would strongly NOT recommend this unless they have their own bathroom space.

Room Renting Pros

This is the easiest to slide yourself into. You don't have to buy a property. You don't have to build an addition. You already have the room, and it's already furnished. If you have a great tenant, then this can be a lot of fun. You can't charge as much as with a separate rental, but since you didn't really have to invest much (if anything), it's a great return on investment.

Room Renting Cons

There really are two primary cons. The first is that you're sharing your living space with potential strangers. I like my personal space, so this doesn't appeal much to me. However, if you have the extra room and don't mind this, you could be making some easy extra money. The second con is that you don't know exactly who you're getting until they're in your house.Really have a strong process for selecting tenants, or it could be a difficult time for a while. This is why this might work better if you're renting to a friend or relative.

* * *

The last one is Garage Rentals. This isn't the same thing as turning your garage into an ADU. Maybe you have a free-standing garage on your property that is underutilized. There's a decent market for people who need to store cars or equipment. This works best if you have it as a separate garage, as it often creates confusion when your garage space mixes with space that someone is renting from you.

Garage Rental Pros

This is pretty passive. People drop their stuff in your garage, and they pay you for it. If you don't have a garage on your property to do this with, it's not super expensive to build one per square foot (again, check zoning, code, and HOA rules). This is because you don't need water or HVAC to the garage like you would in your house. So, if you have an extra garage, this is easy money.

Garage Rental Cons

Same with any construction (if you're looking to build a garage), it can be a headache and cost more than you anticipate. You can also get yourself in trouble if you aren't following the zoning and building codes. One thing to be careful about is that some people look to rent a garage not just to store things in but to run a business out of (maybe fixing up cars or welding things). This often isn't allowed, based on zoning restrictions. It may also cost you money to provide extra security to make sure the renter feels safe storing their things with you (extra locks, security system, cameras, etc.). Lastly, you're not going to make much money from this. You might get anywhere from $150 to $500 per month in my area (more if you live in places with a higher cost of living), based on how big the garage is and if it's temperature controlled.

* * *

Now we're going to move on to ways of investing in real estate that are much less common and are therefore more specialized (and sometimes harder to understand).

Wholesaling

This is an interesting type of investing, because the goal here isn't to hold on to properties. You are essentially the middleman between the original seller and the eventual buyer. I think selling every property you pick up is one of the primary reasons why many investors choose not to pursue this avenue. The other is probably how these properties are acquired (discussed below). By the way, if you're driving down the street and you see a sign stapled to a telephone pole that says something like 'We pay cash for houses' with a phone number listed, that's probably a wholesaler.

Pros

There are two primary pros of wholesaling. The first is that you're getting great deals on properties. A good wholesaler will get properties for 25-40 cents on the dollar.This is because all their deals are off market. They may drive past a house that looks like it's being swallowed by overgrown plants and knock on the door to see if the owner is willing to sell. This is called 'driving for doors', and the assumption is that people who aren't caring for the aesthetics of their property are more likely to be in financial distress. Wholesalers also go onto the county government website and try to find lists of people who are in arrears in property taxes and see if they're willing to sell the property for the cost of the property tax bill plus a kicker to benefit the seller. Wholesalers can spend a lot of time driving for doors or combing property tax lists. They also typically work by sending mail to people on those tax lists to solicit the sale of their property. Some of these campaigns can involve hundreds or thousands of pieces of mail, so it can be time consuming. But wholesalers see it as worth the time and cost, because of the quality of deals they're getting.

The second primary benefit is that you can do as little or as much work to the house as you want to. As a rule, wholesalers don't do much work to the properties (or else it would be a flip). Sometimes they do absolutely nothing, and sometimes they'll do a basic clean-out of the property, which lets them sell for a marginally higher price. So, let's say a wholesaler buys a house that could sell for $150,000 on the open market. A wholesaler finds a property where the owner is behind in property taxes by $20,000, and he approaches the owner, offering $40,000. You may wonder why an owner would ever sell for 27% of what they could get on the open market. Remember that they're behind in taxes, which means they're likely not doing well financially. Financially struggling people often don't have the money to do preventative maintenance on their homes. This means that they would have to pour money into the house to make it attractive on the open market. So, they're not in a great position to sell at market value, and if they just sit on the house, they may lose it to tax foreclosure. The job of a good wholesaler is to provide a way out. In this case, the owner gets to avoid a foreclosure situation (where they'd get nothing for the house), and they get $20k in their pocket. Because the wholesaler does very little to the property, their goal isn't to sell on the open market either. Their goal is to find a property investor who wants to flip or buy and hold. A wholesaler may find an investor who will pay $90,000 for it – an easy $50,000 profit. The reason why it's often not sold for closer to the open market amount is that the flipper needs to have some margin to make money on the sale and the buy-and-hold investor needs to budget funds to fix up the property. Thus, it will take them longer before they get a tenant in, meaning they want to limit their carrying costs before a renter gets in (carrying costs is paying PITI while no renter is in the property). In addition, wholesalers lose money from carrying costs each month they have a property that hasn't sold, so they tend to price to sell.

The last pro I'll cover here is that they are often able to use what's called creative financing. The basic idea is that you're not going through a bank to finance the property. Probably the most common type of creative financing is seller financing.In this, the seller essentially acts as the lender, and you agree to terms with them (length of loan, purchase price, down payment, interest rate, monthly payment). It is rare to have a 30-year loan through seller financing; usually it will be amortized over 30 years (meaning the monthly payment is calculated like you have a 30-year loan), but you're actually only making payments for five years or so with the expectation of a balloon payment at the end of the five-year term. A balloon payment means you'll eventually be getting a mortgage on the property through a cash-out refinance. Since you technically own the property like you paid cash (at least from the bank's perspective), you'll refinance the property and put a mortgage on it. But what happens to the money that was borrowed against the mortgage? It comes to you – and you turn around and pay the owner the remaining amount of the loan (because you're not doing payments for 25 more years). Remember how I said that these niche types of real estate investing can seem more complicated? Although using creative financing is harder to understand, it allows you to buy properties without going to the bank, with very little money down, and lots of flexibility on the terms. By the way, you can use creative financing with on-market single-family homes and multi-unit properties, but the average seller tends to be more interested in getting the whole payout quickly and may not understand seller financing. It's the people who are more desperate who may be more willing to consider creative financing.

Cons

I hinted above that there are some cons that keep investors out. One of them is that some people would never enjoy driving for doors. Count me among them. I hated going door-to-door selling candy bars for fundraising as a kid. I still hate going door-to-door. No thank you.It also takes a lot of time to drive for doors and comb through tax delinquency lists. It can also be very expensive to do the mail campaigns to reach potential sellers. Keep in mind tax delinquency lists may not include secondary contact methods (like phone numbers and email addresses), so mail is the way to do it. According to ChatGPT (by the way, this is a great informational tool for real estate investors), the beginner wholesaler may send 500-2000 mailers monthly, with a cost of 40 cents to $1 per mailer. Easy math means this could cost you $500 to $2000 per month with a response rate that doesn't often exceed 2%. So, if you send 500 mailers, you might expect 10 people to contact you.Keep in mind, that's not how many deals you close from those 500 mailers – that's just people who respond. Industry standard is about 1-2 deals closed per 10,000 mailers. If you send 500 mailers per month, it may take you 20 months to close your first deal and cost you $10,000. It's great that you made $50,000 when you sold the property you closed on, but you probably want to make more than $50,000 in 20 months. And that's after hundreds of conversations with people who responded to the mailers but didn't close. According to the 2% response rate, you'll be talking to 200 people (2% of 10,000) to close one deal. That's 199 rejections and one deal.

So, how do you make more than $50k in 20 months? Send more mailers! That means more work driving for dollars and combing tax lists, printing letters, stuffing envelopes, and dropping them in the mail, more frequent rejection conversations, etc. If you have a team working on this, it's not necessarily more work for you, but most people don't have teams to start. If you're feeling a bit out of breath reading this, then you'll understand why most people don't do this. Additionally, if you remember the idea of carrying costs above, if something happens in the market that depresses it, you might have to drop your wholesale prices (hurting your profits), and you might have to hold on to the properties longer, increasing your carrying costs. Another con to this is it's literally another full-time job doing all this work. Many landlords look to build systems to make their rentals as passive as possible, but this can feel like flipping, in that it's like you've just switched your W-2 job for another one.

Land Flipping

If you're someone who pays attention to detail, you may notice that I've violated my typical pattern of using a bold heading, then listing pros and cons. Why, then, am I doing a new heading that's italicized here? That's because land flipping is an even more niche application of wholesaling. Land flippers are looking for raw, unimproved land that is just sitting. They're often still combing delinquent tax lists and doing mail campaigns. Because the pros and cons are often the same with wholesaling, I'll just highlight a few things here. On the pro side, it's much cheaper to buy raw land. Instead of paying $40,000 for a tax-distressed single-family home, you might pay $4000 for tax distressed raw land. Obviously, you're profiting less per transaction, and you're often holding the property for much longer before it sells. However, your carrying costs are lower, and your sales pitch to the distressed owner tends to be less awkward. It's much harder to get an owner to sell you their home for 30 cents on the dollar than it does their vacant land that they haven't done anything with in years.

Lastly, land flippers often use seller financing to *sell* their properties. We talked about a wholesaler using seller financing to *buy* their properties, but land flippers often sell their properties on terms. They sell that $4000 bit of vacant land for $20,000. Keep in mind that banks don't like financing land, and they don't like giving real estate loans for small amounts. As such, a buyer won't be able to get a bank to give a mortgage for $20,000. That means they'll have to pay cash, which some people who want the land won't have. So, you, the land flipper, use seller financing. You become the bank. You ask for $4000 down (making back your initial investment in one lump sum), then have them pay you 10% interest on the remaining $16,000 over the next five years. That means they're paying you $340 per month for five years. Savvy land flippers will sell as many properties as possible through seller financing, which layers these monthly payments, meaning as some drop off, new ones come on, creating a passive income stream for themselves. It sounds great, but the deal volume tends to be lower, as there are a lot fewer people looking to buy raw land.

Property Development

This is essentially building your own properties. For obvious reasons, this is a very rare place to start, because few people have the expertise or the money on hand to do this as their entry point to real estate.Even so, it's worth exploring for the sake of completeness. I won't be discussing property development from the perspective of building homes that you'll turn around and sell (like flipping). This is usually the purview of established companies with a lot of financial backing that deals with large-scale construction projects, so they save through economies of scale. Very few get into real estate investing this way (unless it's a syndication, which I'll talk about later in this chapter).

Pros

You are in complete control over the types of properties you develop and the quality of property that you're building. This means that everything about the property is a known quantity. You don't have to worry about when the hot water heater will go out or how much life the roof has left in it. If you're building the house (or multi-family building) to keep and rent, you can charge higher rents, because everything is new. You can also avoid the rat race of the open market for properties. No bidding wars, no need to worry about inspections that missed something, etc. You buy the land, and you build it.

Cons

This is most definitely an advanced play in real estate investing. This is not for the faint of heart. If you are a DIYer, then this is going to be a lot of work and take a long time to do it. This means you're spending a lot of money before you start collecting any rent.There is a real risk that if the project goes over budget and falls behind schedule, you may run out of money and have an incomplete house that you can't rent and can't finish. That's my definition of a nightmare scenario. You also really need to know what you're doing to DIY this the right way. You can hire someone to build for you, which will speed up the process and perhaps ensure that the construction is done the right way. However, you have to be a very good project manager to make sure the process is being followed, that people are showing up on time, and that they are doing things correctly. Make sure you have good contractors. Greg (my friend discussed above) hired a contractor to work on one of his properties, only to find out the contractor used one of the draws (a draw is a payment to the contractor in phases that is designed to cover a certain portion of the construction) to take his family on vacation and didn't have the money to do the construction. Greg wouldn't give him another draw until that phase was completed, but the contractor couldn't complete the phase, because he had spent the money that was supposed to pay for materials and labor to complete the phase. I'm glad I didn't have to navigate that. The process is much more complicated, from financing, to the permitting process, to the project management, to the final inspection process – it's not easy. Did I mention that these projects can go over budget and fall behind schedule? In addition, you're involved in every decision. There are a LOT of details that go into constructing a rental, and it can feel overwhelming. As I said, this is an advanced move for a real estate investor. One last comment – again according to ChatGPT, it can be 15-35% more expensive to build a house than to buy it, and you're probably not getting up to 35% more rent from these units.

Commercial Real Estate

I promised above that I would clarify the difference between Commercial multi-family and commercial real estate. As you might remember, Commercial multi-family is considered commercial from a banking perspective and changes the type of financing you can get. *This* type of commercial real estate is buying land or buildings that are designed to support commercial enterprises. There are a couple of ways to do this. One relatively common way is to buy the land and lease the land to the business (called a ground lease) that is constructing their commercial building. They own the building, and you own the land. However, if they move from that building, they're essentially abandoning it, meaning it becomes yours. This happens when there is a reversion clause in the contract, meaning whatever improvements they make on the property will revert to you when the lease is over. This isn't always the case, however. Some contracts require the land to be returned to its original state when the lease is over, which usually involves demolishing the building and returning the land to buildable condition. Another common way is to own the land and building and lease it to a business. You're obviously charging more rent if you also own the building, but the property is more costly to acquire.

Pros

This may be the most passive type of property ownership. This is because of something called a triple net lease (often referred to as an NNN lease). An NNN lease means that the tenant is responsible for three expenses that landlords would otherwise have to pay. These are (in addition to paying rent) taxes, insurance, and maintenance. In other words, the tenant treats the property like they're the owners and are responsible for all expenses associated with it. You literally just sit back, collect the checks, and renegotiate the lease every so many years, usually raising the rent each time. It's hard to get easier than this. And the negotiation process tends to be fairly easy. If you sign a 10-year lease with a business, it usually has several built-in rent increases already in it, and basically every tenant will expect that rent will go up at the renegotiation. A pro that's built into this is that the leases tend to be much longer than residential, giving you nice long-term income. Lastly, the money you make tends to be good, getting a higher rent rate per square foot than you do with residential.

Cons

It is expensive to get into this type of investing by yourself. Even if you're just going to do a land lease, commercial real estate tends to be much more expensive than residential land. And if you buy commercial real estate with buildings already on them, it gets really expensive. For example, Greg told me recently about a land lease situation available on the open market. The person who owns the land is looking to sell it, and a Taco Bell is currently being built on it. The sticker price was $1.1 million. The thing that scares me the most about commercial real estate is vacancy. It's not as bad with land leases. You have bare land, which didn't cost you as much as if you had a building, so carrying costs are less. However, it can be hard to find someone who wants to build from scratch. Even worse is if you paid for the land and building and don't have a tenant. Your carrying costs can be massive. Where I live in Canton, OH, there was an old Family Video store that went out, and the space was vacant for years. Personally, I don't want to mess with that. Another thing that can contribute to vacancy is that your tenant can go out of business. You go from thinking you're on easy street collecting rent to having no one in your property, and you're collecting nothing. Now you've got a building that no one is maintaining, and it's all on you now.It's also not that profitable unless you pay cash. Going back to this land lease with Taco

Bell – the annual rent you'd collect on this to start would be $58,000. That sounds great until you realize that the debt service on this would be almost $77,000 per year. That's not the kind of math I want to get involved with.

We did dabble briefly in commercial real estate when we got a good deal on a house on a main thoroughfare that had been rezoned commercial. The first floor was an office-space type arrangement (that was vacant), and the second floor was an apartment that had been grandfathered into residential use, because it had a tenant in it within the past two years. By the way, it's extremely important that you understand your local zoning laws before you do something like this. We didn't find out until after we purchased it that the upstairs was also considered commercial, and I thought we were in a bad spot, because we were planning on having a residential tenant. It wasn't until I got more specific with my questions with the zoning commissioner that I discovered the 'grandfathered' loophole that allowed us to still use the upstairs as residential. Rachel didn't want to rent the upstairs unit until we got a commercial tenant for the downstairs. She didn't want to rent it to someone with three barking dogs and screaming toddlers when a massage therapist was trying to work downstairs. However, it took longer to rent the downstairs unit, so we were just carrying the cost of the building with no revenue. We ended up signing a lease-to-own contract with a young real estate agent who wanted to get into property ownership. He had similar trouble finding downstairs tenants, and he eventually renovated the first floor and made it into his real estate office. He did a fantastic job, and we just closed the purchase with him several months ago. He got a great property, and we made about $25,000 in the process.

This is the last type of real estate investing that I'll discuss that involves you directly owning the property. That might sound odd, like how can I be a real estate investor and not actually needing to buy the property? Believe it or not, it's true. I'm going to talk about five types of real estate investing that doesn't involve you, yourself, owning the property in the next chapter.

5

What Are My Options? Part 2 - Non-Deeded Real Estate

This chapter covers less common types of real estate investing. Most people are familiar with the ones where you actually own the property. That's not all there is, however. Some people either supplement their real estate activities with non-deeded investing, and some people focus only on this. Here are the most common ways to invest in real estate without owning the property.

Note Investing

There's a fair chance you've never heard of this type of investing before, because it's literally buying debt. The concept of owning debt might sound foreign, but it's not a super complicated idea once you get the basics. Banks own debt, so you'd essentially be operating like a bank. Before I jump too much further into this, I want to repeat what I just said – banks own debt. They don't actually own your property if you have a mortgage. That's a common misconception. You might hear a homeowner say, "I can't wait until my house is paid off, and I'll really own my home." They already really own their home. They own the home, and the bank owns the debt. Legally, the bank can foreclose on a home if the debt service isn't being paid, but that doesn't mean the bank is the real owner of the property. Think of it like this. Let's say you buy a bicycle with your credit card.Does Visa own your bike until

54

you pay Visa back? Of course not. You own the bike, and Visa owns the debt.

Believe it or not, banks often don't keep your debt. They sell it to Freddie Mac and Fannie Mae (these are government institutions that buy residential mortgage debt from banks). Because so many banks sell to these institutions, they have to follow Freddie Mac and Fannie Mae guidelines when issuing mortgages, because they won't buy the debt if their rules haven't been followed. So, if you've been frustrated by all the hoops you must go through to get a loan, it's not actually your bank's doing. Because they want to sell the debt, they have to follow Freddie Mac's and Fannie Mae's rules. So, why would banks want to sell their debt? It's because it takes them a long time to get their money back over the course of a mortgage. Let's say you take out a $250,000 mortgage. At 6.5% interest over a 30-year term, you'll pay over $318,000 in interest on that loan, for a total payment amount of more than $568,000. But banks don't want to wait 30 years to recover all that money. So, they sell the loan (usually after a certain period of time to be able to show that the buyer is paying regularly). They're willing to give up the long-term value of the loan, because they can use that money now and get immediate interest payments on it (perhaps at higher rates than the mortgage they're selling). In addition, because of inflation, getting getting money now and doing something with it can be worth more than collecting money slowly over 30 years. Future dollars just aren't worth as much as dollars right now are. Plus, they've collected thousands in interest before they sell the note.

So, the buyer of the note picks up the debt. If the homeowner sells the house, the note owner is in good shape, because the debt is worth more than what you paid for it. If the homeowner keeps paying on the house, the debt owner collects the monthly payments and gets a big long-term upside by capitalizing on all the extra interest that's being paid over the years. That's a lot of information, but I want you to understand what's really happening with note investing. Ultimately, Freddie Mac and Fannie Mae aren't the only ones who can buy notes. You can too. This isn't the only place you can shop for notes, but check out paperstac.com if you'd like to peruse some inventory and see what this looks like.

Pros

This is a completely passive form of real estate investing. You don't own the property, you own the debt. So, the homeowner is taking care of the property (hopefully). They pay you monthly like they'd pay the bank. In other words, you just cash the check. If the homeowner sells the property, you are often the first lienholder, meaning you get paid first from the proceeds. Even if you don't make much money when the house is sold (the goal is to get back what you paid), you will have been making money each month from the debt service payments. You may wonder what happens if the homeowner stops paying. Since you own the debt, you can foreclose on the property. When this happens, you don't own the debt anymore, you own the property, which you can then sell, rent, etc. Note investing often has a smaller barrier to entry. You can buy a debt note worth $50,000 for $43,000, which is cheaper than buying a property. There may also be opportunities to team up with others to buy portions of notes, rather than the whole note yourself. You can also easily invest in any area of the country that you want to and not have to worry about managing properties from a distance.

Cons

You don't actually own the property. One of my favorite parts of real estate investing is appreciation. The first house we bought as a rental, we paid $145,000.We used our HELOC to pay cash, then we did a cash-out refinance to put a mortgage on the property and get our money back, so we could invest in other properties. We did the refinance about 9 months after we bought it. An appraisal needed to be done, because the bank will let you get 80% of the appraised value in cash out of the deal. It appraised for $185,000. That's a $40,000 increase in nine months. You're not getting that with note investing. Another big downside is that you're only getting paid if the homeowner keeps paying. If they lose their job and fall on hard times, they may not be able to pay their mortgage to you anymore. While non-payment isn't a unique risk to this type of investing (any tenant can stop paying you), as hard as the eviction process is, foreclosure is even harder. And you really need to do your due diligence to understand the laws in your state (or the state where the property is) around foreclosure. In fact, there are some states that restart the foreclosure process every time the homeowner makes even a partial payment. So, you might be two-thirds of the way toward foreclosing, and the homeowner throws $200 your way, and you have to reset the clock. It can be very frustrating and drag on for a long time.

Another con — let's say you found a great deal on a note in Seattle and decided to jump on it (even though you live nowhere nearby). You end up needing to foreclose, and now you've got the property. You might not want to rent it, because you don't want to be a long-distance landlord. You don't have relationships with any contractors in the area to fix it up to get top dollar on the sale. Your best option may be to just cut bait and sell it at a reduced price to get it off your hands. That's definitely not a way to maximize your investment dollars. You can help hedge your bets a bit by seeing if the notes are performing vs. non-performing. Performing notes are the ones where the owner is paying regularly and up to date. You'll pay more for these notes. Non-performing notes are ones where the owner is in arrears and represents a bigger risk to you, the note buyer. These are also cheaper to purchase, and if you can get the owner to pay again, you'll have a bigger profit margin. One last note (pun intended) on note investing. It can be complicated to underwrite a deal (I'll cover this in a later chapter), because you not only have to understand the state laws around foreclosure, you have to evaluate things like the property value, what type of property it is, the interest rate it pays, the unpaid principal balance, the investment-to-balance ratio (how much you're paying vs. how much is left on the loan), the investment to value ratio (how much you're paying vs. how much the house is actually worth), the loan to value ratio (comparing the loan size to what the house is worth), and how many payments are remaining. If it looks confusing to evaluate a deal, it can be if you're not very familiar with these concepts.

Property Arbitrage

Oh no! Another one that sounds complicated! I realize these can be challenging concepts, so feel free to take a breather, hydrate, and take some Tylenol. Remember how I said earlier that when I was on the outside looking in, I felt like people were too vague when explaining concepts, which didn't help me much? I like clarity and specificity. I know I can't give you all the details possible in each of these areas, as a book could be written for each of these topics. However, I am trying to give you enough information to basically understand what's going on in each type and evaluate which ones sound most interesting.

Okay, back to arbitrage. If you've never seen the word arbitrage before, the 'rage' part of it is pronounced like it is in the word 'garage'. Arbitrage is a great way to get into real estate if you don't have much money, but it requires a little 'selling'. Essentially, you approach a landlord who has a vacancy. It could be a single-family home, or it could be an apartment complex that you're targeting. Either way, you have to sell the idea of arbitrage to the landlord. You basically become the tenant, and you sublease the property at a higher rent, and you make money on the difference. There are two main types of arbitraging. The first is with long-term tenants. This is the easiest to get into because you just have to find a tenant. The profit margin tends to be much smaller with this type, because, unless you find a landlord who is oblivious to what rent is going for and is drastically undercharging, you can't charge much more for rent than what you're paying the landlord. The second type is short- and mid-term arbitraging. This is more expensive to get into, because you have to furnish the rentals. However, you're getting a lot more money each month, making this a much more profitable endeavor. Some investors only arbitrage. It allows them to grow their unit count quickly and begin to profit quickly. One final note on this – when approaching a landlord with the arbitrage idea, you need to let them know you're subleasing it. This can lead to lots of problems if they are unaware of what you're doing.

Pros

As I said above, this is a great way to get into real estate if you don't have much money. No matter what type of arbitrage you do, your main cost is paying the landlord rent each month. That's a lot easier than saving for years to get a down payment. In addition, if you're doing the furnished arbitrage, you can make a lot of money on rent. Let's say you're paying the landlord $1200 per month for a 2-bed/1-bath apartment. Often, you can comfortably rent the unit on a mid-term lease for $2000-2400 per month. Another benefit of this type of investing is that you can scale quickly. Let's take a look at the numbers:

Profit and Loss Statement for Arbitrage Example

	Month 1	Month 2	Month 3	Month 4	Month 5	Month 6
Furnishing Costs	$30,000	$0	$0	$0	$0	$0
Rent Paid to Landlord	$5750	$5750	$5750	$5750	$5750	$5750
Total Costs	$35,750	$5750	$5750	$5750	$5750	$5750
Rent Collected	$0	$12,000	$12,000	$12,000	$12,000	$12,000
Monthly Profit/Loss	-$35,750	$6250	$6250	$6250	$6250	$6250
Total Profit/Loss	$-35,750	-$29,500	-$23,250	-$17,000	-$10,750	-$4500

Let's say that it costs you $6000 to furnish a 2-bed apartment. Maybe you have a budget of $30,000 from money you've saved, and you talk the landlord into renting you a block of five apartments. Let's say you negotiate a volume discount, and you're paying $1150 in rent, as opposed to $1200 now. Let's also say that it takes you a month to furnish and get renters in the units. You spent $30,000 on furniture, and you paid $5750 in rent for the five apartments that month, with no income to offset it. Now in month two, you're collecting $2400 for each of the apartments, for a total of $12,000. You pay $5750 in rent for month two, giving you a profit of $6250. That's enough to cover the rent from month one, and you still have $500 left over that you can use to start paying yourself back on the furniture investment. Now, you're profiting each month $6250, and you can attack that large initial cost. As you can see from the table above, month 6 is the last one where you'll be in the negative in total profit/loss. By the time month seven wraps up, you've already made all your money back and then some. You can't recover your money that fast in any other type of investing. That sounds too good to be true, so what's the catch?

Cons

Well, there's not really a catch, per se. It's just not as easy as it sounds. If you arbitrage to long-term tenants, it's relatively easy. You find a tenant, and they stay in the apartment as long as they're paying. You have to do a little property management, but you're not fixing the big issues. If the plumbing is leaking, the apartment complex fixes it, just like they normally would. However, that request may have to come through you, the official 'tenant' of the landlord. Remember, though, you're not making much money this way. There's not much of a 'squeeze', but there's not much 'juice' either.If you do furnish the apartment, it gets much more complex. I don't know if you've ever outfitted a whole apartment, but it can be a lot of work sourcing everything and putting it all together. You also have to be a bit savvy with interior design. Of course, you could pay a designer and buy everything brand new and delivered and put together on site. But all this just gets more expensive. So, it's a lot of work DIY furnishing five apartments. Now imagine building your portfolio to 50 arbitrage units and the amount of work that represents.

Essentially, if you're going to scale, you have to get very process-oriented (create a process that's easily repeatable) and have other people do the grunt work. Also, remember with furnished units, you're dealing with short-term and mid-term tenants. This means you have more turnover. More turnover means more vacancy. More vacancy means less money. Also, you have to find more tenants. Remember that long-term arbitrage tenant situation? As long as they're paying, they can stay as long as they want. Maybe you have turnover once every two years. If you do a mid-term arbitrage, you may have to find somewhere between 2-6 tenants each year. With short-term arbitrage, you may have to find 2-6 tenants per month. It's a bit more work and more pressure – but you're making more money.

You also have sell the idea to the landlords. Remember how I told you that I don't like to sell? That makes this less appealing to me. The landlords may want to know why they wouldn't just find tenants themselves and not have a middleman. There are some ways to sell this concept. First, you can agree to cover any maintenance costs that are less than $200, for example, which saves them money and inconvenience. Second, they don't have to worry about non-payment of rent from a financially unstable tenant, because you're the one paying rent. You can even make it worth their while to agree to a 2-year or 3-year lease. Landlords love steady, reliable payments – and it may lock in rent for longer without the landlord increasing it. Another trick up your sleeve is that you can offer to lease a block of rooms, which saves them the headache of finding multiple tenants. One last trick that you can deploy if they're still hesitant is that you can offer to pay a little over market rent, although I do not recommend this if you're considering long-term arbitrage – you're already not making much per month anyway.

Another con with arbitrage is that you're not making any money on property appreciation, because you don't own anything. That's another major reason why I'm personally not very excited about this. Two more things I'll cover quickly. Make sure you have a really strong contract with the landlord. What if one of your tenants really makes a mess of the carpet, then leaves? You contact the landlord to put new carpet in to keep the unit attractive and rentable and they refuse. That puts you in a bit of a bind, because you can't force the landlord to put new carpet in. If you decided to do it at your own expense, it becomes expensive, and the landlord may start to be even cheaper with you, believing that you'll cover costs like these in the future. If you don't replace the carpet, you might have to lower rent or have a hard time getting a good renter. Ensure that you discuss rent in the contract as well. The landlord may try to raise rent on you, which cuts into your profits. The last point is that if you decide to stop arbitraging, all the money stops coming in. It only pays you while you're working it. You can decide to stop working as a landlord if you own your own properties. Sure, the rents will stop because you sold your properties, but you received a huge payout from the proceeds of those sales. There's nothing like that with arbitrage.

I'm going to add a quick note here about something called co–hosting. This is very similar to arbitrage but with some important differences. It shares many of the same pros and cons, so I won't go into those here, but I will focus on the differences, so that you can better understand what it is and if it's for you. Whereas both will involve you approaching the owner of a property to see if you can use it, arbitrage tends to focus mostly on mid-term rentals, so you can take advantage of the gap between what you're paying the owner in rent and what you can charge in rent. In co-hosting, you're not making money on the differences in rents being charged. You're essentially operating as a service to bring short-term renters to another person's property. Co-hosting is attractive to people who don't have much money to get into real estate and/or who want to make money without the risk of putting a lot of money in. So, while arbitrage and co-hosting are similar, in that you are bringing a renter to another person's property, the short-term renting in co-hosting doesn't require you to pay rent. It requires you to give up about 80% of the revenue to the homeowner. If you keep the property occupied, both you and the owner will make good money. If you don't keep it occupied, then the arrangement will be short. As a co-host, you're essentially responsible for listing the property on the appropriate platforms, communicating with potential tenants, problem-solving for them, ensuring their experience is good, and getting good ratings. It can be a good way to get a feel for real estate without having to make a big up-front investment. Think of co-hosting as being a marketer and property manager for the landlord's short-term rentals, with you keeping a slice of the pie they make.

Hard Money Lender

We've talked about some complicated ways of investing in real estate, so let's take a break and talk about a simple option. As a hard money lender, you're simply letting someone borrow your money. That's it. Of course, it's never that simple, but this is really pretty straightforward.You may remember from the Our Story chapter that we served as a hard money lender to our friend Greg. We gave him the money from our HELOC so he could buy the house at auction. He needed this, because you can't get a mortgage on a foreclosure auction like you can on a house that's on the open market. So, this cash helped him buy the house. We agreed to the payment terms (he was covering our interest payments until he paid us back, he paid us a flat fee for the use of the money, and he was to pay us back on the principal when he did the cash out refinance), and that was it.

Pros

The simplicity of this is one of the major pros. It's extremely straightforward and commonsense. Also, you can charge a higher interest rate. The way the economics of interest rates work is that the riskier the investment, the higher the interest rate. If you'd pay 7% interest on your mortgage, you might pay 10-12% if you're borrowing hard money. Not everyone uses interest rates. We used a flat fee with Greg. It's also very passive for the investor. Write the check and wait for the return money to come your way. You don't need a lot of money to do this. Even if you don't have all your HELOC available to lend like we did, you can lend $10,000 or $20,000, maybe as the only lender or perhaps with a group of other lenders to raise enough money.

Cons

This process is riskier than getting a traditional loan, because the process isn't as regulated. As a result, you must be very careful with your contract, and not many know how to cover their bases this way. One problem that often isn't considered is that the cash out refinance really only works if the property appraises for enough to return all your money. I mentioned this before, but it bears mentioning again. Banks will only give the owner 80% of the value of the house in the refinance. So, if you loaned $140,000, and the house appraises at $160,000, the bank will only give the owner $128,000 to pay you back. That's $12,000 short of what they needed, not counting the interest or flat fee they owe you. You could also find yourself in a non-payment situation, which is why you have to be very careful who you lend your money to. Lastly, if rehab needs to take place on the property, either to flip it or make it ready for renters, the project could linger on and take longer for you to get your money back.

Syndication

Okay, back to the complicated stuff. Before I go too far into this, the last two I describe won't have a list of pros and cons with them, simply because I'm less familiar with these, and I don't want to represent myself as an expert when I'm not. Additionally, these last two are not common at all if this is your first entry point into real estate, with one exception. So, what is syndication? It's a complicated process that has very strict legal guidelines that you need to comply with if you're the General Partner (GP; who sets up and runs the syndication). The GP(s) finds Limited Partners (LPs), who will fund the syndication. It's important to know that LPs are silent partners. They just contribute money and have no role in running the syndication.

Syndications are used to 'take down' really big deals. Let's say you find a 40-unit apartment building for $5 million. To put 20% down, you'd need to raise $1 million for the purchase. Not many have that amount of money laying around. However, you just might be able to find 10 people who can put in $100,000. The basic idea here is that the GP finds the deal, finds the funding, and manages the property. Usually, there is an agreed upon return on investment that is paid out monthly to each of the LPs. So, while the GP often gets something like a 1.5% fee for finding and closing the deal, the GP doesn't' make much during the time the syndication owns the property. The ultimate goal is that in about five years, the property, which has been run efficiently and profitably, is sold again at a profit. The proceeds are then divvied out with about 70% going to the LPs and about 30% going to going to the GP. Running a syndication is a complicated process and should be reserved for experienced investors. In reality, many more people participate as LPs than GPs, although not many people start their real estate journey this way, as it's often reserved for people with a fair bit of wealth.

I mentioned above that there is one exception to people getting into syndications as a first move into real estate. If you work with a financial advisor (or are a knowledgeable money investor), you may have heard of REITs before. These are Real Estate Investment Trusts and work in a very similar way to what I described above but some are more widely available for people to invest in with smaller amounts of money. The main risk with syndications is an economic downturn that doesn't allow the assets to be sold for a profit. So, either the asset is held longer (tying your money up longer than you anticipated) or the asset is sold, and you don't get much of a payout at the end.

Buying Mineral Rights

This is the one I know the least about. I could conceivably have done a bunch of research to present more clarity on this topic, but I have two suspicions that led me to pass on that. Suspicion #1: I really don't think many people are going to be interested in this one. This is probably the most niche type of investing, and most people have either never heard of or have considered it and quite frankly aren't that interested. Suspicion #2: You'd rather spend more time with your in-laws (if you have them) than give me a reason to make these last two chapters any longer. What you're basically doing here is buying the rights to what's under the surface of the land. There may not be anything valuable under the land, but hopefully you've done your research to make that chance worth taking. Because you don't really own anything tangible at first, most don't speculate with this. In addition, state laws vary about how you do this or whether it's even an option. Feel free to 'dig' into this one more if you're curious, but that's where I'll leave it.

6

How to Make Money in Real Estate

If you're reading this book, you are probably thinking about the future of your finances. Maybe you have a lot of money laying around, and you want to know what to do with it. Maybe you don't have much money, but you want to take what you have and turn it into something. There are lots of things to do with your money to help generate a return, and many of them are viable options. For example, you could just keep your money in the bank. That's the safest thing to do, as your bank is likely FDIC insured. That protects up to $250,000 of your money at one financial institution, if they go out of business. While that may be the safest place to put your hard-earned greenbacks, it doesn't give you much return. Banks aren't often in the business of keeping your money up with inflation, so your money will become worth less over time, even as it grows in the bank.

Many turn to the stock market. This is probably better when you have money laying around and you want to position it for retirement. While I won't evaluate the pros and cons of the stock market or pretend to give you investing advice, there's a reason why it's so popular. Since 1926 (which includes the Great Depression and the Great Recession), the stock market has averaged approximately a 10% annual rate of return. Each year is different, and some years show a loss, but it's a pretty good investment over the long haul. That's why the stock market is often real estate's main competition for your money.

Before I talk about why I think real estate is better, I do believe in having a diversified portfolio of investments. This might mean diversifying within real estate, but I also mean that you probably shouldn't have all your assets in real estate. I've been investing in the stock market for a long time, and I'm still contributing to my 401(k). I expect to have a fair chunk of change in these accounts when I retire. In sum, putting money in real estate is a great investment – it just shouldn't be your only one. Now, let's look at how real estate makes you money, but keep in mind that not all of these apply if you're investing in non-deeded real estate.

Cash Flow

Cash flow is your profit at the end of each month. This is what most people are looking for when they invest. You'll hear a lot of people saying how they want to replace their W-2 income with their rental income. This is what investors dream about, including me. Cash flow is the dream, but it can be hard to come by, depending on how you're investing. Cash flow is often geographically influenced. For example, the cost of properties in LA, New York, and Boston are so high that rents can't keep pace. Cash flow is a dream for the new investor in those areas, not reality. If you buy in the Midwest, where property is much less expensive, rent does often provide some cash flow. No matter where you live, however, you have several levers to influence cash flow:

- **Interest rate** – This has killed the cash flow of investors in the post-COVID world. Rates went from historic lows (around 3% on a 30-year note) to over 7%. One of my favorite websites is mortgagecalculator.org. When we get to talk more about underwriting, this website will come in handy. For now, I'll use it to run the numbers on a $300,000 mortgage at 3% and 7% over 30 years and see how it changes cash flow. At 3%, the principal and interest is $1265 per month. At 7%, it's $1996. That's an absolute cash flow killer. Unfortunately, there's not a lot you can do to influence the interest rates, but you can improve your credit score, take out a shorter mortgage (15-year vs. 30-year), shop for lenders, pay points on the mortgage (this is extra money you pay at closing to reduce the rate by a few tenths), or just wait until the rates go down.

- **Price of the property** – This is one of the most obvious levers, but it doesn't make as much difference to cash flow as the interest rate. If we go back to the $300,000 mortgage with the 7% interest rate that gave us a $1996 monthly payment, negotiating the seller down to $275,000 will reduce your mortgage to $1830 per month. It's nice to reduce your payment by $166, but it's nowhere near as impactful as a big drop in interest rates. Don't overlook this, though. Learn to be a good negotiator and do your underwriting effectively, and you can help control costs. You definitely don't want to get caught up in a bidding war like you might for your primary home. Bidding wars erode cash flow quickly. As an aside, if you want better deals, generate relationships that will help you find off-market properties. I'll talk more about this in chapter 10, but if you can avoid the open market, then do it.

- **Type of property** – As I mentioned above, multi-family properties will cash flow better than single-family homes. You may start off with single-family, but savvy investors often move into multi-family to increase cash flow.

- **Down payment** – This works much the same as negotiating down the price of the property. In other words, putting $25,000 more down on the property is effectively the same as negotiating the cost down $25,000, from a cash flow perspective. However, it's not the same when it comes to keeping cash in your pocket to make improvements or putting it toward another house. The optimal play here to increase cash flow is to pay cash and have no mortgage. There's no way to get a higher hit of cash flow. The problem is that this ties up your money, and you can't make other purchases with it. That's not a problem if you're independently wealthy, but I'm guessing those aren't the folks reading this book right now.

- **Rent** – Make sure you do your research on what market rents are in your area. We bought a triplex, and the seller proudly told me that she had raised the rents to $680 per unit and told me that it could probably be raised to $800 when I took it over. Then she had it appraised, and she told me that the appraiser thought we might be able to get $900 per unit. We closed on the property and promptly got $1200 and $1100 for the two open units. I always do my research. I knew that the seller was way off. I knew that the appraiser was way off. That's why YOU need to do your research. Don't just trust what people tell you. Look on Zillow and see what rental units are going for. Look on Facebook Marketplace, but make sure you're comparing apples to apples with bedrooms, bathrooms, square footage, location, and quality of property.

  Once you've gotten some rentals of your own, make sure you're paying attention to rent increases. I can't tell you how many landlords who have owned the rental for decades end up selling at some point, and they are literally leaving tens of thousands of dollars on the table over the years simply by ignoring rent increases. Sometimes the rent is half what it should be. Charging market rent is one of the most reliable ways to help yourself with cash flow. An important point here – the shorter the rental term, the more money per month you can charge. That's why mid-term and short term rentals operate at a much higher monthly rent rate. Finally, you've probably heard about the three most important things in real estate – location, location, location. This is an easy one, because you can charge higher rents in nicer locations. Sure, you've probably paid more for the property too (which eats into cash flow), but hopefully you can compensate for it with higher rents.

- **Property improvements** – The more you fix up a property, the more you can charge for rent. People are willing to pay more when they love what they see. Set your properties up nicely (landscaping, aesthetic improvements) and keep them nice. Property improvements aren't always just skin deep. We added a lot of value by finishing half the basement in one of our rentals, turning an ugly half bath into a brand-new full bath, and adding a bedroom. This is a legal bedroom, because there's a closet and an egress window in the room. We took this from a 2-bed/1-bath, 1000 square foot home to a 3-bed/2-bath, 1500 square foot home that's now worth about $100,000 more than what we paid for it (partly because we negotiated a great off-market deal). We can get a lot more rent from the new configuration than from the old.

Now that we've talked through some levers to improve cash flow, let's look at why it matters, relative to putting your money in the stock market. Remember the 10% rate of return that a good mutual fund can give you? Let's go back to our $300,000 mortgage. Most banks want 20% down on a rental property, which makes the purchase price $375,000. That means you dropped $75k to get the deal. If you put that much money in the stock market at 10% annually, you'd collect $7500 in the first year. If you put that money into a duplex, you might cash flow $600 per month. That's $7200 per year. Once the property is paid off, your cash flow will be MUCH higher than that. So, once you've stabilized the property (meaning that you've done the initial investments to improve the property and you have a regular paying tenant), the return on investment is very similar to stocks, with much less volatility.

Forced appreciation

But you're not just making money from the rent coming in. Let's talk about the house where we added a bed and a bath into the basement. We bought this house for $118,000 in an off-market deal. We can thank Rachel for brokering that. We probably sank about $60,000 in it to fix up the main level, furnish the house (we use it as a mid-term rental), deal with some landscaping issues, fix up the roof and chimney, address some breezeway problems, and remodel the basement. So, we're all in at about $178,000. It's worth somewhere between $210,000 and $220,000 right now. It cost us money, but it was well worth it, because we saw an outsized impact on the value. That's what forced appreciation is. You do something actively to the house to raise its market value. Granted, this doesn't put money in your pocket immediately like cash flow does, but if you ever need to sell the house you will have more money in your pocket or if you decide to do a HELOC on the property, you'll have more money available to borrow.

Market appreciation

This is better than forced appreciation, because you don't have to actually do anything to achieve this, other than to maintain your property. What a beautiful thing this is. I briefly discussed market appreciation above, when I said that we used our HELOC to pay cash for our first rental, then nine months later did a cash-out refinance, and it appraised for $40,000 more than we bought it for. You don't always gain that much money in nine months, but property values will consistently march up over time. This value creator is very dependent on where you live. If you live in Ohio, like I do, you'll never see appreciation like they do in parts of California. However, that doesn't mean you're left out in the cold. I remember listening to a very popular real estate podcast, and the host was talking about how appreciation was so much more important for wealth building than cash flow. That's true, to an extent, and will be discussed in depth later in this chapter, but he was discouraging listeners from buying in markets like mine if real wealth was your goal. The problem is that he wasn't thinking big picture – and I wasn't thinking big picture until recently. Rachel and I were lamenting that we had to sell our house in California to afford paying cash for our house in Ohio. We felt like we needed to, because I was coming to Ohio with an uncertain job situation. We didn't like that a rental here wouldn't appreciate like our old house on the Central Coast.

As a case in point, our house in California is estimated to be worth $235,000 more in 2025 than when we sold it in 2020. It's frustrating that we had to give that appreciation up. Then it hit me. We weren't thinking big picture. I was comparing a now $800,000 house that we used to own with a $150,000 house that I bought in Ohio as a rental. That's apples to oranges. I could buy five $150,000 houses in Ohio for the price of one in Santa Maria. Guess what happens to appreciation over five houses in Ohio compared to one in

California. I believe we're getting better appreciation here than we would have by holding on to one property in a high appreciation market. Quick aside – remember the podcast host who said that this is the way to real wealth in real estate? He's right, as long as you're willing to sell. Some people use buy-and-hold as a strategy. That builds net worth effectively, but your money is tied up in the asset. That's not money-in-your-pocket wealth. There are some who buy and hold for a while, then sell to benefit from appreciation, which they then turn around to invest in other assets. That tends to drive wealth faster, but it's not a strategy that is attractive to everyone. One last statement here – in the last 50-60 years, residential real estate has appreciated at about 5% per year, which will be important for a point I'll make later.

Mortgage paydown

This one is nice because of how passive this is, but it's a slow way to make money in real estate. Your equity climbs each year, because someone else is paying your mortgage. On a $300,000 loan amortized over 30 years at a 6.5% interest rate, you're paying an average of $279 against the principal and $1617 in interest per month in the first year. By year 10 those numbers shift to $501 against the principal and $1395 to interest. By year 20 those numbers shift to $958 to principal and $939 to interest. Year 20 is where you begin to pay more into principal than interest. So, the longer you're paying the mortgage, the more equity you gain each month. But it takes a long time to make much of a dent, because banks frontload so much of the interest. You can accelerate principal paydown by re-investing the cash flow from the business, which eventually frees up more cash flow. If you let your tenants build your equity from mortgage paydown alone, your equity will grow initially at 1-2% per year (less if the interest rate is higher and more if the rate is lower).

Tax savings

This one feels a bit like cheating, in that saving money on your taxes doesn't feel like you're actually making more money. But in my book, a penny saved is a penny earned. If you decrease your tax burden and keep more money in your pocket, it's got the same effect as earning more money. Real estate investing is one of the most tax advantaged places to put your money. Remember my caveat at the beginning of the book. Nothing that I say should be construed as tax or legal advice. Accountants and lawyers hold the last word in these areas. That said, most of your expenses associated with running your real estate portfolio are tax deductible. You get to deduct depreciation from your taxes. If you're not sure what this is, there is an assumption that the building on your property is perishable and that you need to keep making investments in it to replace what wears down. As such, you get to take the property tax-appraised value of the building (not the land), divide it by 27.5 (that's how many years you can depreciate your property), and that's your depreciation deduction. This is a very complicated topic, which is why you'll want a tax professional on speed dial. Some things can't be depreciated for as long. Certain types of property can be depreciated over longer periods of time.You can do a cost segregation study and accelerate the depreciation to most of it being up front. It's complicated – and you don't need to be an expert if you use an accountant. Just know that depreciation helps you when it comes to taxes.

You can also utilize a 1031 exchange (mentioned above) to defer tax payments on capital gains – another complicated tactic that professionals should be helping you with. Even if you do decide to sell a property without using a 1031 exchange, capital gains taxes are often lower than your regular rate of income, if you've held the property for at least a year. The last point I'll make here is that losses in your real estate business can, in some circumstances, count against your regular W-2 income, reducing your overall tax burden. This doesn't happen in all cases, and certain rules need to be followed (like how to get the 'Real Estate Professional' designation). Basically, there's a lot of ways to save money on your taxes in real estate. Make sure you're consulting a professional if you don't have a strong handle on these concepts – you could land yourself in hot water with the IRS otherwise. One last point here: the bigger your investments in real estate become, the more likely you'll want not just an accountant to prepare your taxes but someone who also specializes in tax planning. They will help you navigate your real estate decisions in a way that minimizes damage when the tax season comes along.

Now that we've looked at how real estate can make you money, let's add it all together. While the stock market makes you about 10% per year with the big upside of being passive, real estate can have a much higher rate of return for you. Let's say cash flow can get you 9% per year. Appreciation adds 5%. I won't factor in forced appreciation here, because you won't necessarily be doing this consistently with each property each year. Let's think of it as an occasional bonus to money growth. Mortgage paydown adds 1-2% per year to start (and grows thereafter). Finally, you can save several percentage points on taxes, which functions like it's adding several percentage points to your money. Let's add this up: 9%+5%+1.5%+2%=17.5%. For the sake of round numbers, let's say that forced appreciation adds 2.5%, which brings you to 20% annual return on your money.

Investment Growth Comparison Between Stocks and Real Estate

	$100,000*	$200,000	$400,000	$800,000	$1.6M	$3.2M
Age with Stocks	43	50.2	57.4	64.6	71.8	79
Age with Real Estate	43	46.6	50.2	54.8	58.4	62

*Initial investment

Here's how I arrived at the numbers in the table. The 'rule of 72' says that you divide 72 by your rate of return to see how often your money doubles. If you put $100,000 in the stock market at age 43 (how old I was when I purchased my first rental) at a 10% rate of return, my initial investment would double every 7.2 years (72 divided by 10). You can see how different the numbers are with the rule of 72 when real estate is getting you 20% rate of return annually. My money is doubling every 3.6 years now. Admittedly, this is kind of a best-case scenario calculation, but if you run your business well, you can get close to this. Case in point is that Rachel and my net worth has gone up more than $400,000 in the last three years from our real estate investments.

One final point that shows how effective real estate is as an investment vehicle – there's a general rule of thumb in the investment community (although not everyone subscribes to it) that says you are unlikely to run out of money in retirement if you draw 4% of your savings each year. This is referred to as the 4% rule. So, if you have saved $1,000,000 for retirement, you'll be safe if you draw $40,000 annually. There's also a 60% rule in real estate. This says that if your property is completely paid off, things like insurance, property taxes, income tax, maintenance, vacancy, etc. will take up 40% of your revenue. This means you get to keep 60% as profit. We paid $133,000 for our last single-family home that we've been using as a long-term rental. The base rent we get there is $1500 per month. If that was completely paid off, our cash flow would be $900 monthly ($10,800 per year). So, we'd need four completely paid off properties like this to net $43,200 annually. If we let the tenants completely pay off the properties through mortgage pay down and reinvesting profits into paying off debt, then we'd just need to save $106,400, which is the total amount of the 20% down payment on four properties that cost $133,000 each. What would you rather do, save $1,000,000 for the privilege of withdrawing $40,000 per year or save $106,400 for the privilege of profiting $43,200? I know what I'd rather do.

7

Fix Your Finances

Let's recap where we are so far. You've read our story and hopefully understand that you don't need to come from wealth to be successful in real estate. You don't even need to be handy. You've done some soul searching and worked to figure out if real estate is something that you'd like to commit to (it's not for everyone). You've thought through your 'why', which is essential to keeping focused when things get challenging. You have a pretty thorough understanding of the breadth of ways that you can become involved in real estate. You understand that investing in properties can be a very lucrative way to replace your income, fund your retirement, and achieve your financial goals. Now we're going to talk about a necessary precondition for being successful in real estate investing that is not talked about nearly enough. You must build a strong financial base before you get started. It's just too risky otherwise. So, what do I mean by this? I'm going to talk about four essential pillars in this chapter that nobody can ignore if they want to succeed in real estate.

Eliminate Your Debt

This is so important. Real estate investing is a great way to generate wealth. It's a terrible way to fix your finances. What do I mean by this? During the years that Rachel and I didn't have the means to invest, we were paying down debt and building up our savings. So, when we moved to Ohio, we were poised to take off. We had a strong foundation, and we couldn't have succeeded like we did without it. But if you're investing in an attempt to generate money to overcome the financial issues you have personally, it necessarily changes your strategy.

We bought homes with minimal issues, so we could get to collecting rent faster. We leveraged 100% of our purchases, so we could grow faster. We couldn't have afforded these virtually move-in ready houses without our foundation. Using leverage like we did would be too risky without it. So, people with a lot of personal debt need a different strategy. I've seen the following happen: someone isn't great with personal finances, so they have to buy cheaper houses to get into real estate. To do this, they need to buy fixer-uppers in worse neighborhoods. The fixups cost money, so they cut corners. They're not attracting great tenants because of the neighborhoods. Their properties end up needing more maintenance, because the tenants aren't caring for them as well and their short cuts come back to haunt them. They have more turnover, which creates more vacancy and requires more financial investment to fix issues every time people leave. Sometimes tenants don't pay or don't tell you about problems that could have been nipped in the bud. Finally, the investor is just sick of it all and sells the properties for marginally more than they bought them for and feeling like it was too much of a headache to try again. You don't want that to be you.

You might ask yourself, "Why is Jared saying to eliminate debt, when he leverages his properties 100%?" or "I thought Jared said that Dave Ramsey was very helpful to him in getting their financial foundation strong. Isn't Dave Ramsey against debt?" These are great questions. When I say, 'eliminate your debt', I'm specifically referring to your personal debt. If you're paying $2500 on a mortgage each month, have $1200 in monthly car payments, are paying off your boat in $900 monthly increments, and you have $28,000 in revolving debt on your credit cards at a 21% interest rate, you're not ready to invest in real estate. Please don't take this to mean that then paying off your car means you're home free to jump into investing. You need to have a very healthy relationship with debt, which means you actively work to minimize it, and when you have it, you work hard to pay it off.

In my opinion, it's okay if you have debt against your investment properties, but you must get your personal debt under control and minimal. This might mean you have to learn to delay gratification. This might mean that you have to downsize your life. This might mean you need to have more laser focus in your budgeting process. If you're in this situation, it's no fun to hear this, but it's necessary. Rachel and I never had the boat payment, and we pay off our credit cards in full each month, but we did have the mortgage and car payments. Not anymore. The one exception to this is if you have all your high-interest debt paid off and what you have left is low interest. For example, if you have a $600 monthly car payment, but it's at 0.9% interest, you may just want to keep making payments and put the extra money into something that would make you 20% return (real estate), rather than saving you 0.9%.

But what about Dave Ramsey? I'll get more into this when I talk about our 'Buy Box' (which is the criteria we use to decide whether we'll consider buying a property), but our Buy Box approach has allowed us to de-risk leveraging our properties at 100%. Just to refresh what this means, we have a mortgage that covers 80% of the purchase price of the property, and we fund the 20% down payment from our HELOC. We've owned our properties (on average) for about a year and a half. I just had to complete our personal financial statement for our lender (we do this annually), and this includes looking at the value of all our properties as well as the debt against them. Because of smart investing our loan-to-value ratio is currently 0.75. If we had funded the down payments with cash, our loan-to-value ratio at the time we closed on that property would be 0.80. So, even though we borrowed 100% of the purchase price on all our properties, if we sold them today, only 75% of the proceeds would be needed to pay all the debt against them. The lower the ratio the better, and if you're under 0.80, then banks consider that relatively low risk. So, what exactly is the risk? It's a crash in the market that drives down home prices. If you're 100% leveraged with a house that cost $300,000, and the housing market drops 10%, then the house is worth less than what the bank lent you. They never want to be in that situation. If you put 20% down, then the bank has loaned you $240,000. If the market drops 10%, the house is still worth more than you owe the bank. Their investment is safe.

Back to Dave Ramsey. Here's why I'm not as worried about the business debt that we have accrued:

- **Personal debt drains the power of your income**. The more debt you have, the less you can save, and it serves to handcuff your financial health. It took Rachel a while to really come to grips that business debt is different than personal debt. The mortgages on our properties are not against my income. It's being completely funded by our tenants.

- **Business debt doesn't create as much personal risk**. Let's say that our business got extremely unlucky, and we couldn't pay our debts, and all our properties were repossessed. It would sink our business, but nobody would take my personal vehicles or foreclose on my home. That stays untouched. Sure, I'd have debt on my HELOC, but my income would cover that, as painful as it would be to have to pay that off with no assets to show for it.

- **We don't enter into debt lightly**. We established a very clear Buy Box, and we stuck to it. We did our due diligence underwriting the properties before we bought them. We set a budget for our offers, and we stuck to them. We don't make emotional decisions with our business, and we operate with a clear strategy.

- **Our personal finances our strong**. We have spent years putting our personal finances on sound footing, so that we could weather hard times in real estate, if we needed to.

- **We could have avoided debt, but debt is a powerful buying lever**. If I waited until I saved enough cash to make my first purchase, I'm not sure I ever would have gotten started. It's possible that the appreciation of properties on the market would have outstripped my ability to save for the increasing costs. We got to 10 units in three years, and we did it by using debt smartly.

- **Does debt increase your risk?** Of course it does, but there's risk inherent in anything. If you put your money in the stock market, it could lose value. If you put your money in the bank, you're not keeping up with inflation. Where people get themselves in trouble is when disaster strikes when they're over-extended. Over-extended usually involves speculating (a form of investing in something that appears to have high returns but is extremely risky, due to a lot of unknowns). People get greedy and take chances they should never take. Smart real estate investing isn't about taking chances; it's about reducing risk while executing a solid plan.

So, before you consider jumping into real estate investing, manage your debt wisely. Taking on business debt when you don't have your own under control is a recipe for getting overextended.

Generate a Good Income

I'm not talking about generating a good income with your real estate. Of course, that's the goal eventually. I'm talking about making good money with your primary job. While you can't always control what you make, the better income you make before investing, the more resources you'll have to pay down debt and accelerate your savings – that's creating the foundation I was talking about. If you're stuck in a job that doesn't pay well, you may have to get creative. You may want to pick up a second job long enough to pay off one of your sources of debt, which will free up cash each month to roll into other sources of debt. You may want to apply for jobs with better pay. Some of you reading this book may resist these suggestions. Life is hard enough without having to take a second job. While that's true, every successful real estate investor I know is successful, in part, because of their work ethic. They're not afraid to burn the candle at both ends to make their dream happen.How hard are you willing to work for you dream? Even doing a few DoorDash runs a day to generate extra cash helps (but make sure you adjust your car insurance to cover doing deliveries!).

A good income not only helps you pay off your personal debt faster, but it helps you save more. This extra saving provides a necessary cushion when you decide to start investing. Your income helps show the bank that you're a good risk. Generating a healthy income each year gives you more assets to invest in your business and pay down business debt faster. We do this. We not only reinvest what we make from our business back into the business, but we also use some money from our personal finances, from time to time, to achieve more paydown on business debt. I'll go back to the question I asked above, how hard are you willing to work for your dream? If you want it to fall into your lap, you'll be waiting a long time. Your comfort zone will never get you to investing success. Challenge yourself to be a better employee, to work for that raise or promotion. If it's not happening at your current job, challenge yourself to find one that pays you better. If you can't find one that pays you better, try working a second job, even on a very part-time basis. If you're a single parent and that's just an impossibility, then keep trucking along, working to pay down debt, and consider entering real estate in one of the areas discussed above that requires less capital to get started. We'll talk more about ways to do this below in the Strategy chapter, because there are strategies for folks with lots of money and strategies for those with little. Another reason why income is so important is that many banks will look at your debt-to-income ratio. The less debt you have and the higher your income, the better this ratio will be, and therefore the more lendable you are.

Fix your credit score

According to ChatGPT, the average American in 2025 has a credit score around 700. Although credit scores range from 300 to 850, anything below 620 for conventional mortgage lenders is considered risky. While you may be able to qualify for a VA or FHA loan below 620 (neither of which can be used for rentals, unless you're house hacking – but always check to make sure), many won't lend to you. And if they do, it will be at a high interest rate. About 15% of Americans have a credit score below 620. Your credit score unlocks all kinds of possibilities if it's good and causes all kinds of problems if it's not. For example, with today's rates, if you had a 585 credit score, you'd be paying more than 9% interest on a mortgage, about 17% on a used car loan, and around 30% on your credit cards. If you had an 800 score, you'd be paying about 6.5% on a mortgage, 6% on a used car loan, and 18% on your credit cards. If you want to pay more to buy the same things others are, then be sure to ruin your credit.

Because debt is such an important tool to grow in real estate, you owe it to yourself to build your credit up to reduce the rates you'll be paying to borrow and increase the odds that you'll be approved for the mortgage. If you have some major dings on your credit, such as bankruptcy, it can take up to seven years for that to fall off. Here's the basic idea, pay your credit card balances in full each month, pay your bills on time, and don't keep opening and canceling credit cards. The credit agencies want to see that your credit lines have been open for a long time. This is also where paying off your debt becomes important. The more debt you have and the less credit you have left (having $18,000 on your credit card with a $20,000 limit, for example), will drive down your score. If you see anything that isn't correct on your credit, report it to the agency that you're using to look at your score. They can work to fix the error, which may improve your credit. Some credit cards and banks allow free access to your credit score. Otherwise, you can use an app like Credit Karma.

Save Money

One of the most important things you can do financially is to build a cash cushion for yourself. If you keep playing too close to the edge, one day you will fall over it. That's what happens when people don't have much in reserves and rely on everything going right to get started in real estate. It never happens that way. We bought a house once that we thought had a relatively dry basement. It turns out we thought wrong. We called our water proofer after we got water in our rental, and he waterproofed it for us. That was an unexpected expense. However, when he was in the basement fixing the water problem, he noticed that one of the walls was slightly bowing in. He said that it's not that uncommon when there's a gravel driveway for the pressure of vehicles to compress the ground, which pushes against the wall. And the next thing you know, the wall is starting to bow. He said that it could be 25 years before it starts to collapse, but unless we wanted to rebuild the wall, it should probably be addressed sooner rather than later. We gave him the go-ahead, and he put steel supports against the wall to keep it from moving any more.

When we went to bed the night before the rainstorm, we had no idea that we were in for thousands of dollars of repairs. This is the life of a landlord. It is absolutely necessary that you have a cash cushion if you don't want to go over the edge financially. Of course, the amount of cushion you have is related to the type of investing you're doing. If you're arbitraging, you might only need $5000 to $6000, because the apartment owner takes care of the big problems. You just may need to replace some furniture if it gets damaged and have a few months' rent on hand, if there's a vacancy. If you've purchased a 20-unit apartment building, you might more than $100,000. Probably the thing that scares me the most about real estate is seeing people jump in without this cushion. It shows poor risk management and questionable judgment, and the whole ship may sink. I think this is one of the biggest areas of risk to your investment dream if this isn't managed well.

Hopefully I've painted the picture of what your financial life needs to look like to go into investing responsibly. While it might be tempting to just jump in and get your dream moving, if you don't have a good financial foundation, then it might all go up in smoke. This may be a frustrating message for some of you who have some work to do in this area. It's no fun to wait. Believe me, I waited almost 18 years. But it is SO MUCH BETTER if you do it right.

8

Creating Alignment with Your 'Partner'

Another necessary precondition is alignment with your 'Partner'. Without this, your investment business and relationship can go down the toilet. So, who is the partner I'm referring to? This is your spouse or significant other. I'll get more into the idea of a business partner later, but if you have a special someone who is going to be on this journey with you, there must be alignment. Things can get ugly otherwise.

I mentioned above that our first real estate investment was a house flip that I purchased at the county sheriff's auction for homes that had been foreclosed from property tax delinquency. We weren't allowed to inspect or even go into the house before the purchase. I went out to the property with Greg to get the lay of the land, but there was so much we couldn't see. I decided to go ahead with the purchase, but Rachel was not on board. As the project ran behind schedule and over budget, she became more agitated about it and pushed for solutions. Some things couldn't be easily solved, like the plumber who we couldn't get to show up to install the boiler. This issue lingered for months and ultimately threatened our completion timeline. There was a lot of anxiety, disagreement, and attempts to control an uncontrollable situation. In other words, it wasn't the happiest time in the Detter household. Ultimately, we flipped the house and made about $30,000, which was more than a third of my income for the year. You may remember from a previous chapter that this was during a difficult time professionally for me, so that money came in really handy. We were at a conference several months after we sold the house, and I heard Rachel talking to others about it. She represented the whole project like it was a failure. I was shocked at this, as, despite challenges, it was very successful for us and a much-needed financial shot in the arm at a difficult time. It was good insight for me, in that Rachel's level of stress regarding this project literally blocked her from seeing it in anything but a negative light.

I took this to heart, because I knew that if our investing was going to be successful, I would need both of us to be on the same page. In fact, this was table stakes for success. The main reason for this is that Rachel is more important to me than my investing. So, if she pulls out, I pull out. I'm sure I'd have to deal with some feelings of resentment, but I have my priorities straight. I learned that there were several things I needed to do well to keep this business partnership thriving with my wife.

Paint a Compelling Picture

One of the most powerful motivators is to find out peoples' WIIFM. This acronym stands for What's In It For Me. If I wanted Rachel to add a bunch of stress to her life with no obvious benefit for her, real estate would be a tough sell. I spent a lot of time talking with her about the sacrifices I had made for the family over the years, going to work, doing a lot of business traveling, etc. This was my chance to capture some of that back. Succeeding in our investments would reduce the time she was acting like a single mother. It would allow us to have a financial foundation to see our boys more often when we are empty nesters. It will allow us to spend more time together. It will provide a source of wealth for our boys once we're gone. It will provide a solid financial foundation for her if something were to happen to me. I also spent a lot of time highlighting the benefits for me, as I hoped she would care about that as well. If real estate investing works like I want it to, it would cut 7-10 years off the length of my career, allowing me to retire (or at least semi-retire) early. That is a big deal for me. She could see how excited I was about it and how motivated I was to get started.

Communicate Frequently

But I didn't just communicate in the beginning. Many times when you're thinking of taking a big step forward in your life, it's not a matter of one or two conversations. Rachel had to 'marinate' in the idea for a while. We would look at houses on Realtor.com together and talk about whether they might be good for rentals. I would walk through the underwriting math with her to show what could be made. Even though I was the impetus behind our rental journey, she needed to have her questions answered and really understand what this new 'adventure' was all about. My job was to help eliminate uncertainty, educate her on what I was learning, and bring her in on conversations with other investors I would meet. In fact, this last one proved valuable, because I think Rachel saw me as a biased source of information. So, I tried to involve her with as many people as possible to hear what they had to say about their investing experience.

Take One Step at a Time

Some people can handle being thrown into the deep end and being forced to sink or swim. That is NOT Rachel's style. She would pull the plug too quickly if I overwhelmed her. So, we started with the flip that she didn't want. I think my mistake here is that I went too fast in the 'picture painting' and 'communicate frequently' stages. This created misalignment when she felt like she was tossed in the deep end of the flip. I wanted to do better the next time. So, I had to ease her into the process. Instead of buying a rental property, we served as a hard money lender to our friend Greg, so we could watch the process of buying, fixing up, refinancing, and renting. The process went a little longer than anticipated, but it went pretty smoothly and turned into a profitable property for Greg.

Lending to someone was a step further into the investing world. Then we began to look for properties ourselves. As described in chapter 1, we got under contract with a multi-unit. Rachel was uncomfortable with this. She thought it was too far away (about 30 minutes), and she didn't want to jump into a multiple tenant situation immediately. The stress she felt about this was worth noting. Fortunately, the owner wouldn't release the profit and loss statements that the bank needed to fund our mortgage, so we backed out. I realized that as much as I wanted to start with a multi-family property, if I was going to have Rachel on board, we needed to start with a single-family home. We bought one, and it went relatively smoothly. The initial plan was to buy one rental property every three years, but I quickly realized that the pace was never going to get me where I wanted to go. Because I felt like the plan needed to change, I went back to the first two steps above, so I could bring her along with me in the accelerated plan. Lo and behold, four months later, we had our second property. As much as she perhaps didn't want to admit it, she was beginning to enjoy parts of what we were doing.

Find What Interests Them

Once I saw what she liked about real estate investing, I could lean in and begin encouraging her in these areas. For instance, Rachel loves connecting with new people. She's very outgoing and enjoys talking. I figured out very quickly that the people side of investing was motivating to her. She wanted to get to know the tenants and build a good working relationship with them. She also likes doing nice things for them, such as creating a welcome basket and occasional gift cards for things like Christmas, although this has gotten harder as our portfolio has grown. The downside to this approach is that Rachel feels more hurt when a tenant takes advantage of our generosity.

Besides the people, both of us have always been interested in looking at houses. We'll be driving home from church on Sunday afternoon, and we'll see an open house sign. Our kids always groan when we hit the brakes and turn around to see the open house. This gives us an excuse to look at houses, even when we're not buying. You might wonder why we look when we're not planning to make a purchase. It's because we're doing market research. We want to see the quality of what's out there and what people are asking for it. It also gives us ideas about what we might like in future purchases. It turns out Rachel REALLY likes looking at houses. She's gone from being very skeptical about growing our real estate business to looking at properties daily on Realtor.com. In the meantime, Rachel's comfort level with real estate began to increase, and she was willing to buy a triplex, then a duplex.

Create Systems to Reduce Stress

Although Rachel has become much more comfortable with our real estate investing, there are times when she wonders why in the world I got her into this. It's in these moments when I start to consider what we could do to make things less stressful for both of us. Ironically, Rachel isn't always open to this. Sometimes she doesn't like to give up control, even though it keeps her too involved. I'm trying to help her understand the benefits of not overcontrolling things. For example, we just recently put our tenants on a platform that reminds them to pay rent on time, so she doesn't have to keep texting reminders to them. She would get tired of doing this each month if it looked like some tenants weren't going to pay on time. Now the system is sending reminders, so she doesn't have to. Currently, I'm trying to talk Rachel into using cleaners between tenants, rather than doing it herself. That's the goal of experienced investors – to run their business largely through systems, rather than doing everything themselves. I'll touch on this a bit more later, but this is not a book about how to make your investing activities more efficient; it's about how to get into investing in the first place.

Let Them Lead the Way

Once she got hooked, I realized it was very important for me not to just take for granted that she would keep pace with me if I took off. When she was ready for a multi-family property, we bought one (then two). The decision to move into mid-term rentals was a 'we' thing, not a 'me' thing. When she was concerned that we were growing too fast, I quit looking online at properties. I didn't want to be tempted. Turns out she kept looking, though. When she said that she thought we needed to pause with buying and pay down some debt, I agreed. I didn't push anything at that point.

I was glad she was on board with the nine units we had. I went back to step two and began to communicate with her a lot about what strategy we were going to use to accelerate debt pay down. We began to talk about possibly doing more mid-term rentals. At one point, she said that she would love to own a nice brick bungalow. Shortly after these discussions, Rachel found a brick bungalow up for auction with a local auction house. I let her decide if we went to see it (she wanted to). I let her decide if we wanted to bid on it (she wanted to). I let her decide how high we went on it (which she did). We ended up winning this really nice house, and we're turning into another mid-term rental. Notice what happened here. Amid our plan of paying down debt, we grew our portfolio with exactly what my wife wanted (a brick bungalow), and I didn't even have to push for it.

Admittedly, I have my doctoral degree in psychology, and I've been trained as a hostage negotiator. Some might say that I have an unfair advantage in getting people to do what I ultimately want them to do. Our friend Greg, who I have mentioned several times so far in this book, said that he thinks it's funny watching me operate at home. He said that I let Rachel think she's in charge, but I'm pulling the strings in the background, getting things to work out like I want them to. I'm not saying I don't have an unfair advantage, but this isn't simple manipulation. It's about understanding how people operate and creating real unity and alignment in the most important relationship in making this real estate journey successful. I couldn't do this as effectively without her.

But what if you're a single person and don't have a special someone to build alignment with. That sure saves you the energy and effort needed to do what I had to do to build alignment, but you might not be doing it alone forever. Even if you're well into your real estate investing journey by the time that partner comes on board, they may not know how to operate comfortably in this new arena at first. They might find it confusing or stressful, which means you'll have to come back to this chapter and reread it. What happens if you have a significant other who just isn't interested or perhaps actively resists it? I can't say for sure that they'll ever come around. However, what I do know is that they won't come around if you're arguing about it. Take it from a psychologist, arguing only cements you in their head as the opponent, and we're emotionally invested in not seeing things from the perspective of our opponent. You're only making it harder for yourself if you argue about it.

Your goal is to have a campaign of your significant other 'marinating' in the idea over a long period of time. Personally, I have said things like, "I would love to own rentals someday" or "I'm going through a stressful patch at work. I just can't help thinking about how much I'd like to cut some years off my working life." I might make statements like, "I'm not trying to talk you into anything right now, but if we ever did pick up a rental property, what do you think you'd want it to look like?" If they accuse you of trying to force something on them, you might just reply, "That's not my goal. I'm just dreaming out loud, and I think that's a healthy thing for couples to do." An approach like this gets the other person used to the idea that you're dreaming of real estate investing. It gets them 'marinating' in the idea. The longer they marinate, the less foreign the idea is. Be patient and use the steps I described above. I would rather be patient and reach my goal than push too hard too fast and lose alignment or lose my partner.

9

Getting Started

So, let's assume that you've decided that real estate investing is, in fact, for you, you've clarified your 'why', you've put your finances in order, and you have alignment with whomever you need to have alignment. There are a few things you need to get a good handle on as you get started down the pathway toward your first investment. Don't skip these things. Getting clarity in these areas will help you be much more successful once you get started.

Reread Chapters 4 and 5

Now is the time to get very clear on the type of real estate investing you're interested in. Look at your finances, reread the pros and cons and determine where your entry point is. If your finances allow you to take down a bigger target, you may want to think about house hacking, buying a single-family home, or a multi-family property.If your finances don't allow that yet, you might want to consider arbitraging or note investing. You don't want to do anything that's misaligned with your ultimate goal, however. For example, if you sink $45,000 into a debt note but you suspect that you'd be ready to house hack in two years, you probably don't want to jump into note investing and tie up that money. You may want to arbitrage for a couple of years to raise funds for the duplex purchase. It's so important that you figure out where you're going to start, so it can take you where you want to go.

Determine How Active or Passive You Want to Be

Here's the rule of thumb on this: the more active you are managing your investments, the less money you're spending on others to do it for you. However, DIYing costs more time, sometimes significantly more time. Ultimately, this may be an economic decision; it was for us. Property management companies often take 10% of your monthly rent and charge one month's rent to find you a tenant. If you do it yourself and charge $1500 per month, your revenue is $18,000 per year on that property. If you use a property manager, they'll charge you $1500 to find the renter and $1800 over the course of the year, meaning it will cost you $3300 to have someone else do the work. Sometimes it's worth it (although there can be issues with property managers) but leveraging 100% of the purchase price of our properties, we just couldn't afford to eat up all our cash flow.

From a time perspective, you may be in a dual-income situation, and both of you working doesn't allow you enough time to manage properties. This is an important decision and shouldn't be made without thinking it through in depth. While we aren't using property managers, we are moving away from DIYing everything. We have a great group of contractors that we use to address issues. It's not as expensive as property management, and it doesn't require the time commitment like we did in the beginning when we were more hands on. It's extremely important to be realistic here and know your limits. Don't be an amateur electrician or plumber – it's just not worth it. It's really irritating every time we have to fix what someone did poorly inside a house.

What Kind of Landlord Will You Be?

My wife's cousin told us about a problem she had with her landlord before moving from Cincinnati to stay in our mid-term rental while between jobs. She rented from this landlord for four years, never caused a problem, took care of the property, and always paid on time. When her job situation became uncertain and might require a move, she asked the landlord if she could go month-to-month, instead of signing another year lease. Her landlord said she could, but she would double her rent. That definitely wasn't going to work. She put in her 30-day notice and asked the landlord if there might be some flexibility at the back end to add a few weeks, if needed, which the landlord agreed to. When she found out she needed that time, she alerted her landlord, who promptly said that she couldn't extend, because she already leased out the property. She had to leave when her lease was up. So much for four years of being a good tenant. Don't let this be you. This is the kind of landlord who is only in it for the money. Remember how I said in the Finding Your Why chapter that money should not be your why? That's because it leads to this type of behavior. Treat people with dignity. You may have to set boundaries. You may have to ask people to leave. You may need to evict someone. That's fine, because you're running a business, but always treat your tenants with dignity.

This isn't the only thing you need to decide – you need to decide how you're going to treat your properties. Some people will do as little maintenance as possible to increase cash flow. One potential tenant we talked to said her landlord wouldn't fix the air conditioning issues and never fixed a leak in the roof that was leaving stains on the ceiling. Don't let this be you! Of course, you need to be smart about the investments you make in your property and operate on a budget, but you shouldn't be a slumlord. One of our former tenants had a young son with cancer. She let us know that a tile had fallen from the bathroom wall and there was mold behind it. It turns out they were peel-and-stick tiles and not real ones (they looked convincing!). We inspected a few more and saw the same issue. As a result, we remodeled the bathroom, to include putting a fan in to keep the mold issue from recurring. We have another property that had very steep steps going upstairs. During our showings to potential renters, we heard that this was an issue for some of them. Then we had a family come through who decided to rent it, but one of them slipped down the top part of the stairs during the viewing. We knew we had to do something about it, so we rebuilt the stairs to make it more visually appealing and safer. We could have gotten away with not doing either of these projects. However, we did it for three reasons. First, we felt like that was the right thing to do for our tenants. Second, it improves the value and rentability of the homes. Third, it reduces our liability risk by fixing issues.

Because we're 'high touch', responsive landlords, it allows us to rent toward the top of the average range in our market.

Consider Real Estate Jobs

If you're not quite ready to pull the trigger yet on buying a property (or investing in general), but you'd like to gain some experience in the industry – or perhaps make some more money – you may want to consider a job in real estate. Some people do this by getting a real estate license, so they can sell houses. Obviously, selling houses will help you learn about the industry, create relationships in the real estate world, and save money when you serve as your own Realtor. These relationships can help you learn about properties before they hit the market, find good inspectors, contractors, etc. Also, if you have your real estate license, you can charge people for acting as their property manager (at least in Ohio). Another option is to work for a property management company. You'll learn about finding tenants, landlord laws, and property maintenance. You could also become an appraiser or inspector of real estate. Again, learning about and developing an expertise in real estate would come in handy when you're doing your own investing. It's a powerful combination to make extra money and learn about real estate at the same time. Plus, this income may allow you to quit your job and focus on something you like more.

Draw From the Cash Flow or Reinvest

This is a big decision. The dream for many investors is to live off the cash flow and not need their regular job. But that's often not where investors need to start. Let's say you're cash flowing $30,000 from your properties. You could draw this from the business and use it to supplement your income. Maybe you'll put this in the stock market and pad your IRA. Maybe you'll use it to fund the vacations you've always wanted and pay for some nicer cars. If you do this, then you're using real estate to help you live the lifestyle you want. While that's perfectly fine and what many people dream of, that's not my goal. I want to reinvest that $30,000 back into the business. If one of my mortgages is $90,000, then I'll be able to pay that off in less than three years (because the tenants are also helping pay it down). That may free up $850 per month ($10,200 per year) that I can roll into paying off more debt. The next year, I'll have $40,200 to put toward properties. Maybe I have another unit with a $120,000 mortgage. I'll be able to pay this off in less than three years and add another $12,000 to my cash flow. Now, I've got $52,000, and I'll pay off my $150,000 mortgage on another property in less than three years. Maybe that frees up $14,000 in cash flow, and now I'm looking at $66,000 per year in cash flow. Less than nine years of reinvesting my cash flow into the business, and I'm massively closer to retiring early than I would be if I was using the money to supplement my lifestyle. Another way to reinvest your money is to build up some savings for a down payment on your next property. You're growing your cash flow that way too. I'm not saying one is better than the other, but you need to figure out which one matches your goals – and stick to it.

Keep Buying or Pay Down Debt

This is another important decision to make, but it doesn't need to be a one-time decision. We 'sprinted' for three years getting to 11 units, then selling two, then picking up another one, as well as flipping a house.Rachel had decided she wanted to focus on debt pay-down now. Then she decided she wanted to pick up that 10th unit (the brick bungalow). Now she's back to wanting to pay down debt. Not everyone likes to pay down debt. Some are more aggressive investors and want to grow their portfolio as big as they can. We don't want to overextend ourselves, from a debt position, and we have a limited amount of money to invest. In addition, we don't envision our real estate journey will take us to owning 100 doors. So, paying our properties down is a great way to increase cash flow and get me closer to not relying on my salary to live comfortably. Again, this decision is important, but you may change your stance on this as your strategy changes.

How Long Will You Work Your Job?

Some people want to quit their job as soon as they start investing in real estate. This is very risky, as cash flow is hard to come by at first. Depending on how much you need to invest in the properties, it may be several years before you turn your first profit. Sometimes people will continue to work their jobs but figure out the minimum amount of money they would need to live on to quit. Once they hit that, they walk away. Again, this is a risky strategy, as you're not leaving much cushion in your personal life, and you're not able to use your profits to support the business – like buying a new furnace when it goes out. So, often the smart thing to do is plan on continuing in your job for a good while. This does a few things. First, it allows you to reinvest all your profits into the business, because you don't need them to support your personal finances. Second, you can take from the excess (if you have any) on the personal side and throw it into the business to help achieve your growth or debt pay-down objectives faster. Third, it's important to note that banks like income from a regular job. It makes it easier for them to loan to you. Don't make it harder than you need to on yourself to grow your portfolio.

Know Your Landlord Laws

It's extremely important that you know the laws that govern property ownership when it comes to rentals. You can get yourself into a lot of trouble if you don't know or ignore these laws. There are lots of relevant statutes that govern being a landlord, but perhaps the most important to pay attention to are the ones that determine whether the state is a tenant-friendly or landlord-friendly state. I live in Ohio, which tends to be a landlord-friendly state. I used to live in California, which is a notoriously tenant-friendly state. They make it hard to raise rent in rent-controlled areas. Also, you're not necessarily allowed to just not renew someone's lease. You must be able to prove that they have violated the lease in one way or another. The longer a tenant has been in place, the longer the lease termination needs to be. So, if they've been renting from you for more than a year, you have to give them at least 60 days' notice. What I'm about to write isn't to scare you off from investing in tenant-friendly states, but you need to be aware of the laws and risks. These are real stories (fortunately not mine).

In 2020, a couple bought their dream home in Riverside, California. This occurred during the pandemic, and once they closed on the house, the former owner refused to leave. Even though he wasn't a renting tenant, he was protected from getting kicked out, due to the non-eviction laws that were being put in place. This left the couple with no choice but to engage in a lengthy legal battle that took 15 months before they were finally able to gain possession of their house.

Another California family left for an extended vacation and came back to find that squatters had been living in their house for weeks. Apparently, California doesn't consider this breaking and entering? They were told by police that this was a civil matter, not a criminal one. This meant that the homeowners needed to treat it like an eviction, which meant the squatters were legally allowed to stay in the house until the eviction process was complete. If you don't think that's insane enough, if that family had forced the squatters out and changed the locks to prevent them from coming back in, the squatters could sue them. You heard me correctly – depending on how long the squatters have been in place, they have tenant law protection, even though it's not their house, they have no lease with you, and you never granted them permission to be there. It's not just California where this can happen. A similar case happened in Colorado.

Admittedly, these examples weren't rental situations, but it shows which way these states lean. Try this on for size as further evidence of the challenges landlords can get themselves into in these tenant-friendly states: in California, if you want to sell your rental property, you're not allowed to end the tenant's occupancy for the sale. This can be a problem, as it might limit who is interested in the property, and you might not be able to maximize its value. Even if you do legally end the lease (like if you or a family member are going to occupy the property or if you're going to remove it from the rental market), you may have to help pay relocation costs for the tenant. That's why some landlords simply do a 'cash for keys' arrangement, where they pay the tenant to voluntarily leave. Additionally, if you have a tenant who allows someone to live with them, even without your knowledge, for 30 days or more, California treats them like a tenant, and you have to go through the eviction process with them. Unfortunately, this has created a niche cottage industry in California, where people will go from property to property as squatters or have unauthorized people move in with them simply to put themselves in a position where they can force a cash for keys negotiation. According to ChatGPT, these types of buyouts have cost landlords in LA a total of $142 million from 2019 to March 2025, with some people asking as much as $25,000 to leave.

That sounds a bit overwhelming to me. Where I live and invest (Ohio), it's more of a landlord-friendly state. I can choose not to extend a lease, even if they haven't violated the lease, as long as I give proper notice and I'm not participating in discriminatory practices. So, I can ask a tenant to leave if I feel like I'll get more value from the home sale by doing so. I hear this a lot from potential tenants – I'll ask why they're looking, and they'll say they were given 30-days' notice, because the landlord is selling the property. Even in Ohio, you run into trouble getting rid of unauthorized people who have been in your property for more than 30 days, but the Ohio eviction process is much less problematic than California. In addition, if it's less than 30 days, the police will intervene, due to criminal trespassing. So, do your research to make sure you understand now to navigate tenant law.

One last point on knowing the law – it's not just the states you need to educate yourself on. There are Federal statues in place to protect tenants from discrimination. It's important to know what these laws are, because you can be sued. There are courses online that can help educate you on these laws. I took one of these through a platform called TurboTenant, so you may want to check out this or similar courses, because it's not all common sense. For example, smoking is considered a disability. So, if you advertise your property by saying, "non-smokers only," you would be considered discriminating against someone with a disability. There's a way around that, however, by advertising "no smoking on the property." Some of these regulations can be head scratchers sometimes, so it's better to over-educate yourself than step in something that you didn't intend.

Get Very Clear on Your Buy Box

I teased the idea of a Buy Box earlier, and we'll discuss it in depth here. Your Buy Box is the clearly defined criteria of what you're looking for in a property. If it's outside that Buy Box, then you probably shouldn't buy it. If it's in your Buy Box, then you should consider researching the property, underwriting it, and perhaps putting in an offer.Your Buy Box is what guides your purchasing-related activity, so it's super important to have a lot of clarity here. What my Buy Box is shouldn't necessarily dictate yours, due to different economic realities between us, different geographic locations, the strength of the housing market, etc. That being said, I will walk you through what our Buy Box is and why we landed on those things. While we might someday purchase outside of these criteria (we did once and ended up selling it, which I'll talk through in this section), we're sticking with our plan now, because it's working for us. Here's our Buy Box:

- **In Perry Township** – This is the township in which we live. Our kids go to the schools here. We're part of the community, and we know it well. We know what the regulations are, who to talk to about zoning or code issues, and we know the market. This puts us in a strong position to be effective landlords here.In addition, many people who are displaced from their homes for fire and flood issues want to stay in the same school district while the house is being repaired. This puts us in a great position to meet the needs of families in Perry Township. The other big benefit is that all our properties are within a seven-minute drive of us (give or take). We love that. I was on a call with another investor who was driving down to Maryland from Pennsylvania to deal with a tenant issue.That's not what I'd want to do.

- **Two to four-bedroom units** – This is our Buy Box specifically for our long-term rentals. Our goal was to accommodate families and be able to charge a higher level of rent. Our Buy Box is different for multi-family, as you're looking mostly at two-bedroom units. Our Buy Box with mid-term rentals is 1-3 bedroom. This is because some traveling medical professionals or temporary corporate workers often come alone. So, there's a robust mid-term rental market for 1-bedroom or studio properties. The 2–3-bedroom properties will accommodate most families or couples who need mid-term accommodation. If you go four bedrooms or higher, you are potentially looking at higher vacancy with mid-term rentals, which we don't want.

- **Less than $7500 in short-term renovations** – While we may invest more money in a property over time, we don't want to invest much up front. That's because part of our model is to get tenants in and paying quickly. We don't want carrying costs of a 3-month renovation before we start collecting rent.Our most recent purchase will need waterproofing done in the basement, but not before tenants come in. We're looking for cosmetic fixes, like repainting, reflooring, and minor updating. As such, most would consider the houses we buy as nearly move-in ready. We are willing to flex on this for our mid-term rentals, as we want to make the property as nice as possible and competitive with others in the area. We also have the expense of furnishing the whole house, which slows down the occupancy process.

- **Houses we would have lived in at one point in our lives** – We want to provide a high-quality renting experience for our tenants. We've seen other rental properties owned by various landlords, and sometimes we walk away with an 'icky' feeling. The properties are not always well taken care of, look shabbily updated, and are properties that we would never want to own. We want our properties to represent our brand well. If we don't have a feeling as we walk through a property that we would have lived in it at some point in our lives, we won't buy it, period.

- **No nasty basements** – I'm going to say something profound here: nasty basements are nasty. It's too much work to fix them up, and even when you do, it's like putting lipstick on a pig. We don't like nasty basements, and tenants don't like nasty basements. No nasty basements.

- **About 10% below market value** – This is a big part of our Buy Box and a major reason why our loan-to-value ratio is so favorable, even though we've financed 100% of the purchase price of our properties. We don't allow ourselves to get wrapped up in bidding wars and spend more money than we want to. I've heard it said (and I believe it) that your money is made on the property at the purchase. We really want to buy well. I think there's only one property (our duplex) that we bought at market value. Shortly before writing this, our banker wrote to say that our appraisal came back (part of the bank's due diligence process before funding our loan) on our most recent acquisition. This is his direct quote in the email, "I do not know how you do it, but you always get good properties below value – and no one else does. Congrats!" That's music to my ears. We perhaps could have grown faster if we weren't as picky here, but we want to grow well, not just fast.

A couple of additional points are worth noting. First, you can have different Buy Boxes for different types of investments. We're willing to invest more up-front money in a mid-term and take longer to get it ready before a tenant. We're willing to invest in more bedrooms for the long-term rentals. Your Buy Box might change over time. We changed our Buy Box to pick up a commercial duplex (zoned commercial first floor with a grandfathered residential upstairs apartment). We got a good deal on the property but decided we didn't want to dabble in the commercial space. We eventually sold the property and made a profit on it. That was a spur of the moment Buy Box shift, and, though it worked out for us, deflected us slightly for a while from our goals, with the money tied up in the property. As a result, we decided we need to keep operating within our original Buy Box. My goal is to eventually try varying our Buy Box with location – I'd love to own a vacation property that we mid-term rent while we're not there. I'll talk more about buying out-of-town properties in chapter 13.

One final point before ending this chapter on getting started. I remember what it was like to be on the outside looking in, wondering if I'd ever be able to make that leap. I'd read books about super successful investors and listen to podcasts with guests who had 'made It' and accomplished their real estate and lifestyle goals. It can be very tempting to compare yourself against them, and it can be very discouraging. There is something in psychology called Social Comparison Theory. This says that we tend to compare ourselves against others, but we do it consistently in one direction – up. We don't compare ourselves against poor people and feel good about ourselves for being middle-class. We compare ourselves against wealthy people and feel like a failure. We don't compare ourselves against less attractive people and congratulate ourselves for being above average. We compare ourselves against beautiful people and feel like we're not attractive.

Sometimes I use the example of pulling up to a stoplight in the middle of three lanes. To the left is a 1984, dull, metallic gray Ford Tempo with a bumper pushed four inches to the side, no antennae, a blower that doesn't blow out hot or cold air (it just seeps out at you), and it dies when it comes to a full stop. If that description sounded very specific, it's because that's what I drove for a year in graduate school, and Rachel refused to be seen in it. In the other lane is a brand new, beautiful top of the line Lexus (I've always wanted one). I'm much more likely to look at the driver in the Lexus and wonder what he or she is doing financially to afford that car than I am to look at the Tempo and be glad that's not what I'm driving.

In your real estate journey, you're more likely to feel like you're not doing it right if your operations aren't as sophisticated as someone else's or if they're growing faster than you, etc. I heard a great quote one time that I may be slightly paraphrasing, but it went like this, "Don't ever compare your journey to someone else's destination." The person on the podcast might have 'made it' in real estate, but they had their journey as well, and that's what prepared them for success. Without the journey, there is no destination.

10

Buying Your First Property

When you're finally prepared to buy your first property, it's a very exciting time. It's fun to look at the available real estate on the market and dream about what you could do with them. However, you still have a lot of work in front of you. Let's cover some steps that you'll need to take while you're working on making your first purchase.

Have Patience

While real estate is a lot of fun and can be very rewarding, there are times when it can be immensely frustrating and requires a lot of patience. Depending on where you live, if the market is heating up, you may find that you're competing with a lot of other homebuyers and/or investors, and you just can't seem to win. There are other times when the market is stabilizing but the interest rates are up, and you're tempted to wait until rates come down. But you have no idea when that will be. Maybe you're looking for a multi-unit property, but there doesn't seem to be any good ones available.

Trust me, it's better to be patient and get the right property than to rush in and end up with buyer's remorse. Remember the adage I mentioned above – your money is made at the purchase. Buying right is what helps you make money.Imagine that you get impatient, are sick of losing out to others who bid higher, and you decide to go all-in on a property. Great, you won. But now you have no margin on the rental, and you're doing a whole bunch of work managing the property for no profit. It's not really moving you forward financially, and now all your money is tied up.It is much better to be patient.

Don't Wait For Opportunities, Create Them

This might sound like it contradicts what I just said about being patient, but it doesn't. The section above was about not compromising out of impatience. This section is about not sitting around doing nothing when traditional routes to property ownership aren't cooperating. Not everyone starts with owning as the first step in real estate investment. If purchasing seems beyond your reach, consider co-hosting or arbitrage. Just because it isn't your ideal doesn't mean it can't work for you.

Another major way to create opportunity is to network. I've heard several successful people in real estate say, "Your network is your net worth." You can't do this alone. We own a triplex, because I did some networking at my local chamber of commerce. We own our first mid-term rental, because my wife got to know one of our neighbors. We flipped a house, because we got to know another neighbor. This second neighbor has also promised us first dibs on his house when he moves out or passes away. We're not waiting for opportunities to come to us. We're finding them.

Talk about your desire to get into real estate to as many people as possible. Ask people you know (even by posting on social media) if anyone is considering selling their property. If you can broker an off-market deal, you can negotiate lower prices, because you're saving the seller on Realtor fees. Although it didn't work out, Rachel and I saw a derelict property in a beautiful location, found out who owned it through the county auditor website, and stopped by when we saw he was home. Turns out he was (very) slowly fixing it up for his son, so he wasn't interested in selling. But you have to be willing to put yourself out there like this to find opportunities.

Location

Location, location, location. You've heard the old real estate adage. It may sound overused, but it's extremely true. Location can determine how much market equity your property enjoys, and it's not just LA versus Canton,

OH. It's choosing the nice parts of Canton versus the down-and-out parts of Canton. You can buy a 4-bedroom single-family home in less attractive parts of Canton for $50,000. If no improvements are made to the property, you'd still be able to buy that property for around $50,000 several years from now. We have chosen our property locations carefully, and you may remember that one of our properties appraised for $40,000 more than we bought it for only nine months later. Location also determines to a large degree what you can charge for rent. Location also influences, although not guarantees, how tenants will treat the property. If a renter moves into a nice neighborhood with pride of ownership, it's harder for them to let it look run down without feeling embarrassed about it.

It's important to introduce the idea of neighborhood grades here. 'A' class neighborhoods are high-end, new, and close to great amenities. There tends to be low crime here and houses are largely owner-occupied. These properties are expensive to buy and are largely about appreciation, rather than cash flow. 'B' class neighborhoods are middle class and where a lot of investors aspire to own. While not affluent, these neighborhoods tend to be safe and have good schools. The houses are also a bit older and will have more upkeep, in general. These neighborhoods tend to mix appreciation and cash flow well. You're also getting a more even mix of renters and homeowners.

'C' class neighborhoods are older homes in varying condition. The schools and amenities tend to be less desirable. Some of these neighborhoods feel safer than others. Renters tend to predominate more than homeowners, which means there's more occupancy turnover. Because the houses are older, there tends to be more maintenance and sometimes significant renovation to update them. You may find that tenants are at more risk of missing rent payments and/or taking worse care of the property. While the rents are lower here, so is the cost of the property, so the benefit of these houses starts to lean more toward cash flow than appreciation. 'D' class neighborhoods are in distressed and rough areas of town. The houses are typically cheap and dilapidated. Crime is high and amenities are poor. You'll find few homeowners here, as most are renters. Prepare yourself for more evictions and vandalism in these neighborhoods, which may also result in longer periods of vacancy. This is more where the traditional 'slumlord' landlords tend to operate. Because properties cost so little, you're looking at little to no appreciation, so you're looking at cash flow being the primary benefit.

In case you're wondering why certain neighborhoods vary between cash flow and appreciation, here's the logic behind it. Property values tend to vary more widely than rents do. Using Canton, OH as a for-instance, I could buy a $300,000 house and charge $2500 in rent in an 'A' class neighborhood. This fails the 1% rule of investing, which says that you'd ideally like to get 1% of the property cost in monthly rent ($3000 in this case). But I'm not getting $3000. I could buy a $150,000 house and get $1500 per month in a 'B' class neighborhood. Now I'm hitting the 1% rule. Or I could buy an $80,000 house in a 'C' class neighborhood and charge $950 in rent. Now I'm doing better than the 1% rule.

So, home prices rise faster than rent in high-end neighborhoods, while home prices are lower relative to rent in low-end neighborhoods. This means it's harder to generate cash flow in more expensive properties and easier in less expensive ones. This gets extreme in very expensive areas. If you live in LA or New York, you may be losing money each month in rent but seeing a lot of appreciation. The point here is that you can make it work no matter where you buy (A, B, C, or D-class neighborhoods), but it has to be aligned with your strategy, and you must know what you're doing with your strategy. In other words, don't buy a 'D' class property if you don't want a lot of fix-up every time a tenant leaves and a lot of tenant-based headaches. Also, don't buy an 'A' class property and expect to be swimming in cash from the profits you're making each month.

Tolerance for Doing Management/Maintenance

This one ties in very closely with the types of neighborhoods I just described above. I said that you have to be strategic with what you choose. This, in part, should be decided based on your tolerance for DIY management and property maintenance. If you buy in a 'D' class neighborhood, I don't think a property manager will want to touch it. If they're getting 10% of your $800 rent each month but dealing with a lot of vandalism, property problems, and evictions, it just won't be worth it for them. Also, the properties tend to be like older cars, where even minor accidents can cause them to be totaled by the insurance companies. That's because the cost of fixing them can be more than the value of the car itself. In some of these 'D' class neighborhoods, the properties just aren't worth paying a lot of money to contractors to fix up, because you'll never recover the cost in appreciation. So, plan on being very handy if you buy in these neighborhoods.

We do our own property management, but we don't like to DIY maintenance. So, we tend to buy in 'B' class neighborhoods. While these houses do require some maintenance, they generally tend to be in good shape and relatively well cared for. This limits the maintenance costs for us. Since our tenants tend to be gainfully employed and have good credit, we're able to manage our properties without too many problems. We did need to evict one tenant, and another tenant quit paying us, all while misleading us about why they weren't paying (and promising to pay). We didn't renew their lease, which forced them to leave, and they skipped town after stealing $10,000 from a relative. Needless to say, I don't think we'll be getting our rent from them. We currently have a great group of tenants and are thankful for them – it sure does make our lives easier.

Financing

Obviously, the dream for any investor would be to self-finance – in other words, paying cash. Not many can do this, but it does provide some advantages. Paying cash means closing faster, and sellers like that. If you've ever seen the Truth in Lending disclosures when you close on a house you're financing, you'll end up paying twice the purchase price of the house when you factor in interest, if you pay over the course of a 30-year mortgage. It's a massive expense. So, paying cash saves you massive amounts of money over the long run.

The main drawback of paying cash is that it's a slow way to grow (unless you're independently wealthy). Imagine that it took you 15 years to save the $200,000 needed to pay cash, and you finally pull the trigger. Congratulations! Now you have to do it all over again just to get your second house. Of course, you'll be able to do it faster, now that you have rent coming from your first property. That's not the way we wanted to do it, however. We wanted to grow faster, so we used leverage. Now we own 10 rental units in three years. If you're tracking the risk-reward balance with financing, you grow faster with debt, but it kills your cash flow relative to paying cash. If you're like most people, you'll have to use financing, and I think that's generally a good idea if you want to grow like we did. You'll learn more about financing options in the next chapter.

Risk

There is a lot of risk in real estate, so much so that I have a whole chapter just on how to de-risk your investments. Here, I'll just talk about some common risks you should pay attention to when you're looking to buy your first property.

- **Being too impatient** – I mentioned this above, but it's worth repeating here. Don't let impatience lead you to buy a property that's not going to be good for you.

- **Not having your finances in order** – I also mentioned this above, but it bears repeating. Probably the riskiest thing you could do is not having enough financial cushion to deal with challenges that crop up, because they will.

- **Not doing your due diligence** – Let's say that you don't want to own your own properties, and you decide to invest in a syndication opportunity. Make sure you do your research. You don't want to be scammed. Even with reputable opportunities, you need to understand the risks and rewards, what the expected earnings are, and how long before you'll realize a significant return on your money.

- **Tying up your money** – Be strategic about what you put your money into, because you might not like how long your money is tied up. It might limit your growth options. For example, you can hop into syndications through things called Real Estate Investment Trusts (REITs). You can do something similar by investing with the Fundrise platform, but your money is often tied up for five years or more before you can get it back without penalty. Whatever you do, do it with your eyes wide open.

- **Not contracting well** – You don't likely have to worry about this with banks and Realtors, because the contracting process is so formal and regulated. However, if you buy a property and will have tenants, you need to make sure you have your bases covered. You can introduce a lot of risk if you don't know what your state laws allow in leases or if you leave out important clauses that would protect you. Even if you don't buy a property and decide to co-host or arbitrage, you will be entering into an agreement with the property owner. Make sure they don't leave you high and dry by not doing the work that will keep the property attractive for the tenants you'd like to put in it. All these things need to be in the contract.

Underwriting

We'll cover this in more depth in chapter 15, but underwriting is essentially the process of running the numbers to ensure that the property will perform financially like you need it to. This involves doing research into what you could reasonably purchase a house for, what you could likely get in rent, what type of vacancy percentage you're looking at, etc. The idea here is to know your market and to do the calculations to determine whether each property is likely to be successful for you. It's great practice to underwrite properties you're not even that interested in buying. Get good at this process, and it will serve you well in making your first investment a good one.

I would also strongly recommend being conservative in your underwriting. Here's what I mean: Let's say you run across a $200,000 house that could ultimately sell for anywhere between $180,000 and $215,000, depending on how many people end up being interested in it. You think it could rent for anywhere between $1750 and $1950.Some people are overly optimistic and run their numbers on a $185,000 purchase price and $1950 in rent. That is decision-making on best case scenarios, which I don't think is wise. It's much better to make sure it still works if you buy it for $215,000 and rent it for $1750. If it works in the worst-case scenario, then everything better than that is gravy for you.

To Pet or Not to Pet

This is a major decision you'll need to think about before getting your first property. While it can be lucrative to be pet-friendly, it also creates its share of issues. Because dogs and cats are the most popular pets, I'm speaking more about them than things that live in terrariums or aquariums. Here are a few drawbacks to allowing pets:

- **Wear and tear** – Pets destroy things. Dogs chew them up, and cats scratch them up. I can always tell when people have cats, because the carpet on the stairs is shredded. Cats like to stretch on the steps and will claw the carpet in the process. If you furnish a unit, it's your furniture that the pets are destroying, not the tenants', so it can cost you more money over time to rent to tenants with pets.

- **Smell** – Oh, the smell of pets. The tenants get nose-blind to the odors over time, so it doesn't bother them as much. Good friends moved into a rental one time, and it smelled like dog. They complained about the odor to the landlord, who had the carpets cleaned. It went from smelling like dog to smelling like wet dog – it only made it worse. This is why we tend to use luxury vinyl planking (also known as LVP) in our properties and not carpet. We also use washable area rugs to help with this. And if you've ever smelled cat urine in a house, it's a very distinct odor...

- **Noise issues** – Cats aren't so much of an issue here, but dogs can cause problems. This is more of a risk in multi-unit situations, where a dog won't stop barking, and there's only a wall separating rental units. This can be a problem even in a single-family home if a particularly loud and barky dog is disturbing neighbors. That's why we have a noise clause in our lease with pets.

- **Yard mess** – This is worse with bigger dogs, but they will leave unpleasant land mines in the yard. If you are going to mow the lawn, you won't want these around to step in and get smashed in the mower wheels. If you pay someone to mow, they're not going to like it either. Plus, it's just gross having turds all over the lawn. You're avoiding this largely with cats, because of kitty litter. Lastly, dogs tend to find their favorite spots to pee, which can kill the grass and plants over time.

- **Aggression** – Dogs can be aggressive. In fact, one of the biggest causes of homeowners' insurance payouts is dog bites. The news has stories of aggressive dogs all the time, and you want to make sure you don't get into trouble as a landlord because you didn't do your due diligence on the pets coming into your property. Many will deny that certain breeds are more aggressive than others (they are often coincidentally the people who own those breeds), but the truth is certain breeds *are* more aggressive than others. Statistics show that Pit Bulls account for about 23% of all bites, about 50% of dog-related maulings, and 67% of fatal attacks. Rottweilers, German Shepherds, and Mastiffs add about 20% to that fatality total. So, you have four dog breeds that account for almost 90% of the fatal attacks. Given that there are between 200 and 400 recognized breeds, and countless mixed breeds, this is a massive overrepresentation of aggressiveness in these four breeds.

The clincher for many who allow pets, but not certain breeds of dog, is that many homeowners insurance policies won't pay out in a liability claim if you've allowed certain breeds in your properties. That leaves you exposed. The other thing to consider is that it's not just people being attacked that you should be worried about. Dogs also attack other dogs, which can cause its own share of problems. It's not just biting that's the issue either. Dogs will often chase people, even if they don't bite.

Combine being chased with the dog barking aggressively, and that can be a scary experience for someone. I won't just pick on dogs, as cats can be aggressive too; they just tend to cause less damage when they are.

So, you have some thinking to do about pets. We had decided that it's worth the issues to allow pets in our properties. There are several reasons for this:

- **It reduces your turnover**. Not all landlords allow pets, so when tenants find one who does allow their furry friends, they tend to stay longer. Less turnover reduces between-tenant costs and ensures a reliable stream of income.

- **Pets allow you to collect more money**. We're currently collecting $600 per month extra in rent from tenants with pets. That's because we charge $50 per month per pet. We also charge a one-time $300 non-refundable pet fee when someone signs a lease with us.This helps offset the issues described above.

- **It reduces your vacancy**. Allowing pets opens up a much larger pool of people who can occupy your property. This is particularly important if you're doing mid-term rentals. A lot of vacancy can kill your profits, and if people have a house fire, they're going to be bringing their pets with them.

Because of this, we've decided to allow pets. We just make sure our lease is very clear about pet-related expectations.

One final note on pets, and it's a frustrating one for me – emotional support animals. A quick point of important information. By law, you aren't allowed to reject an applicant because of emotional support animals, even if you don't allow pets. You can't charge them for pets, and you can't charge a one-time pet fee. You can reject an applicant for other reasons if they have one of these animals, but you can't reject them for the animal. Unfortunately, there's a lot of fraud involved with 'emotional support animals'. As a psychologist, I've had an insider's view of this problem. Ultimately, for a pet to be considered an emotional support animal, they have to be certified as such.

Many people with emotional support animals have no need of them, and many certifiers will certify any animal simply because you're paying them to do it. There literally have been therapy clients of mine who I would never approve for an emotional support animal (due to lack of any emotional need), who have reported that they've gotten one and found a certifier with a reputation for certifying everyone. As a result, there are a lot of renters who will have their animals certified just to avoid having to pay extra for them. It's fraud and a big scam in many cases, but how are you going to challenge them and prove that they don't need an emotional support animal? Now, as a landlord, you are allowed to make them show the certification. However, I know of landlords who have requested this, and the tenant or applicant will say that it's against the law to ask for that. This is most certainly not true, and you can and should ask for the appropriate paperwork. Just be aware of the laws around this, as you don't want to get yourself in trouble inadvertently.

Inspections and Home Warranties

Some people swear by inspections, while others see it as an unnecessary expense. We started off getting inspections when we purchased our personal homes, just to make sure we weren't getting ourselves into a problem. When we bought our first rental, it was during that weird time during the COVID pandemic, when house prices were skyrocketing, and buyers could get themselves into ridiculous bidding wars. We were working with a seasoned Realtor (Greg), who was also experienced investing in real estate. So, we decided to make ourselves more competitive with the seller, and we waived the inspection. Since then, we've gotten relatively experienced spotting problems, and we've only had an inspection on a potential property once. It was an older duplex, and I noticed some things that sent up some yellow flags. We got under contract on the property, but we didn't waive the inspection. Turns out it was a good decision. There were enough problems with the property that we backed out. Sure, we would have uncovered things in other properties prior to the purchase if we had inspections done, but none of them would have kept us from buying the property.

Sometimes getting an inspection can help you with the negotiations process, as uncovered problems can help you drive the price down. However, this won't work as well when there's a lot of competition for the property or when the price is already listed under market value. Because we buy our properties under market value in the first place, these inspections won't help us much.

To sum this up, I recommend getting an inspection if you're relatively new to buying real estate. If you're experienced and have a good financial cushion to cover unexpected fixes in the property, you can get away without them. With the money we save by not doing an inspection, we have our plumber and electrician come in after the purchase, and we put that money toward what needs to be addressed. One way to protect yourself if you skip the inspection is a home warranty. This will cover different components of the home if they go out, like an HVAC system. You need to do your research on home warranty companies, because they're not all created equal. Sometimes you have a fight on your hand getting them to pay out. You can also try to negotiate with the seller to include home warranty coverage for a year. We've done this before, but we don't pay for home warranty coverage on our properties on our own.

Inheriting Renters

One final point of discussion in this chapter – it's often the case that when you buy rental properties, you're inheriting the renters. While it's nice to buy a property that will generate rent immediately, I prefer buying a property that is vacant. There are a couple of reasons why. First, you have no idea what you're getting. You didn't vet the tenants, so you don't know much about them. Sometimes the landlord hasn't been in the property for 20 years, because the tenant has been there that long. When you visit these properties, it's clear that nothing has been updated during that time, and you've got some renovations on your hands when the tenant moves out. Second, it's harder to evaluate the health of the property. When it's vacant, you can see more defects. When there's a tenant, their stuff blocks your view of many of the problems. Third, and this a huge issue for us, landlords with long-term tenants are TERRIBLE at keeping up with market rent.

We looked at a triplex one time where we would be inheriting three tenants who were paying about half the market rent. That gives you a difficult choice. You can either pop rent up to what the market will bear but put your tenants in a bad position financially, or you can take one for the team and make a lot less on the property, so you don't feel like a jerk to the people you inherited. We've decided that it's not our ethic to buy a property and double the rents. We walked away from that opportunity. As a quick aside, you legally must abide by the leases you inherit. If you inherit month-to-month leases, then you can give them a 30-day notice of rent increase once the property is yours (at least in Ohio). However, some sellers recognize that they're putting their tenants at real risk by selling. They'll help them (and really hurt the buyer) by signing their them to another year-long lease at their low rent just before selling. As the buyer, you must abide by the agreement until the year lease is over. If you run into that situation in a property you really want, I would use that to negotiate a lower price, if possible.

There's a lot in this chapter to consider before buying, but once you've done it a time or two, it starts to feel like driving. Go back to your 16-year-old self and how stressful everything was when you were behind the wheel – so much to pay attention to and so much pressure. Then a year later, you're totally relaxed and it's no big deal. That's the way it is with real estate, so don't let this chapter discourage you at all.Use it to help you determine how you want to operate.

11

Financing Your Property

We touched on financing above, but it's worth doing a deeper dive here, because of the complexity of the topic. Let's talk about your options.

Paying Cash

Not many can do this, at least until you're an extremely advanced investor, but many don't like the cash option if they can avoid it, due to the tax advantages of having a mortgage. As I mentioned above, cash makes you a more competitive buyer, which is a big advantage in hotter markets. You're more competitive, largely for two reasons: 1) you can close faster, because you don't need to go through all the hoops with a mortgage and 2) you're viewed as less risky, because you can't back out of the sale from the financing falling through. Paying cash also really helps increase your cash flow. Keep in mind that paying cash doesn't mean your monthly cost of ownership is zero. You'll have insurance and property tax. You'll also have maintenance and capital expenditures (new HVAC, new roof, etc.). However, paying cash in my area would increase my cash flow by $600–800 per month on my properties. But remember, paying cash slows down your growth, because your money is tied up in the property. So, if you want to finance, let's look at some options.

Residential (Conventional) Mortgage

Most people think about residential mortgages as the ones you put on your own personal house, and that's true. This *is* how most people finance their own homes, but that's not the only way this option can be used. Let's look at some relevant information on using this type of mortgage to finance rentals.

- **Number of units in a property** – Residential mortgages are for properties that have between one and four units. So, this type of financing can be used for single-family homes, duplexes, triplexes, and quadplexes.

- **Underwriting criteria** – Banks will look at your personal income, credit score, and debt-to-income ratio (DTI) before deciding on your loan. Most people know what personal income and credit score is, but not everyone is clear on what DTI is. Basically, banks want to know that you're making a lot more than what you owe on things. You may know someone who makes a lot of money, but they have loads of debt. Banks don't like that. They typically like to see that your housing costs are no more than 28% of your gross monthly income and all debt is no more than 36% of your gross monthly income. Also, if you're a contractor (1099 tax status) or self-employed, banks like to see at least two years of tax returns before financing a loan.

- **Down payment** – This is where a residential mortgage is very advantageous.You can get into a house with as low as 0% down with a VA or USDA loan and as low as 3.5% with an FDA loan. That can make it much more affordable to get into a property. However, keep in mind that the lower the down payment, the higher the monthly mortgage costs.The higher the mortgage, the lower the cash flow. So, low down payment isn't always helpful if your goal is cash flow. Outside of these programs, banks will allow people with good credit, solid DTI, and good income to put as low as 5% down. However, if you put less than 20% down, you'll have to pay private mortgage insurance (known as PMI) each month, which is you paying for insurance that protects the bank against you defaulting on your loan.Once you get to 20% paid down (through the monthly payments), you can often petition the bank to drop this.

Before we move on, what are VA, FDA, and USDA loans? VA loans are for those who are Active Duty in the military and military Veterans. So, if this isn't you, it is not an option. If it is you, keep in mind that VA loans can't be used on primary rental properties. However, if it's a multi-unit property (remember, it's got to be 4 units or less) and you plan to live in it for at least the first year, you can use a VA loan. FDA loans are for people who wouldn't necessarily be able to qualify for a conventional loan, due to low savings or limited credit (often with first time homebuyers). Like the VA loans, you can't use it to buy a rental, unless it's a multi-unit property and you plan on living in it for at least the first year. USDA loans focus on homebuyers in rural areas and can only be used to finance single-family homes that you plan to live in, so it can't be used to fund rentals.

- **Interest rates** – Residential mortgages typically allow for lower interest rates and often allow them to be fixed, meaning they won't shift over the course of the mortgage. This is an attractive benefit of these mortgage types. While this can change as the interest rates go up and down, residential mortgages are typically 1-2% lower than commercial rates.

- **Loan terms** – Residential mortgages allow you to pay over a 15-year term, which allows even lower interest rates but higher monthly payments or up to a 30-year payment term. Many use 30-year terms, because it lowers the monthly payments, even though the interest rate is higher. For example, as of this writing, 15-year rates are around 5.8%, while 30-year rates are around 6.7%. So, on a $300,000 home with 20% down and 6.7% rate over 30 years, your mortgage will be about $1550 a month. The same house with a 5.8% rate over 15 years, you'll have a mortgage around $2000 per month. You might wonder why people take the shorter loan if it costs that much more per month. There are two reasons. First, you own the house free and clear much faster, which means your profit levels go way up after 15 years. Second, on that 30-year loan, you'll be paying $317,000 in interest.On the 15-year loan, you'll pay about $120,000 in interest. Some people just don't like forking over $200,000 extra to the bank.

- **Appraisals** – Every property that is going to be financed needs to be appraised. This is because the bank doesn't want to finance a property that's worth less than you're paying for it. If you paid $400,000 for a house that is worth $350,000 and you stop paying on the house, the bank will be upside down on the property immediately, meaning that they couldn't get all the money back that they loaned out. The reason why residential mortgages will sometimes allow 0% down is that the VA or USDA program is backing the loan. This means that if you default on it, these programs will cover the banks. If you're not using these programs, banks require more down payment (at least 5%) and you pay the private mortgage insurance.

Appraisals for these loans are made by comparing your property to similar properties in the area that have sold recently. If the most a 4-bed house in your area has sold for in the last six months is $400,000, and you just got under contract with a 4-bed house very similar to recent sales, but you're under contract at $450,000, you might be in trouble. The property 'won't appraise' from the bank's perspective, meaning they would be loaning you more than the house is worth, and they just won't do it unless you fork up the difference in the down payment. So, if you were going to put 10% down ($45,000), you'd have to find an additional $45,000 to have the bank fund it. That's because the house will only appraise for $400,000, which they would finance. Ten percent down of that amount would leave $360,000, which would be the amount of the loan. If you're under contract at $450,000, the only way the bank would finance it is if you get the loan amount down to $360,000, which now requires a $90,000 down payment. That's why most real estate contracts allow you to back out with no penalty if your funding falls through.

- **Ownership** – You can put the property under your own name. While this is nice (because of the benefits above, like lower interest rates, lower down payment, etc.), it has three drawbacks. First, liability passes directly to you. If a tenant sues you, they can go after all your assets. Second, you're limited to how many mortgages you can own under your own name, primarily because it skews your DTI. Typically, the most you can have at once is 10 mortgages. While that may be fine for some, others may want to grow their portfolio beyond this amount. Third, all your real estate financial transactions impact your personal credit. If you want to get a new car, they're looking at all your real estate debt when making that decision.

- **Prepayment penalty** – Residential mortgages typically have no pre-payment penalty. This means that if you make extra payments, the bank doesn't penalize you for paying the mortgage off early. While this is typically the case, it never hurts just to make sure.

- **Loan process** – With residential mortgages, it is typically a painfully slow and arduous process. Within the past few years, banks that were underwriting conservatively would take up to 45 days to process the loans, and the amount of information necessary to complete the process can be painful.

Commercial Loans

While residential mortgages are a popular option, another one that savvy investors will consider is a commercial loan. As with anything, there are pros and cons to each type, but this is the direction that Rachel and I have decided to go. Below, I'll cover the same topic areas as I did with residential mortgages, so you can easily compare and contrast.

- **Number of units in a property** – If you plan on getting a loan and the property has five or more units, it's going to be a commercial loan. It doesn't matter if people will be living in it as their residence – you need a commercial loan. The astute reader may have noticed that we have commercial loans on all our properties, but none of them are five units or higher. That's because you can also get commercial loans on properties that are four units or less. We used a commercial banker through our LLC, and since we're a business entity, we can get a commercial loan.

- **Underwriting criteria** – This is one of the reasons why people choose to do commercial loans on their properties, no matter how many units there are on it. These loans can be underwritten on net operating income (NOI) and debt service coverage ratio (DSCR). NOI is essentially your gross income from a property minus all the operating expenses (property taxes, utilities, maintenance, insurance, any management fees). In other words, this is how profitable your property is before looking at things like the mortgage payment. You don't include the mortgage payment in NOI, because it is then used to calculate DSCR. You basically take your NOI and divide it by the debt you have on your property. So, if your NOI is $15,000 per year, and your debt service is $15,000 per year, then your ratio is 1. Banks don't want to finance that, because if your operating expenses go up, then you're losing money on the property. So, anything 1 or lower is considered a problem, and the bank won't likely underwrite the loan. Banks commonly like a DSCR ratio of 1.25 or higher. So, if your NOI is $20,000, and your debt service is $15,000, then bank will like that, as the ratio is 1.33.

One last thing to note here (and I love this about commercial loans) – banks are willing to factor in investor experience when deciding whether to underwrite a loan. As an example, since Rachel and I have a strong relationship with our commercial banker, who has done all our loans, we have a strong payment record, and he knows we're running our business profitably, he might be willing to extend a loan with a DSCR of 1.1, for example. He would be much less likely to do so with someone who was purchasing their first rental property.

- **Down payment** – One of the drawbacks of commercial loans is that they often require 20-30% down. That's because the government isn't backing these loans like they do with VA, FHA, and USDA. The bank is taking the risk on commercial loans, so they de-risk the loan for themselves by requiring a bigger down payment. That makes it harder for them to get upside down on the loan if the market crashes. That's why banks care about something called the loan-to-value ratio (LTV). I mentioned this above when I pointed out that, although we finance 100% of our loans, our LTV ratio is 0.75. Banks like to see 0.8 or lower on these loans. That means that if you buy a $300,000 property and put 20% down, the bank is loaning you $240,000. Your debt ($240,000) is 80% of the property value ($300,000). Even if the market dips by 15%, the property is still worth more than they loaned to you, which provides a safety net for them. While it's no fun trying to save 20-30% down, it helps you on the back end with better cash flow, as your mortgage payment is lower.

- **Interest rates** – Let me tell you a secret about interest rates (although you may already know this). Interest rates reflect the level of risk a bank is taking. I remember when I was younger asking someone why lenders charged people with poor credit higher interest rates. It only increases the likelihood that they won't be able to afford the payment. Why would they set someone up for default? Doesn't that put the lender at more risk? To a certain degree it does. However, it also protects the lender. It does this in two ways. First, lenders in the real estate space always have collateral. In other words, they can take the property back if you don't pay. That means they're not looking at a total loss if you default. They take the property back, sell it, and reclaim (hopefully) the amount that was owed. Second, by charging higher rates of interest, they're collecting more money quickly. This helps provide a cushion if the person defaults. So, if a borrower defaults after five years of payments, the bank has collected loads of interest payments to help cover any losses the default may cause them. That's why mortgages are so front-loaded with interest versus equity paydown. It's not that the banks are just taking advantage of you. Banks are protecting themselves from default.

That said, commercial loans are considered riskier. With a residential mortgage, there's all sorts of due diligence about you, your credit score, your debt levels, your income (and income history). All this helps the banks quantify your risk level very reliably. However, with commercial loans, there's more outside of your direct control. You may know that you always pay your mortgage payments, but you can't always control if your tenants pay regularly. You can't control whether market rents are moving up or down or some of the factors that influence occupancy. Because of this, commercial rates are usually 1–2% higher than residential rates.

One more thing – commercial rates tend to be fixed for a shorter period of time, then adjust themselves to the market rates. At my bank, we have the option to choose three- or five-year fixed rates. After this term is over, they adjust to the going commercial rates and are fixed again for three or five years. Because rates are higher now, we're choosing the three-year rates in the hope that they'll drop, and we can lock in lower rates when the term is up.

- **Loan terms** – Commercial loans tend to have more 'moving parts' to them than residential loans. First, they often have the fixed rates for shorter periods of time, like I mentioned in the paragraph above. Second, it can be difficult to find a loan for 30 years, depending on your market and the bank you're using. For example, our bank goes up to 25 years on the repayment of the loan. This obviously will increase the mortgage payment versus a 30-year loan. Third, some banks amortize the loan over 25 or 30 years, but the loan length will actually be 5-10 years and will require a balloon payment at the end. If you've never heard of that, you're not alone. In a residential mortgage, there's no difference between the loan length and the amortization (payment schedule) of the loan. That's not true with some commercial loans. They will amortize the loan over 25 years (which means they set up the payment schedule like you're paying for 25 years), but the loan is only for five years, for example. Once the five years is up, the loan comes due, and the bank is looking for a balloon payment. This means they want the rest of what is owed to them all at once. This is often worked around by simply refinancing the loan. This is great if the interest rates have dropped. It's not great if they've climbed. Plus, every 5-10 years you're paying the closing costs on the refinancing. That's why we like our current arrangement, where our loan term of 25 years matches the amortization schedule, so we never have to worry about that.

- **Appraisals** – If you're buying a property with 1-4 units on a commercial loan, they'll still appraise it like they would a residential mortgage, by looking at similar properties nearby that have sold recently. However, if you're going to buy a property that has five or more units, they actually look at whether the property can pay for itself with its revenues. This introduces a concept called capitalization rate (or cap rate). Cap rates are calculated by taking the NOI and dividing it by the purchase price. Remember that NOI is your profit before taking account your debt payment. If your NOI is $15,000, and you paid $100,000 for the property, then your cap rate is 15%. This is a fantastic cap rate, by the way. If your NOI is $15,000, and you paid $300,000 for the property, then your cap rate is 5%. That's not terrible, but it's not great.

When you go to buy a commercial property (either a 5+ unit residential property or a property that will have a business run out of it), the listing will often show the cap rate and NOI. That is used to calculate the purchase price. If a property's NOI is $20,000, and the cap rate is 7%, then the property will be listed for sale at $285,714, which is the NOI divided by the cap rate. Let's say you find a way to make the property more profitable, and the NOI goes up to $30,000, divide this by the cap rate, and the value of the property goes up to $428,571. That's the interesting thing about commercial properties – it becomes more valuable on the open market the more profitably it's run. So, banks aren't looking at comps here, they're looking to see if the property is priced correctly based on cap rate and NOI.

· **Ownership** – You're much less likely to see a commercial loan in someone's personal name. You're likely to see these owned by an LLC or another business entity. That's what we do. All our properties are owned by our LLC. The major benefit of this is that you're not capped at the 10 mortgages limit, like with a residential loan. While financing can be stricter if you have more loans or a certain debt amount, there's not that hard cap anymore. In addition, the debt is against your business, not you, so none of the business debt impacts your personal credit. Lastly, the LLC (if that's the business entity you choose) can help protect you against liability incurred by your business operations – but you have to follow legal guidelines for the protection to stay in place (more on this in chapter 15).

· **Prepayment penalty** – Commercial loans often have prepayment penalties. It varies by bank, but using our bank as an example, there's a 5% prepayment penalty in the first year of the loan, 4% in the second year, etc. all the way through the fifth year, after which there is no prepayment penalty.

· **Loan process** – It can be easier to get a commercial loan compared to residential loans, particularly if you have already worked with the bank before. All my bank wants to see is my new tax return each year, an updated personal financial statement (they provide the template), and the current rent rolls, which is showing them how much in rent I get from each property. It's much easier than the process that residential loans go through each time.

Just a couple more notes about bank financing. First, banks don't love land purchases. You typically have to put a higher percentage of the cost down (often 30-50%), they do shorter loan terms (often not longer than 15 years), and they charge higher interest rates. Second, banks don't often like to finance smaller purchase amounts. So, if you find a flip property you won at auction for $35,000, you're going to have a hard time finding a bank to loan you that amount. It just isn't worth it for them. These two factors often make small land purchases very difficult to finance – it's raw land and below the purchase price threshold to finance. However, if you plan on building on the property right away, you can get the bank to finance the land and construction costs together. With the higher interest rates we're seeing now, some people are not building their own, they're turning to newly built homes, because the builders can offer financing much lower than banks do. While banks are offering 6-8% right now, some builders are offering financing as low as 3.9%.

Non-traditional Financing

Don't despair if you run into trouble with traditional financing. You can consider tapping into other forms of personal debt. We did this when we used the value of our house to get a HELOC. You may point out that we had our house paid off at the time, and many don't have that same advantage. However, you don't need to have your house paid off to get a HELOC. Let's say you have a $300,000 house and still owe $200,000 on it. When you apply for a HELOC, the bank will do an appraisal, and they will give you up to 80% of the value of the home, minus what you still owe. So, 80% of $300,000 is $240,000. If you owe $200,000, then you'll be able to access $40,000 of your equity. If banks require 20% down, you can use that money to buy a $200,000 rental. If you can't access any money this way, you can look for opportunities to use creative financing, which was discussed briefly in chapter 4. You can also look for private money. This is about borrowing from hard money lenders (who will have higher interest rates), or you can look for investors to help you afford the properties. Many books have been written about how to finance your properties, so I won't go into lots of detail here. Just know there are multiple options available to finance your first property.

Finding a Partner

There's one more option here, which isn't even a form of financing technically. It's using partnerships to fund purchases. This looks like financing from the outside, in that you're using third parties to cover most of the costs. And you're often paying something like a mortgage, but it's actually a distribution of the profits to the different equity owners. We did this on our first flip, in that my parents helped fund it. There are pros and cons to using partners. The pros are that you'll be able to get into a property much faster than saving on your own. In addition, some of your partners may have an expertise that you don't have that could be important in your business (like a lawyer or construction contractor). In addition, there's often no debt on the property, particularly if you can find enough partners to cover the whole purchase price.

Many people love the option of using partners to fund real estate purchases. I'm a little leery on it. My biggest issue with it is that I don't love the idea of sharing ownership of a property with someone, particularly a property I plan on keeping. I'd rather own the whole thing myself.Remember, I'm in real estate primarily for cash flow, to eventually replace my income. Thus, I don't really feel like divvying my cash flow up to different parties. Some people disagree with me and use partnerships a lot, and that's fine. I think that people prefer partnerships primarily for two reasons: 1) They don't have enough money to get started in real estate and 2) Their primary goal is growth and not cash flow. Those are great reasons to use partners, but neither of them lines up with my goals. In addition, remember my 'why's. One of them is to leave the business to my children to help generate wealth. Another is to provide for Rachel financially if I were to pass away. I wouldn't want other people involved in how things get passed on to our kids or impacting how wealth is distributed to Rachel. Partners can be a great way to get into real estate and accelerate the growth of your business, but it also needs to be handled very carefully if you're going to be successful with it – more on this in the next chapter.

12

Finding (and Keeping) Your Team

One thing that irritates me is when people describe themselves or are described as 'self-made'. You'll hear people called self-made millionaires, for example, and it's just not true. Nobody is self-made. Anyone who is successful has had people help them out along the way. Nobody does it by themselves. That's why it's so important to find your team – the people who will help you become successful in your real estate journey. I'm going to list some people below who may be important parts of your team and why it's so important to find the right people – and keep them.

Your Mentor/Coach

Not everyone has a mentor or coach, but this person can be extremely valuable to your growth as an investor. Unfortunately, I've gone without a mentor for most of my life. The good news is that I love few things more than learning, and I'm a self-starter, so I've been able to be successful without one. However, there are times when I wonder if I have some blind spots that limit my success in one way or another. If I was being consistently mentored or coached, I might be growing in areas where I'm currently stagnant. In my opinion, you're always better off with one than without, if for no other reason than to have an objective 3rd party as a sounding board. If you can find a good one, they're worth their weight in gold.

One point I'd make quickly here is that the best mentors or coaches are the ones who are a little bit ahead of you. It's very tempting to want to find a mentor who is a multi-millionaire many times over and who owns 300 rental units. However, these people have often forgotten what it's like to buy their first property, and they may be giving you advice based on how they're operating now. I remember listening to a well-known real estate podcaster consistently giving advice to new investors about how it's smarter to invest for appreciation than cash flow. Appreciation is where the real money is, even if you have to take a small loss or break even. Go for appreciation.

However, if you're a first-time investor, you're not typically thinking about appreciation. You want to supplement your income and perhaps eventually replace it. The average Joe needs cash flow. The rich get to shoot for appreciation without needing the cash flow. That's why I'm writing this book now, three years into my rental investment journey. I remember well what it feels like to be on the outside looking in, and I'm just around the corner from you, with everything I've learned in the past three years still in the forefront of my mind. This means that as you grow, you may need to find different mentors or coaches. The mentor with eight doors is a great place to start, but they're perhaps not the right person when they're still at eight, and you're sitting at 14. You might want to find someone who is in the 25-50 door range at that point.

Your Partner

I have a chapter on this above, so I won't rehash everything here. But I will expand the scope of what it means to have a partner. Above, I was largely referring to a significant other who is doing the real estate journey with you. The major upside is that you don't have to do it all yourself. That's a huge relief. Rachel is the property manager (largely because I'm still working full-time and doing a fair bit of traveling), and she pays the bills. When we find a property, I'll do the financial analysis and underwriting. I do the bookkeeping and our taxes. I set the goals and cast the vision for the business. In a sense, I'm the CEO and Rachel is the VP of Operations. I couldn't be as effective without her and vice versa. However, this isn't the only type of partner out there. You may literally have a business partner – someone who invests with you to help get you off the ground quicker. Many investors have a business partner, so it's not rare. Here's some quick advice if you want to have this person as part of your team:

- **Choose your partner very carefully** – Just because they're excited about real estate and want to jump into it with you doesn't mean they're going to be a good partner. Maybe you're more of a careful, conservative investor and your partner is about moving quickly and taking risks. Over time, you're going to think they're a loose cannon, and they're going to think you're a stick in the mud who is holding them back. Even worse, you might find a partner who ends up cheating you or cutting corners that puts the business at legal risk. It's extremely important that you find someone who is aligned with you. Keep in mind, however, that alignment doesn't mean that they'd do everything like you would.It's actually helpful to have diversity of thought.

- **Don't feel like you need to stick to one** – Many investors have had more than one partner. Maybe an investor likes long-term rentals, whereas another likes short-term rentals. Maybe you want to do both and would see benefits from partnering with both people – one with your long-term and one with your short-term. Maybe you invest with one person for smaller purchases and another for bigger purchases. Maybe you start off with one partner and work together for a few years, then switch to other partners. If you're investing in different geographic locations, maybe you'll have partners in each place. All of this is very common. Don't feel like partnership is a marriage. Choose the right partners for the right properties and the right season of your investing journey.

- **Find complementary skills** – It's nice to have a partner in your business venture, but it's even better when they are good at different things than you are. I've heard it said that if your partner thinks just like you do, your partner is redundant. I'm not sure I completely agree with that, because you may be bringing on a partner for their money, not their thinking.

That being said, unless your partner is a silent one (meaning they're just bringing money and you make all the decisions), you'll want to find someone who has a different skill set than you do. This is why Rachel and I do well together. I look forward to spreadsheeting our profit and loss and doing the taxes. Rachel likes to connect with people and set up our furnished rentals.

· **Communicate consistently** – There's no substitute for regular communication. Again, if you're dealing with silent partners, and you're making all the decisions, it's a little different – but not much. You may find yourself in need of more money, and the silent partners might be willing to open their wallets if you've been keeping them in the loop. No matter what, meet regularly, talk often, and involve each other in decisions.

· **Contract well if you want it to end well** – It's extremely important that you have a solid contract between you and your partner. This shouldn't just be written up between the two of you and signed. This should be crafted by a lawyer who has experience in real estate law. Perhaps the most important part that needs to be contracted well is how the partnership will be dissolved. You don't want a fight on your hands if things get soured. How the partnership is supposed to end is just as important as how it begins.

Your Contractors

These are the lifeblood of your success, particularly if you're not a DIYer. I'll do some manual labor around our properties, but I'm not super handy. This means that our contractors are extremely important in our strategy of maintaining nice properties. It's very important that you find good ones, because many landlords have horror stories about contractors. There are several major things you need to be careful of with contractors, so do your due diligence:

· **Used licensed contractors when it matters** – I can't tell you how many times we've had to undo what DIYers or unlicensed people did in homes. So, we have chosen to use licensed contractors in these areas. Their knowledge and expertise have been invaluable, and we have them inspect our properties after closing and fix whatever needs to be fixed. If you're a bigger real estate operation, you may even hire a general contractor to manage your properties. If that's the case, you may not be interacting much with the sub-contractors. If you're smaller (or haven't started yet), then you're likely going to be managing these folks, so having people you trust and work well with is such a blessing. Fortunately, mostly due to Rachel, we have a great team of experts who give us no cause to complain. We don't give them cause to complain either, and this is super important.

Here are three rules we live by with these members of our team, if you want them to keep working with you: 1) Pay quickly, 2) be thoughtful, and 3) be generous. We have a contractor who does a lot of our remodeling. He was recommended to us, and he stepped in when we needed a basement renovation quickly. This was the first project we used him for. He knew we were on a budget, and it turns out he adjusted his pricing for us to meet the budget. We paid quickly with the materials, so it wasn't coming out of his own pocket for long. We stopped by several times during the project to bring him lunch or snacks and a drink. When he gave us his final bill, and we saw that he had given us a deal to fit our budget, we gave him an extra $1000 to say 'thank you' for a job well done. This is our approach, and it has served us well.

We tend to be the first in line with our contractors when we need something. They're very responsive, because we take care of them. I wouldn't have it any other way. If you find a good contractor, don't nickel and dime them. Don't be cheap with them. One more thing – some landlords like to hoard their good contractors, so that others don't take up their time. I've found this to be inconsistent with our ethics. In fact, we've gotten our contractors tens of thousands of dollars of work through referrals, and they have most definitely appreciated it. Rachel got our carpet guy so many referrals during a financially difficult time in his life that he'll do just about anything for us.

- **Be clear with your contracting** – Similar to what I said above about how important it is to contract well with your partners, it is extremely important to be clear with your contractors – when the project starts, the scope of the project, the cost of the project, when it will be completed, etc. Anything that's unclear opens you and the contractor up to being frustrated and unhappy. You want to minimize how often this happens. One of the most important things to have clarity on is the scope of the contract. What happens all too often is that you start off with a bathroom remodel, then decide you want some work done in the kitchen. The problem is, you know exactly how much the bathroom remodel was going to cost, but you don't get clarity about what the extra work is going to cost. When the work is done, you get the bill and end up surprised. Neither you nor the contractor wants to be in this situation. Everything you add or change should be accompanied by a new or updated quote. I'd rather be clear up front than surprised afterward.

- **Make sure they are showing up when they're supposed to** – This is one of the most frustrating parts about contractors, when you don't have a good one. First off, it's hard enough to get them to reply with a quote, let alone show up when they're scheduled. What probably happens is they pack jobs too closely together, and they don't get the previous one done in time for your project to start when it should. However, sometimes they just forget. Even when they do show up, they're not always on time, and sometimes they leave early.It helps to work with trusted, responsible contractors – that's probably the best way around this. Short of this, it's not inappropriate to remind them the day before when they're supposed to start work. However, sometimes they just don't show up or respond. We once had a rogue plumber that held up our first flip for months by not getting back with us, no matter what we tried. The problem is that he had ordered the boiler for the basement (not all plumbers do boilers, so we were stuck with him), and it was sitting in a warehouse that was only open to contractors, not the general public – so we couldn't just go get it. After much frustration, gnashing of teeth, and lots of messages, he finally finished the job, but it was hardly worth the frustration. Many people attempt to solve this problem (with varying degrees of success) by putting penalties or rewards in the contract for timely completion of the project (or lack thereof). For instance, I've heard some real estate podcasters build in a 5% incentive for on-time completion, which they said made a big difference on their projects.

· **Be careful with your money** – There are two financial mistakes that you can make with your contractors. The first is to pay them the entire amount of the project up front. I've heard stories about contractors who take the money and run. You've lost the entire amount, and nothing gets done. The second mistake is to make the final payment before the project is finished. This massively disincentivizes the contractor to finish the project. We've learned this one the hard way. The best way to do this is in what are called 'draws'. This is when you draw a certain amount of the budget out to pay the contractor. Usually, the first draw is to pay for materials. It's often best to ask for an itemized receipt for the materials, so you know you didn't get ripped off. If you want to avoid this, you can have the contractor tell you what materials to pick up, and you can do it yourself. I don't like doing this, as I know the contractor will be able to find what they're looking for more efficiently than I would and will have fewer returns from accidentally getting the wrong thing. So, we ask for receipts.

Don't be surprised (or offended) if they have a mark-up on the materials for their time and gas. That's perfectly normal. Just talk about this ahead of time, so you're both on the same page and that you're comfortable with the mark up. The second draw is usually to pay for the labor. This is even more true if the contractor is paying people to help on the job.

He or she doesn't want to get in the hole for thousands of dollars to the subcontractors without knowing when they're going to get paid. The third draw may be the last one. Even if the contractor asks for this before the project is complete, don't do it. In fact, make it part of your contract that the last draw happens only when you are satisfied with the final result. They want to get paid, so they'll be motivated to finish if the money is waiting for them at the end.

- **Get references** – While it's better than nothing to get references from the contractors themselves, this isn't my favorite. Maybe they did a job for their uncle at a discount, to buy them off to give good reviews. They're stacking the deck with their own references. Even be careful getting referrals from local home-improvement stores. A random employee at a Menard's gave us the referral for the rogue plumber. What we like to do is use our own network to drum up contractors. We put a post on Facebook asking for an electrician that someone has used before, and we'll put our criteria on there – licensed, responsible, on time, good communication, reasonably priced. We'll often get a few names, and a few other responses that will be something like, "Wow, I used that guy too, and he was amazing." Once you get several people in your network affirming someone's work, they're probably worth a try. Also use your in-person network. Our neighbor, who worked with me on our first flip (and who's very handy – he did our personal basement renovation) referred us to our plumber. Our plumber referred us to his uncle, who did the basement renovation in our mid-term rental and who also re-did the stairs in one of our single-family homes. They are both valued and trusted contractors.It's an amazing thing to have trusted, competent people on your team – they're worth their weight in gold.

Your Lender

Not all lenders are created equal. I recently listened to a podcast, where the guest talked about needing to make a PowerPoint presentation for a bank, so they could understand what mid-term rentals are. If that's the situation you find yourself in, that's probably not your bank. Here are a few questions to help you evaluate potential lenders when you're looking at banks:

- **How often do you work with real estate investors who have a lot of diversity in their portfolio?** This is a good question to ask, because it will help you figure out if you're dealing with a bank that's never heard of mid-term rentals before or a bank that knows the rental business.

- **Do you typically give portfolio loans or conventional loans?** I mentioned this above, but most banks will give you a mortgage then turn around and sell it to someone else, most often Fannie Mae or Freddie Mac. As a result, they have very stringent rules for loans that make the process of getting one difficult. We work with a bank that is a portfolio lender (also known as a bank that gives in-house loans, balance sheet loans, or non-conforming loans). This means they keep the loan as part of their lending portfolio. That gives them more flexibility with their lending criteria, how many loans they're willing to give you, and what types of properties they'll finance. You're likely to find portfolio lenders at local banks or credit unions. While you may pay higher interest rates, I think the flexibility is worth it.

- **Where is the nearest branch that has a mortgage banker/commercial banker?** It's extremely frustrating to get a person on the phone in Portland, Oregon when you're in Portland, Maine and are having a problem with your loan. These people don't know you, don't know your situation, and perhaps don't know what's going on. The more local your banker is, the more likely you can have a phone call with the same person for each transaction and even stop by to deal with issues.

We have a great relationship with our lender and have enjoyed someone who is a phone call, email, or text away. He provides great service and communicates well with us. As I indicated above, we like the banks that do portfolio loans. We appreciate the flexibility they have and their willingness to work with investors. While it's true that you may have other lenders besides the bank (family, friends, hard money lenders), these may help with some properties and not with others, and often your goal is to pay them off or buy them out as quickly as possible. As a result, they may not be a consistent member of your team, so they won't be covered here.

Your Insurance Agent

Don't overlook this important piece to your puzzle. Most of us aren't experts on how much coverage we need, or even what type of coverage. If you're just looking to save a few dollars, you might end up with coverage that will only pay for the depreciated value of your roof, not the full replacement value. That could leave you on the hook for thousands of dollars that you didn't expect. Your insurance agent can help you understand what your insurance covers and what it doesn't. You might have restrictions on what dog breeds your insurance will cover. You need to know this, and your agent can help you understand what you need to know. Your agent will know the difference between covering the purchase price of your house if it burns down and covering the rebuilding cost of your house – those are two very different things. Think of your insurance agent as an indispensable consultant to help you de-risk your property.

Also, consider going with an independent agent. These are agents who have access to multiple insurers and can do comparative shopping to get you the best coverage for the price. If you have a State Farm agent, for example, they'll only quote you State Farm prices. That's why we go with the same independent agent for all our properties. Again – he's nearby (I met him through my local Chamber of Commerce), and we have developed a great relationship. If they are truly going to be a member of your team, you shouldn't be contacting them through the customer service line or through an anonymous email account.

Your Realtor

Not all Realtors are created equal. Some do a great job selling a house. They have strong networks, pay attention to detail, and are strong marketers.

Some do a great job helping you buy a house. They're proactively scouring listings to find the deals and pass them along to you. They're leveraging their network to find off-market deals or pocket listings with other Realtors (pocket listings are ones that haven't been listed yet and the seller's Realtor is shopping around privately first). Ideally, you'd find a Realtor who is strong in both areas, as you may want to sell some of your properties eventually. However, you'll be looking to buy before you sell, so there are a few things you'll be looking for in your Realtor:

- **They're 'investor-friendly'** – This is really important, and it doesn't mean that they're friendly with investors. It means that they regularly work with investors and are ideally investors themselves. Don't overlook how important this is. A regular Realtor might be thinking about the fact that you don't have kids, so the school district doesn't matter as much. An investor-friendly Realtor knows that your renters might have kids, and the school district matters to them. They'll know where the district lines are and how much that makes a difference, not just in the purchase price of the house but in the rental price as well. They'll know what to look for in a house that might attract or turn off a potential renter. They might have tips for marketing your rental and how to evaluate applicants. They may even have recommendations for potential contractors. So, don't go with your cousin who just got their Realtor's license two months ago. There's a huge difference between someone who is licensed to help you buy a house and someone who is experienced enough to serve as a valuable consultant.

- **Local** – We used to live in Santa Maria, CA. It's in northern Santa Barbara County, about an hour north of Santa Barbara. In the grand scheme of things, it's not that big of a stretch to think that a Realtor could operate reasonably effectively anywhere within a county, and that's generally true. However, as an investor, you may be looking for some specific things. Realtors in Santa Barbara are used to catering to the rich and selling multi-million-dollar properties. Because of how expensive things are there, they're likely working more with primary homebuyers, as most renters aren't looking to rent a $3 million dollar home. So, I would much rather work with a Realtor based in Santa Maria. They know the market better and are more likely to be aware of the nuances of the rentals in the area. I recently took a vacation with my family out west, and I decided to meet with a Realtor in Prescott, AZ to learn more about the area. I didn't know anyone, so I went on ChatGPT and typed in 'investor-friendly Realtors in Prescott, AZ'. One of the options was a Realtor based out of Sedona but who also did business in Prescott. No thanks – I went with a Realtor who lived in and whose whole professional Realtor career was in Prescott.

- **Connected** – I touched on this above, but an ideal Realtor will know other Realtors, other investors (who may be looking to sell), property managers, contractors, etc. There is so much value to be had simply through the connections of an experienced and well-regarded Realtor.

Your Home Inspector

As you read through this book, you'll see that Rachel and I have used inspectors before, but it's been on a minority of our purchases. This has been because we've gotten more comfortable recognizing a good house from a bad house ourselves and have a strong team that can address issues they find when they do their post-purchase inspection (like our plumbers and electricians). In addition, most of our purchases occurred in the post-COVID competitive environment. This is notable, because people often use inspections to find issues and use them to negotiate down the purchase price after getting under contract. With a lot of competition, there are usually buyers who are willing to waive their inspection, which means you're now a less attractive buyer if you have an inspection contingency. Right now, the competition has slowed significantly, and it may be worth it to us to get an inspection to be in a stronger negotiation position.

While we don't have an inspector as part of our team currently, I've discovered that I like watching short videos on social media that home inspectors put together to show what to look for. You may find these videos a valuable resource as well, not necessarily to replace an inspector but to educate yourself. There's one in particular who I follow on Facebook (Inspector Preston), and he offers the following steps to ensure you're getting a good inspector:

- **Don't make your decision based on price** - The good inspectors know their worth, and the bad inspectors are just looking for business.

- **Good inspectors allow you to attend the inspection** - They know their job is to be a consultant for you, and being there to discuss the findings as they see issues not only helps you understand the house better but what should be deal-breakers. Those who don't let you do this may be trying to cover up that they do shoddy work.

- **Ask if they've passed the NHIE** - This is the National Home Inspector Exam. It's a difficult test and ensures a higher level of competency. If the inspector is unlicensed, that's a major red flag. If they just have a state license, they might not be as knowledgeable.

- **Ask the inspector if they use thermal imaging** - This helps them see if there is water leaking where it shouldn't be in the house. This is an extremely important way an inspector can find those hidden problems that you'd miss otherwise.

- **Ensure that the inspector does a roof-level inspection** - Many inspectors just bring binoculars or take pictures from ground level and zoom in to see if they can detect any problems. This is drastically inferior to them either getting up on the roof, using a drone, or using a camera on a pole that gets to the roof level.

- **Ask if they're an interNACHI member** - This is an international organization of home inspectors that has strict criteria for ethics and standards of practice. You're more likely to get someone who is ethical and knows what they're doing this way. You can go on nachi.org to find inspectors in your area.

- **Ask if they have a crawler robot** - Believe it or not, inspectors, if they can't easily access an area, they can put 'Not readily accessible' on the report. This gets them off the hook from getting into crawl spaces and nooks in the attic. If there's a problem there, you'll never know about it ahead of time, unless they have these robots to send in to these spaces to see any issues, even in the small spaces.

- **Take a look at their Google reviews** - Inspectors can't control these, so they're more likely to be based on real performance. Look for high ratings and recent reviews.

Real Estate Attorney

This may not be part of your team in the beginning, depending on where you start. If you set up an LLC, you can do that with or without an attorney. You can pick a site like LegalZoom to create the document for you. However, when you get into more complicated partnerships, you'll want an attorney. If you're doing syndications, you'll want an attorney. If you're doing a 1031 exchange, you'll want an attorney. On occasion, some people who do off-market deals will use attorneys to write up the documents. We haven't taken that route, as we've used the title company to supply our documents for off-market deals. So, an attorney isn't part of our team yet, but at least we understand when they should be.

Accountant

Speaking of people who aren't on our team yet, you may want to consider an accountant. This member of your team isn't like a lawyer, where there are some situations where you need one and others where you don't. A tax accounting of your business activities will need to be completed each year. It's just a matter of whether that's you or someone who is an expert.So far, it's been me for our business. I can't necessarily recommend this for most people, for several reasons: 1) This is an extremely difficult thing to figure out from scratch. If you have no experience with doing your own taxes or the tax code, this is probably not the time to DIY. 2) You can run into big problems if you don't do this correctly. The government doesn't like it when it looks like you're screwing up your taxes. 3) There are a lot of moving pieces to get this correct. You must be on top of a lot of things to be reasonably good at doing your own taxes.

I feel comfortable doing my own taxes for the following reasons: 1) I had been doing it for years on TurboTax before getting into real estate, 2) I do a lot of our personal budgeting and financial tracking and have for our whole marriage, 3) I keep good records, and 4) I am a learner. I listened to a lot of podcasts on real estate taxes to wrap my head around what I needed to know to do things correctly. In fact, I set up a meeting with a real estate accountant to figure out whether I was out of my depth. I asked an important question, "What are three things that DIYers often mess up with their real estate taxes." After listening to his answer and being on top of all three, I felt pretty comfortable continuing on as my own accountant. Again, this isn't for most people, and a good accountant would serve you well. As our investments become more complicated, I may need more than just someone to do my taxes. I may need a tax advisor – someone who helps me plan my strategy and business behaviors around how it will impact my taxes. That's not something I'm expert enough to do for myself.

As a quick aside, you may find that the daily or weekly keeping track of expenses gets a little overwhelming. If that's you, that's okay. You may just need to hire a bookkeeper. This helps make sure that the expenses are recorded and that they are current. You might find yourself scrambling before tax season, trying to patch together your business finances. That's no fun, and that's what a bookkeeper is designed to help you avoid. I put this under the accountant section, because sometimes your bookkeeper is through your accountant's office.

Property Manager

We don't use a property manager as part of our team either. You may be starting to notice a theme. Please don't hear me saying that these people are less important members of your team. These folks can be indispensable if you've designed your business to include them. We currently do our own property management, and we do this for a strategic reason. You may remember that we finance our properties with 100% leverage. This means that if we want to make any profit, we can't afford to pay a property manager right now. They often charge up to one month's rent to find you a tenant and 10% of the rent to manage the property each month. That's not money we want to give up.

In addition, I mentioned earlier that we see ourselves as high-end landlords. I'm sure there are great property managers out there, but I've heard enough horror stories that I don't think anyone would match our ethic with tenants. That being said, I didn't get into real estate for us to be property managers. Eventually, I'd like to spend more of my time running the business than managing properties. Whether this involves using property managers or hiring someone as a go-between with our tenants and contractors, I'm not sure yet. However, many people who do end up stepping back from active property management have one thing in common – they've hired a virtual assistant.

Virtual Assistant

A virtual assistant (VA) is someone who could live anywhere in the world who you hire (usually part-time) to do things in the business that aren't a great use of your time. I don't love connecting the utilities after we buy a property. This would be a task I'd love to hand off to a VA. Some VAs do bookkeeping, some do scheduling, some receive communication from tenants and coordinate with you and a contractor to get done whatever needs to get done. VAs can even scour the internet for properties that fit your Buy Box. They can really do whatever you want them to, as long as they're qualified to do it.

Just know that not all VAs are built the same. It's kind of like dating, in that you may have to go through several before you find a good match. You increase the odds of finding a good one by being thorough in the hiring process about understanding their areas of expertise, setting a clear business/communication rhythm, and by being very up front about expectations. They're not mind readers, so they won't know exactly how you want things done. We haven't gone in this direction yet, but I could see us headed there some day.

* * *

You may find circumstances where there are other members of your team that aren't described here, and that's okay. I just wanted to describe perhaps the most common. Keep in mind that you don't succeed unless you have a good team. Find good people to put on your team, and treat them well. Be good to them, and they'll be good to you. That's the recipe for success here. Don't take them for granted, and let them know how much you appreciate their contribution to your success. If one isn't good, switch them out. It's not disloyal to do that. Loyalty isn't blind, and it runs both ways. Be loyal to the person, if you choose to, but don't turn a blind eye to bad work or poor ethics. That's not what loyalty is for.

13

Near or Far

This will be one of the most interesting decisions you have to make as a budding real estate investor – where, geographically, will you invest. If you're involving yourself in a syndication, acting as a hard money lender, or buying debt notes, it may not matter so much where the property or properties are that you're investing in. However, if you're doing something like arbitrage, flipping, or renting to tenants (short-, mid-, or long-term), you may be tempted to pick up properties close to where you live. It's important to understand that it doesn't have to be this way. You can flip, arbitrage, or own rentals anywhere – you just have to manage things a bit differently. Let's look at some of the differences and what you might need to consider when making this decision.

Investing Nearby

This is a no-brainer for most people starting off. Many don't like to bite off more than they can chew, and your first investment can feel complicated enough. It's hard to think of investing out of town as dipping your toes into the real estate pool – it feels more like jumping in with both feet. So, most investors start in their own neighborhood, so to speak. We'll take some time here to explore the conditions under which you may want to spend more time focusing nearby:

- **You haven't developed good processes yet** – One of the major differences between investing locally and investing out of town is the way the business is run. You can drive by your rental to pick up a check each month if you want to. You can't do that if you're in Miami and your rental is in San Diego. You can sit down at Starbucks to review a printed lease agreement and have the tenant hand sign it if you're five minutes from your rental. You can't do that in Minnesota if you live in Iowa. You're relying on tighter, more advanced processes when your property isn't local. You can be a bit more relaxed and flexible with your approach with a nearby property. So, if you haven't fine-tuned your processes yet and are in a figure-it-out-as-you-go-along position, it's probably better to start off locally.

- **You'd prefer not to learn from mistakes** – You know yourself best. If the thought of making a big mistake keeps you up at night, then you probably want to start locally. Understand what I mean by this; hopefully we all learn from our mistakes, but some of us really don't like to make them. We get nervous about the thought of screwing something up and missing an important detail. We work to minimize risk, not lean into it. While making a mistake isn't bad, per se, not all mistakes are created equally, and it can be much harder to recover from a big one if that mistake happens halfway around the country. If you don't have the stomach for that right now, then don't start there.

- **You don't have much of a network outside of town** – It's extremely risky to get yourself involved with a property in an area where you don't know anyone or have a limited network. Just because your mother's second cousin (who you've never met) lives in Milwaukee, that doesn't mean you're ready to make that move. Remember how important your team is to your success, if you don't have a team (or any member of the team) in a location, you probably want to stay away. Even if you don't have a team locally yet, it's easier to find and refine that team, which means it's less risky for you to invest nearby.

- **You have limited tolerance for complexity right now** – If your life is busy, and you don't feel like you have much tolerance for added complexity, then you might struggle with owning properties remotely – maybe. This is an interesting one, because it's not as straightforward as the other ones. What I mean is this – if you're successfully running a property from a distance, you can't actively manage it yourself. This probably means you have someone managing it for you and/or you have more advanced systems and processes. Also, if there's an issue, it's harder for that to fall directly into your lap, meaning you won't have to do what I did one time and show up in person to balance a wobbly ceiling fan. You can't do that yourself if you're a long-distance investor. You can send someone else to deal with it. So, it sounds like long-distance properties can be easier. Well, they can be if you're set up right. However, if you don't have advanced processes or a reliable team, things do fall back on you, and you might find yourself boarding a plane to figure out why the roof is leaking and vet a roof contractor you've never met before. I mentioned in a previous chapter how I was on a phone call one time with another investor as he was driving from Pennsylvania to Maryland to deal with a property issue. That doesn't sound like fun to me.

- **You tend to worry a lot** – For the sake of relationship, I won't call Rachel out here, but there's someone in my life very important to me who tends to worry a lot. Let's define worry for a moment. It's an application of our imagination, where we take situations outside of our control, and we visualize bad outcomes. Read that again and chew on that sentence for a moment. Let's say your 16-year-old daughter is late coming home from a birthday, and it's now past her curfew. Let's also say you don't have a tracking app set up on your phone, so you're not sure where she is or why she's not answering her phone. You've called her friend and found out that she left a little while ago. You might find yourself pacing back and forth imagining worst-case scenarios. The problem with this is that it doesn't help solve the problem, and it just makes you miserable.

Worrying is one of the most pointless activities you can engage in.You're subjecting yourself to emotional torment, ruining your present for a future that may never happen. While it's true that your daughter may have gotten in a car accident, your worrying doesn't make it less likely or fix the issue if she did.

Some people are wired to worry more. The good news is that there are ways to manage this effectively, but that's beyond the scope of this book. For the time being, it's important to determine if you're a worrier, and if you are, you'll probably recognize that long-distance investing gives you lots of reasons to lose sleep at night. Until you get the worrying better managed, this may not be a great place to start. One last note here, if you're going to consider long-distance investing and have a significant other, you both need to be on board. You don't want to force a worrier into this and generate misalignment.

· **You haven't done much research in other markets** – They say ignorance is bliss, but this isn't true for long-distance investing. What you don't know will definitely hurt you with investing. I talked above about doing research on the landlord laws in the state you're considering for your properties. You don't want to figure out after you've purchased the rental in San Francisco that it has rent control regulations. You don't want to discover that the short-term rental you just purchased in Denver could result in a felony charge if you use it that way (under certain conditions). You don't want to salivate over the reasonable prices in Texas only to find out that they make up for the lack of state income tax with extremely high property taxes. You don't want to buy a condo in Florida only to find out that you're getting hit with a huge assessment from the HOA for safety and maintenance issues that are now required by law to be fixed. By the way, all these are real issues that investors have run into. I wouldn't dare to invest in an area that I hadn't been very thorough with my due diligence and consulting a local expert.

Investing Far Away

Now that we've reviewed some reasons why you may want to stick with local investing, let's take a look at some situations that may cause you to look farther away than your own backyard.

- **You live in an expensive market** – Now we're getting to an important point. I live in Ohio, and I'm well aware that not all markets are as affordable as where I live. In fact, I've lived in some of those expensive markets. If you live in Orange County, CA, for example, and you're trying to buy your first property, Orange County may not be the place to do it. It's not impossible to invest locally in expensive markets, but high housing costs are one of the major reasons why investors look elsewhere.

- **You have good mentors who can help you** – Being a long-distance investor is not something you probably want to tackle without the help of someone with experience in the area that you need it. It turns out the Realtor I connected with in Prescott, AZ has experience with property development. He buys land and partners with a friend who is a general contractor. They build duplexes, then sell them. If I was interested in moving into property development, I would likely be having lots of conversations with him. If possible, you want to learn from the mistakes of others, rather than make them yourself.

- **You have connections in other markets** – This is a big one. If you don't know anyone where you are investing, that's a recipe for things being much harder than they need to be. I'll talk more about my interest in Prescott shortly, but I was specifically looking for a Realtor who was investor-friendly. It turns out he also has experience in property management and construction. If I were ever to decide to invest in Prescott, he is a great way to get my foot in the door with vital relationships.

Remember the chapter about finding (and keeping) your team? If possible, you don't want be blind dating people to see if they're going to be good for you. Either choose markets where you have connections or take the initiative to begin creating connections. There are lots of ways to do this. You can do what I did and use ChatGPT to find a Realtor. You can attend an investor conference and get to know people there. You can use online investor forums and begin to network there. Believe it or not, Facebook is a great way to build your non-local network. You can do this by joining investor groups on Facebook, but an even more powerful way to do this is to use connections you've made over your lifetime and see where they're living and who they know.

· **You've done good research on other markets** – A long-distance investment shouldn't involve guess work. Let's say you buy a house in the relatively expensive market of Denver, CO. You're willing to pay higher prices, because you plan on using it as an Airbnb. You close on the property, and immediately start furnishing it, only to find out that it's against the law to have short-term rentals in Denver – and there are some significant penalties for using it this way illegally. Now you've gotten yourself into a bind that you would have avoided if you had done some research.

Let's say you buy a completely fixed up, beautiful duplex in Phoenix, only to find out that the neighborhood isn't great, and you can't get the rent needed to cover your costs. Let's say you buy a nice, 5-bed historic house, hoping to rent to families, who you believe will likely stay put, providing stability to that property. Then you find out the neighborhood was nice 30 years ago, and the schools currently have a reputation for being a bit rough. Thus, the families are moving into other districts, and you now have a big house that's sitting empty. If you're going to invest long-distance, you have to know what you're getting into.It's just too risky otherwise.

- **You have the financial and schedule flexibility to travel** – There are people who invest all over the country who have never once set foot on their out-of-town properties. That's because they have good teams and systems in place to help de-risk the purchase. However, if you're just starting out, you'll likely need to get on location to meet your team, see the property, oversee the operations, and do some problem-solving. This all takes time and money. If you don't have much of either (and you don't have well developed teams and systems), then you'll likely create more problems than it's worth with long-distance investing. However, if you have some of this flexibility, it can go a long way toward helping you feel more comfortable with the investment and manage operations more effectively.

- **You're a bit of a risk-taker** – Stepping out into the unknown is not for the faint of heart. If you're likely to stay up at night worrying about whether your contractor understood your latest text about the renovation change you decided to make, then long-distance investing probably isn't for you. If you're someone who likes to tackle challenges and see the opportunities in risk, then you'll likely stomach the stress of something that's outside your line of sight most of the time.

Let's be clear on this – long-distance real estate investing is riskier than investing locally. I read a book once on the topic by a well-known investor and real estate influencer, who spent a fair bit of time trying to convince readers that long-distance investing didn't represent any significant extra risk. I didn't buy it for a minute (although there is good advice in the book). You tell me what's riskier, giving driving instructions from the passenger seat or from the trunk, where you can't see anything. The answer's obvious. It's clearly riskier to invest far away (from the trunk, where you can't see things directly), but people do it for a reason. Based on your strategy, there may be opportunities in other places that your local area doesn't provide. For example, if you've always dreamed of owning a vacation rental, but you live in Hooker, OK (a real place, by the way), you'll need to look elsewhere. So, if you're a risk-taker, that's great. Go ahead and buy a property far away, but don't do it unless...

- **You have better processes (or are willing to invest in them)** – If you're going to invest somewhere other than where you live, you've got to have good processes and systems. It's just too much work and too risky otherwise. I heard some good advice on a podcast once. They said to treat your portfolio like you have 100 doors. What they meant by this piece of advice is to automate as much as you can. You have to create processes that allow you to scale your portfolio without overwhelming you with work. You might point out that you only want to buy one long-distance property, so why worry so much about systems and processes. It's because distance makes the management much harder. If you're doing some renovations locally, you can just stop by and talk with the team about what you want them to do. You can't necessarily do that with a place that's 1000 miles from you. You need to develop ways that streamline communication channels. You know the old trick for getting money to your contractors – putting a check under your welcome mat and telling them to pick it up when they can? You can't do that with long-distance investing. The more advanced your systems are, the less likely the property will be a chronic headache.

I'm sure there are other factors, but that should give you a head start to think through whether local investing or long-distance is where you want to start your journey. The nice thing, though, is that no matter where you start, you don't have to stay there. I hate cold weather. I've always been this way. I absolutely run cold, and I'm always looking for heat sources. When I lived in Texas, we were invited over to a friend's house who had both a pool and a hot tub. It was summertime, and I started off with the pool. I thought it was too cold, so I went for the hot tub. In Texas. In summertime. That's just how I am. But I live in Ohio.

Rachel doesn't really want to move from Ohio, so how do I navigate my cold aversion and my desire to be someplace warmer? I dream about having a vacation property someplace warm, or at least warmer. We've talked about the East Coast, like somewhere in the Carolinas. I also love Arizona. I have since a family vacation when I was 19. So, let me circle back around to the Prescott story. My oldest son goes to college in Phoenix, and the trip through Prescott I was describing above was part of the big family road trip that led to him being dropped off at college. He's studying Sports Management in the very sports-heavy market of Phoenix. So, there's a reasonable possibility that he'll be staying out there after he graduates. Since I'm someone who thinks ahead, I wanted Rachel to see Prescott and to have a real image in her head when I talk about it. Phoenix is too hot for her. Given that Prescott is 5000 feet in elevation, it's about 20-25 degrees cooler in the summer than Phoenix. It's up in the mountains of central Arizona (I love the mountains). It's got lakes and national forest nearby. It's a beautiful location.

I don't know if it will be in Prescott, somewhere on the East Coast, or somewhere else entirely, but I would like to be a long-distance investor someday. The challenge for me is that the strategy we've used so far doesn't work as well with a long-distance investment. First, we wouldn't want to use it as a long-term rental.We wouldn't be able to take vacations there if it's always got a tenant in it. That means we'd either have to use it as a short- or a mid-term rental. I'm reluctant to do a short-term rental, because it's more work and riskier, in case the location I choose decides to legislate against them. That means the mid-term rental approach would likely work best.

This brings up the second issue. Pretty much any place we'd want to buy would be more expensive than Canton. Let's take Prescott, for example. I can't get a nice 3-bed/2-bath for $195,000 there. It would be more like $400,000.Remember how we use 100% leverage to buy our properties? We don't have loads of cash sitting around to make a 20% down payment, so we use our HELOC. This cuts into our cash flow, and we're going to need cash flow if this property is going to pay for itself. We're not well off enough to plop cash down for a vacation property, then let is sit vacant when we're not there. It would need to make enough money to cover its costs. It's harder to cover costs on a $400,000 mortgage (100% financed) than it does with a

$320,000 mortgage, if we put 20% down in cash.

You might ask why we don't just do what we've done here locally with mid-term rentals and replicate it in Prescott. There's a great website out there for mid-term rentals called Furnished Finder. It's the site we use to advertise our mid-term rentals, and it allows landlords to do research on what the market is looking like where you might want to set one up. As of the date of this writing, there are 39 mid-term rental houses in Canton, adding four more if you're okay renting a single room. There are 269 mid-term rental houses in Prescott, adding 52 more if you're okay renting a single room. That adds up to a lot more competition in Prescott than Canton. Perhaps there's demand to match it, but I'm not super comfortable understanding the competition well and not knowing much about the demand. In other words, buying a long-distance rental right now feels too risky for us, particularly because we're trying to set up a scenario where we have lots of cash flow to fund my retirement. I wouldn't want to buy a long-distance property, only to have it underperform and eat up all our profit.

This chapter illustrates some of the challenges of long-distance investing. We're not there yet, but hopefully we will be someday. Even if it seems too much for you to bite off right now, just put the idea in your back pocket and come back to it sometime later. You might just find that your circumstances have changed. Or you might want to consider using other peoples' money to buy the property or go in with a partner. I'm not enamored with either of those ideas right now for us. Perhaps one day we'll get there. Maybe you'll get there sooner than we will. I hope you do!

14

Learn How to Negotiate

Negotiation is a vital life skill. It's something we do all the time, but not all of us are good at it. When I was in graduate school, we only had one vehicle between Rachel and me, and we needed another one. My mother-in-law discovered that her elderly neighbor had passed away, and they were selling her 1984 Ford Tempo. She bought it for us for $300, because we didn't really have the money. It was a wonderful gift, but it was an ugly car. The antennae had been torn off, so it got half a radio station. The blower didn't work, so the heat and AC just seeped out at me. The back bumper was knocked about three inches to the right. It was a dull metallic gray, and the engine died every time I came to a full stop. I learned to cope with that last feature of the car by feeding it a little gas while I had my foot on the brake. Oh, and Rachel refused to be seen in it. But it got me around for a year before it died. We decided to upgrade, so we went into a dealership and let them know that we had a non-functioning car for a trade in. Since we didn't have much money, I wanted to get as much for the trade-in as possible to offset the cost of the car. I was hoping for somewhere in the range of $500-750. When the salesman asked what we wanted for the trade, Rachel jumped in and said, "Well, it only cost $300, so that would be fine." I looked at her in horror and wondered silently whose side she was on in this negotiation. Unfortunately, the words had been spoken, so the salesman quickly agreed and took the car off our hands. I'm still not happy about that outcome.

Some people like to negotiate just for the fun of it. They'll go to garage sales and haggle just to see how cheaply they can get things. I'm all for getting things cheaply, but I don't get a rush out of the negotiation process. However, I've discovered how important good negotiation is in life. Much of what I learned about negotiating was from my time as part of the hostage negotiations team (HNT) with the San Antonio Police Department. As one of three psychologists in the psychological services office, we were all part of the HNT. While we weren't the ones on the phone during negotiations, we had to be trained as hostage negotiators. We served an important purpose, as we interpreted psychological data about the person and situation that was unfolding. We helped the primary negotiator understand the person on the other end of the phone, and we worked to find ways to de-escalate the situation and ultimately get it resolved peacefully. While I won't go into detail about these types of negotiations, I learned that good outcomes happen from being prepared and having a plan. If you try to 'wing it', you'll find yourself being reactive, and good outcomes don't happen that way.

The good news is that negotiations in real estate aren't life and death, and you can learn to navigate them effectively without going through hostage negotiation training. Let's first explore the types of things you will likely be negotiating, then we'll talk through how to be an effective negotiator.

- **Contractors** – If you remember from the chapter above about finding and keeping your team, you want to be very careful about negotiating with contractors. You absolutely don't want to be cheap. Their time is valuable, and you don't want a reputation for nickel and diming them and ultimately underpaying. So, I would be careful about negotiating too much on price. However, there are a few times to negotiate. First, some contractors will have a different cash price than if you're paying by some other method. Ask about this, as this is the one way to talk about price without leaving them feeling like you're driving the price down. You can also negotiate bundled services. For example, it's typically cheaper to have your plumber fix all the plumbing issues at once, rather than address them piecemeal as issues create problems. Also, if you own more than one property, having them work on both together can give you some wiggle room with price. A final point made in a previous chapter – you can purchase the materials you need, instead of the contractor purchasing it. There won't be any upcharge that way, but you'll need to know what you're getting.

· **Property owners (if arbitraging)** – If you don't have the money to purchase your own property, you might choose to arbitrage. In that case, you could be negotiating with those property owners. The obvious thing you'll be working on is keeping costs down. While many owners will have little trouble filling their vacancies (thus making them unlikely to drop rent for you), that doesn't mean there's nothing to negotiate. Check to see if they have any 'move-in specials'. If they do, capitalize on those. If you're going to arbitrage more than one unit, you may be able to haggle on price. If you're willing to take on a longer lease term, you may be able to haggle on price. This is an important lesson to learn. Just because someone won't budge on the rent price they're charging you, doesn't mean there aren't ways to get them to move by pulling other levers.

· **Rents** – If you buy a property and inherit a tenant, you may find yourself negotiating on rent, particularly if the rent is below market. As the landlord, you hold the advantage in those negotiations. We inherited a tenant well below market rent. We didn't want to raise it immediately to what we could get on the open market, because we can't imagine what it would be like to be living peaceably in your home, and a new landlord swoops in and crushes your budget, forcing you out – upending everything in your life. We raised her rent from $740 to $850 per month, then told her we would leave her on a month-to-month lease (in case she needed to find a different apartment to fit her budget) and said that we would raise her rent $100 per month each year until she was at market rent. She was upset and said that she would be looking for another rental. More than 18 months later, she's still in place, and she's paying $950 per month in rent. I suspect her research on other rentals let her know that she's still getting a good deal. While this example might seem like a very one-sided negotiation, the tenant was trying to pull some levers, like threatening to leave. You might have a tenant offer to mow the lawn for a reduced rent price, etc. So, while rent is typically fixed, there is room to negotiate.

- **Payment to Realtors** – Many people already know this, but you can negotiate with Realtors regarding their compensation. It's common for them to start at 3% of the purchase price. We often shoot for 2.5%. We don't really want to go much lower than this, because it can demotivate Realtors to give you their best effort. Let's say that you're a Realtor, and a new client approaches you to represent them in buying a house. They let you know that they only want to pay you 2%. You have other clients who are giving you 2.5% or 3%. Who are you going to focus on the most? Who are you going to respond to the fastest when they text you with a property they want to see? Negotiate them down a little, but don't push them so hard that they aren't motivated to work with you anymore.

- **Price of real estate** – This is probably the most obvious thing you can negotiate.Just because the property is listed at $475,000 doesn't mean that's what you have to pay. This is where your Realtor should be earning his or her pay. A good Realtor will operate like a consultant for you to help you understand the market. If it's a seller's market (meaning prices are getting pushed up amidst lots of competition), you may have to put an offer in that's above asking price. If it's a buyer's market (meaning prices are steady or dropping, and there's more inventory than competition), you can get away with offering less than asking price. If the house has been sitting on the market for a while, you can risk a lower offer. You can use an inspection to give you leverage to lower the price or ask for other concessions. Again, an experienced Realtor can help you figure out ways to negotiate on price.

There's no way I could cover every situation where you might be negotiating, but that gives you a sample of the types of things you can do some haggling on. But perhaps even more importantly, let's talk about some principles of negotiation. These should help guide you in the preparation, which is where negotiations are won or lost. Before we get too far, we need to cover some definitions that are going to be an indispensable part of your negotiation preparation.

BATNA

This stands for Best Alternative to a Negotiated Agreement. This is essentially your plan B if plan A doesn't work out. Let's say that I want to buy a property, and I've become a little obsessed with it. Once I found this one, I stopped looking at other properties. I start to get a little worried that other people will outbid me, so I instruct my Realtor to submit a bid for $10,000 over asking price. In my desperation, I end up paying more. Let's say it's the same scenario but I'm a savvier negotiator. What I'll do here is find two other properties that I'm interested in. I'll use these as price comparisons to guide what I think the property is really worth to me. If I don't get that property, then I've got two more that I'm interested in. Desperation and lack of a plan B will lead to overpaying for properties. Remember, your money is made or lost at the purchase. Buy smart, and it will make you more money than desperation buying that leads to overpaying. This isn't just about buying houses, though. Always get more than one quote for a job. Having another quote gives you a plan B. With no plan B, you're left to pay whatever price the contractor is asking. If you can't negotiate a successful agreement, you must know what your plan B is.You're in a weaker bargaining position otherwise.

Resistance Point

This is also known as the reservation point. This is essentially knowing your budget and sticking to it. There are times when Rachel and I really wanted a property, and we walked away from it, because we had made an offer that was at our resistance point, and they came back and asked for our best and final (which happens when there's more than one competing offer).

We already gave our best and final and weren't going to increase it. While it hurts to lose a property that we liked, it hurts more to get swept up in the emotions of it, overpay, and end up with buyer's remorse. If you're looking to arbitrage an apartment unit, do your research and see what the going price is. When you negotiate with the owner, know what the highest price is that you're willing to pay, and don't go past it. If you're going to be a smart investor, you've got to negotiate strategically, rather than just caving on the plan when emotions kick in.

Bargaining Zone

This is the space between your opening bid and your resistance point. If you're selling a property, your opening bid is the list price. Hopefully, you also know what your resistance point is, which would be the lowest offer you'd accept. Theoretically, then, anything between the opening bid and the resistance point would be an offer you would consider accepting. If you're the buyer, the bargaining zone is between your initial offer and the highest price you'd be willing to go on the property. It's important to know that the bargaining zone can shift over time. Let's go back to the seller's position here. If they're not getting any bites on the property, they might lower the list price. They also might lower their resistance point after a while, just to get the house sold. That's why savvy investors often look at the houses that have been on the market the longest. They know that the bargaining zone is often shifting for those sellers, sometimes significantly.

ZOPA

This stands for Zone of Potential Agreement. This is the overlap between your bargaining zone and the other side's bargaining zone. If you have a positive bargaining zone, it means that you have an overlap between bargaining zones, and a ZOPA exists. For example, let's say a seller has had their house on the market for 35 days, and they just lowered the asking price from \$524,000 to \$499,000. While you probably don't know it, their resistance point is \$465,000. So, their bargaining zone is anything between \$465,000 and \$499,000. Let's say you do some underwriting on this property and believe it's actually worth about $485,000 (which you decide is the highest you'll go), but you want your opening bid to be $455,000. In this case a ZOPA exists, because we have a positive bargaining zone. We have overlap in our two bargaining zones between $465,000 and $485,000. That means if I'm the only potential buyer on the scene right now, we're likely to get the deal done when the offers move somewhere in that zone.

A negative bargaining zone is when the bargaining zones don't overlap. In other words, we don't have a ZOPA. This might happen if I love the house, but I'm limited on funds. I put in a low-ball offer of $450,000, because that's all my bank will approve. I'm below the $465,000 reservation point of the seller, so no deal is getting done here. However, remember that bargaining zones change. If the house is on the market still at 75 days, it might be worth floating that $450,000 offer again. A final point on this – sometimes you can overcome a negative bargaining zone if the deal is sweetened in one way or another. That's where good negotiators get deals done. They figure out what factors are at play besides price and start to bring those in.

Let's talk about how we do that now by looking at the four steps to effective negotiation.

Step 1: Evaluate Your Side of the Negotiation

This is where things like BATNA and reservation point come in. What is your overall goal? Is it to be a smart investor and buy good properties in line with your strategy? If so, then knowing what your reservation point is becomes very important. If you get caught up in the emotions and overbid, you've actually worked to undermine your goal. Be clear on what your goal is in the negotiation. Another question to ask yourself is what issues are involved? By 'issues' I mean things that impact the negotiations. Maybe you have cash to buy the property; maybe you don't. Maybe some things need to be fixed with the property and that impacts your bargaining zone. Maybe the property is on septic and a well, and you don't love that. Figure out what that dollar amount is for each of these issues to you. Given that wells and septics can go bad and cost a lot of money to fix or replace, this might shift your resistance point. Maybe it's important to you that the seller pays for a home warranty, which would cover system failures during the first year of ownership. Know what these issues are and know how important they are to you. Figure out your BATNA. Figure out your resistance point. All of this is part of your preparation.

Step 2: Evaluate Their Side of the Negotiation

Everything that you just did for your side, try your best to do that for the other side. What is their goal? This might appear obvious, but it might not always be. The goal for selling a house of a deceased person is often different than the goal of a person selling to relocate. The estate of a deceased person often wants to sell quickly and is willing to take a potential hit on price, which is why they're often sold through auction houses. The goal of someone whose property has been on the market for 150 days is different than someone whose house was listed last week. Try to put yourself in their shoes to understand what their goal is. What issues are involved for them, and how important are those issues? We've lost houses to people paying cash. We had an equal bid with no contingencies but lost out because another party could close 10 days faster. Apparently, speed to close was an important issue for these sellers. You might not have direct access to these answers, but your Realtor can probe a bit with the other Realtor. What is the other side's BATNA? If the house was just listed, they probably have a good BATNA (meaning there's a fair chance others will be interested and potentially putting in offers). If the house has been on the market for 150 days, it's pretty clear that others aren't that interested, and they probably don't have a great plan B (other than just keeping it listed) if they can't reach an agreement with you. Try to determine what their resistance point is.While it may just be speculation, it can help drive your strategy.

Step 3: Evaluate the Situation

This is an important step and shouldn't be overlooked. The first rental we bought, we found a house we really liked in our school district. Our goal was to not lose the house. We really wanted to get our first rental. But we didn't want to go in blind. We knew that it had just been listed, so we figured there wouldn't be much wiggle-room with offers. This is also when potential buyers are the most active. We also went on the county auditor website to research the property, looking at things like how long the current owner has had the property, who owns it, how up to date they are on their property taxes, etc. In this situation, we discovered that the house was owned by the estate of a deceased person. This usually means that they're wanting to sell the house quickly. With this knowledge, we formulated our strategy around the three things that any seller is evaluating in the offer of the buyer: quality, speed, and price.

Let's dig a bit into these important factors in an offer. Quality is about how good your product or service is (or in this case your offer). In real estate, the more concessions you're asking for and contingencies you have in your offer, the lower quality it is. Speed is about how fast you can bring the deal to close. Price is whoever is offering the highest price. Usually, satisfying two of these three will represent a good offer to the seller. For example, let's say that you're a manufacturer, and you make widgets. You have a competitor whose widget is higher quality than yours. Does that mean you're going out of business? No, it means you need to produce and deliver them faster at a cheaper price. If you can't compete on quality, compete on speed and price.

In this case, because our goal was to not lose the property, while not overpaying, we decided to focus most on speed and quality, but not lose sight of the price. We knew there would be competition, as it was fairly priced and new to the market. So, we decided to offer asking price. However, our HELOC was untapped and more than enough to pay cash for the house. We also asked for no contingencies or concessions. A cash offer and no contingencies/concessions makes for a high-quality offer. We also agreed to close in three weeks or less (which was possible because of the cash offer). We weren't sure if we had the highest price, but we wanted to be a sure bet (quality) and a fast close. Remember, we assumed a fast close would be important, due to the estate selling the house. Our Realtor also made a savvy negotiation move, in that he presented our offer in the afternoon and said that we would need an answer tonight or we would pursue other alternatives. This was a good move, because he figured there would be other competition.

He wanted to put pressure on the sellers to hop on the full-price, sure thing and not delay to consider other offers. The strategy worked. They accepted our offer that night, and it was our house three weeks later.

Here's the important takeaway – the more you know about the situation, the more you know which of the quality, speed, price levers you need to lean into, and which one you can relax on.

Step 4: Evaluate the Negotiation Relationship

Your relationship with the other party needs to be evaluated to determine which tactics can be used in a negotiation. For example, if you're buying a used car, and you'll likely never deal with the salesperson or dealership again, you're free to use more pressure in the negotiations and take a harder line. The other side might not enjoy the experience and may not want to work with you again, but since you're not likely to conduct repeat business there, that doesn't matter much – as long as you're achieving your objectives. Again – how you treat people is important, so don't put your objectives ahead of treating people with dignity. Now, if you're a supplier who will have repeat business with a company, you're not as free to be difficult in the negotiations, because you don't want the other side to stop doing business with you.

You might think that real estate is like doing business with a used car salesperson, in that the odds of doing repeat business with someone are low. That's not always the case, however. If you're in a smaller town (or operating consistently in a single township like we are), you're likely to run into the same Realtors at different times. If you gave them a hard time before, they may be less likely to advocate for your offer to the seller. Believe it or not, you may run into the same sellers at different times (usually real estate investors who are purging their portfolio over time), and you don't want to have a bad reputation. This means that you need to conduct yourself respectably and demand that your Realtor does the same. If your Realtor is engaging in underhanded tactics to get you properties, people won't want to do business with your Realtor anymore, and this puts you in a bad spot. The same is true if you're negotiating with contractors or even your Realtor.

When negotiating for a property, sometimes you can build relationship by writing a letter to the seller and submitting it with the offer. If you're a local investor who takes good care of the property and has a mission of caring for tenants, sometimes passing this knowledge on to the buyer in the letter will give you an edge over an out-of-state conglomerate buying up local real estate to put money in the pockets of their already-rich investors. It doesn't hurt to try. It also helps to get to know the tenants (if there are any) of the property you may be buying. Although we didn't get this property, we put an offer in on a duplex. When we went to view it, the tenants were home. Rachel got to talking to them (for a loooong time), and she established good rapport with them and discovered that she had conducted some minor business with the husband when we bought our first mid-term rental. They ended up advocating for us to the seller, because they wanted us as their landlord. Although it didn't work that time, if the landlord has a good relationship with their tenants and cares about them, that kind of advocacy can make a big difference.

Negotiation Tactics

Let's talk about some specific tactics that you can use when negotiating. I'll focus more on negotiating a property purchase here, but you can use these tactics in other situations as well. Let's dive in:

- **How you pay** – Remember, the purchase price isn't the only thing you can negotiate.How you pay can make a difference.In the example above, we made a cash offer from our HELOC. We're going to win in a situation where we offer the same amount of money, but the other party has to finance. I know you can't always be a cash buyer, but if you've got the money available (either sitting in cash, in a HELOC, or from investors), this is a big tactic to use.

- **Concessions** – Again, price isn't the only thing you can negotiate. For some reason, sellers can overly fixate on the price they're getting for a house. Maybe it's psychologically comforting to have a bigger number on the offer sheet. Maybe it feels like a negotiation win if they get the price they're looking for. That's fine, and you can use it to your advantage. Remember in step 2 of prepping for negotiations, where you're supposed to understand the other side? If they won't budge on price, act like price was your most important thing as well. Then when you give ground, ask for a concession. In reality, price might not be your most important factor, but if you act like it is, when you give ground and ask for something less important from them in exchange, you've turned the negotiation in your favor, even just a little bit. For example, if someone won't budge on price, have your Realtor communicate to the other Realtor that not budging on the asking price really puts this property just out of the budget range, and the buyers will have to consider whether they're motivated to meet that price. Now the sellers might be sweating just a little bit about losing a potential buyer. Then have a conversation with your Realtor about asking for the seller to pay for a home warranty and a few thousand toward closing costs. Ideally, the seller will be relieved that they won the price point negotiation, that the potential buyer didn't back out, and if it costs them a little bit in an area that's not as important to them, then they might give ground here. The seller gets their price, you got a better deal, and it's about giving ground strategically to get ground back somewhere else. Ideally, you'll know what's most important to you, you'll have a good guess what's important to them, and you'll trade concessions in a way that gives you what you want without the seller feeling like they've given up something important to them.

Sometimes it takes a little creativity to figure out what concessions might work.For example, maybe you noticed a piece of furniture or an appliance that you really liked that the sellers were planning on taking with them. Feel free to ask for that furniture or the appliance if you meet their price point. They might even be relieved not to have to move the washer and dryer. As another example, every once in a while, a seller will need to rent back the house they just sold to you if the place where they're moving isn't ready yet. Instead of charging them rent during this time, you may be able to negotiate a lower purchase price. The added benefit to you is that property taxes are often based on the sale price of the house, so you've just lowered your property taxes for a few years that way. Be creative and try to find unique ways to generate give-and-take discussions in negotiations. Your Realtor might also be a good source of ideas for this – have the conversation and see what you can come up with.

- **The double offer** – I really like this tactic. It's not guaranteed to work, but it's worth trying. Essentially, a seller expects that there will be some sort of negotiation (unless there are loads of offers, and they just take the highest one). So, if the asking price is $600,000, and you offer $560,000, the seller understands that you should be expecting a counteroffer from them. They might counter $585,000, then you might counter $575,000, etc. The double offer reduces the likelihood of a counteroffer – but you have to be more careful about the offering price. So, instead of offering a price you know they're going to reject and counter-offer, hopefully you've done some research into their perspective to see what they really value.

For example, if it's not a new listing, odds are, they're going to value getting the sale done slightly more than price. While it feels good to get near asking price on a property, if it's been on the market a while, the initial flurry of interest has passed, and they're likely starting to get worried. Let's say a property has been on the market for six weeks, and you decide to make an offer. Asking price is $450,000. You know an offer of $410,000 is, at best, going to be counter-offered. Remember $410,000, if it's your initial offer, shouldn't be your resistance point. Let's say that number is $435,000. So, anywhere between $410,000 and $435,000 is your bargaining zone. You'd prefer to get it closer to your initial offer, so you begin to think about a double offer. Here's what that would look like – you have your Realtor present two offers simultaneously to the seller. Your first offer is $410,000 with no closing cost assistance. Your second offer is $420,000 with $10,000 in closing cost assistance. Notice that both offers are essentially worth about $410,000. If the seller is savvy, they might take the first offer, for several reasons: 1) It is a lower sale price, so it's more likely to appraise for that amount or more (which is important if you're using financing), 2) Asking for closing concessions could signal you need some financial help with closing, which may not inspire confidence, 3) They're paying more in Realtor commissions at the higher price, so their net proceeds at closing will actually be better with $410,000. However, many sellers like the idea that they got a better price. So, if the seller is thinking this way, they'll like the $420,000 offer.

So, what are we really doing here? In negotiations, unless the mafia is making you an offer you can't refuse, people take for granted that there are at least two options. If you only present them with one (like your initial offer), then they feel like they are free to create a second option (like their counteroffer). However, if you present them with two options, they're going to feel less free to throw a third one in the mix. Essentially, you're creating a psychological pull toward one of the two options you presented, instead of them creating one of their own. However, if you're a smart negotiator, you won't leave it there. You recognize that getting the house sold is probably more important than price right now. They're looking for someone who can get the deal done, so they don't want to lose an interested party. So, what could cause a deal to fall through? Contingencies. If you get the house inspected, and there are things you don't like, you can cancel the deal. So, when making the offer, you can instruct your Realtor to say that either of these offers, if taken, will be associated with no contingencies. However, driving the price up from that point will represent a riskier investment from you, and you'll want to add at least an inspection contingency. You've asserted a lot of pressure on them now to accept one of your two offers without making a counteroffer. Because they know if they make a counteroffer to drive the price up, even if you accept a higher counteroffer, it will come with an inspection contingency, which means it's no longer a sure thing from their perspective. If you haven't picked up on this by now, there's a lot of psychology that goes into effective negotiations.

- **Gaining leverage** – A good negotiator will have several levers to pull during the process. If you find the property of your dreams, become psychologically committed, then develop a fear of losing it, you've given away all your levers, and you'll overpay for the property. As I mentioned above, do as much research as you can on the property and owners to find out what's important to them. If you know that selling quickly is important, then they're probably willing to budge on price. If price is super important and there's not a lot of current competition, then get an inspection done. If there's a lot of competition, then this contingency can make you a less attractive buyer. However, with less competition, an inspection can work wonders in the negotiation process. First, it protects you and the investment you're about to make, in that you'll have a clearer idea of how risky the investment is. Second, everything wrong with the property is a potential lever in the negotiation process.

Even if the property is being sold 'as is', which basically every property claims to be, if the inspection report says that there's mold in the attic from a roof leak and that there is evidence that wood-eating insects were in the garage and may still be, you can get an estimate for how much these will cost to fix, and use that to reduce the price of the house. While they don't *have* to adjust the price for these things, this inspection report puts the seller in a tricky position. They and their Realtor have to fill out a property disclosure form (that is available to all potential buyers) that spells out anything that is or has been wrong with the house. Many sellers don't know the whole history of the house, and so they just put 'don't know' or something similar in many of the categories. However, if you find something in the inspection, like mold and wood-eating insects, and they decide to back out of the sale rather than make concessions to you, they now must include on their property disclosure form what you found in the inspection. They can't say they don't know anymore. This may scare away potential buyers or make them more likely to get their own inspection to see just how big of an issue these things are. Maybe it's a safer bet to just make concessions and sell it to you. This is a big lever you can pull.Once you've been around the block a few times, you start to know what to look for and can make a list of issues to negotiate with even without an inspection. But if you're newer to the game, these inspections can really give you ammunition for negotiating.

Negotiations is a very interesting topic to me, and there's probably lots more that I could mention here, but it would involve me getting too much in the weeds. So, I'll close out the chapter with a few more pieces of advice:

- **Understand that you're not always negotiating with the sellers**. There are some Realtors who manage the negotiation process without giving the sellers all the information. For example, if you give a bit of a lowball offer, the Realtor may not even present it to the sellers. They get paid on commissions, and they may not want their clients to sell at a low price. That's one of the reasons why I like off-market negotiations better than through Realtors – I know my messages are getting through.

- **Make sure you have a good BATNA**. If you're too sold in one direction, you start to feel desperate. Once you're desperate, you've given away your leverage.Have several options available to you if you can't make this deal work. Also, do some research into the seller's BATNA. Like I said above, if the property has been on the market for a while, the seller's only option besides the deal is simply to let the property sit longer. That's a weak BATNA for the seller, so you know you've got some leverage there.

- **Do a lot of research on your opening offer**. Research says that the opening offer plays the role of an anchor in negotiations, meaning that it influences where the final price ends up more than the counteroffer does. So, when you make the first offer, make sure it's a well-researched one. Study the comps for the property that have sold in the last six months. You can even tell the seller that your offer is based on recent comps. This doesn't play as well if the house is brand new on the market, when the offers will cluster much closer to the asking price. However, if it's been on the market any length of time, don't be afraid to make a lower offer, as this pulls likelihood in your favor that your anchor will steer the price in your direction.

Just be careful about making an offer that's too low. That might get you a flat refusal, rather than a negotiation. One last note on this – if a property has been sitting for a good long while, don't be afraid of making an insultingly low offer. The worst they can say is 'no'. Best case scenario, they'll enter a negotiation with you, and at that point you know they're desperate to sell. Even if they have shut down your offer with no counter, come back to them each month with the same offer. It might just start to look more attractive to them the longer the property sits.

- **Shut down 'bad asks' immediately**. If the seller makes some demand in the process, like asking you for closing cost concessions that you just can't afford, say 'no' immediately and without any sort of counter. Just let the denial hang out in space there for a while. Your firm response with no counter-negotiation shows that they just crossed into a non-negotiable. The problem comes when you act like you're thinking about it for a while before you say no. That gives the seller an idea that you almost caved and can push you in this or another area, if you won't give in to this request. In other words, your hesitation gives the impression that their 'ask' was 'on the table' for a while. Once you take it off the table, they will want something in return for removing that item from the negotiation. Don't give them that leverage.

- **Don't reveal your resistance point**. Remember, this is the highest amount you're willing to pay, as a buyer. You can reveal this (or at least hint at it) in several ways. First, you make a high offer. This means asking price or above, particularly when the market is competitive. If your opening offer is too high, you're not negotiating well, which could signal to the seller that you're starting off at or near your resistance point. Second, you move up quickly in the counteroffer. If you offer $410,000 for the house we were referring to above, and they counteroffer $440,00, you're hinting at your resistance point if you move too quickly close to their amount. So, if you counteroffer $435,000, you've moved a long way off your initial offer and closer to theirs, which indicates your resistance point was close to their asking price.

If you're savvy, you can shield your resistance point through a technique called the escalation clause. We used this technique to buy our primary home. We really liked the house and didn't want to lose it. However, we didn't want to be overzealous and offer too high. So, we made an initial offer that was close to asking price. In truth, we were willing to go $10,000-15,000 over asking to get the house, because it was such a good deal. Our Realtor, Greg, suggested the escalation clause, which will automatically offer $500 over the highest offer until it hits our resistance point. Our house was listed for $249,900, and we bid $249,000 with an escalation clause. It turns out there was another offer for $250,000 – but they didn't have an escalation clause. We were willing to pay up to $265,000, so our clause kicked in, and our offer became $250,500, which was $500 above our competitor's bid. We got the house without having to overbid. Without this clause, the fear of losing the house may have forced us to 'reveal' our resistance point by overbidding, close to the maximum we would be willing to pay.

- **Finally, make sure you don't skimp on planning for the negotiation**. I am a firm believer that they are won or lost in the planning process. Do your research, and make sure you prepare adequately. If you go in with a BATNA that could have been strengthened beforehand, then you've gone in weak. If you haven't discussed with your Realtor as many possible levers as you both can think of in the negotiation process, you'll likely miss an opportunity to be creative and drive the outcome toward what works best for you. If you go in unprepared to the negotiation table, you're more likely to make the negotiation about one thing (like price), and you'll find yourself being reactive, which usually means you're either giving way more than the other party and/or you're being more emotional than you need to be — and emotions never put you in a strong position when negotiating.

I'm repeating here an old (and true) real estate adage that the value of your investment is determined at the sale — and you most influence the sale by negotiating effectively. Some people are naturally more comfortable at the negotiation table, and others feel less comfortable there. The good news is that everyone can learn to be an effective negotiator, and this often happens to those who plan well!

15

De-risking the Start-up

If you're like most people, the thought of investing in real estate is both scary and exciting. If the scary part is bigger for you, then you may never take the leap. But since you're reading this book, there's a good chance that the exciting part is drawing you in more than the scary part is driving you away. The good news is that there are things you can do to reduce the risk of investing in real estate. With that in mind, here are some things within your control to help de-risk your investments, particularly when you're just getting started.

Negotiate well

I won't go into much detail on this, as we just covered negotiations. The main point is this – if you negotiate well, then you're getting a better price (which automatically de-risks things), getting better terms (like you can get with owner financing), or getting important concessions (like a home warranty). Get good at negotiating, and you're laying a good foundation for reducing risk.

Your lease

Your lease can be your best friend or your worst nightmare, from a risk perspective. A well-written lease can protect you against all sorts of issues. We created our first lease on our own, based on what we wanted it to say and some research I had done into leases, as well as borrowing a lease from Greg. When we bought our triplex, we were given the existing leases of the current tenants, and we found out from the seller that her lease had been written by a lawyer. As I was reviewing this lease (and incorporating parts of it into our lease), I came across a section that would have protected us from some shenanigans that a previous tenant did to make things difficult for us after we let her know she was being evicted. The verbiage in the lawyer-written lease really would have come in handy and saved us time and money. So, not only might you be missing something if you write a lease yourself, you might also be adding something that, at best, isn't legally defensible and, at worst, illegal and could get you into trouble. There are companies out there like Rocket Lawyer that can help you create legal documents relatively cheaply. There are also real estate specific websites that can help you craft leases compliant with your state's laws, like turbotenant.com and furnishedfinder.com. Even if it costs you a little bit of money, having a legally defensible and comprehensive lease is worth the cost.

Choosing properties

Choosing properties can be a lot of fun, but you have to do it right if you want to reduce your risk. The most obvious way to reduce your risk is to get an inspection. This helps protect you from unexpectedly walking into a money pit. I mentioned previously that Rachel and I don't typically get inspections done. This is because we've been around the block a few times and know some things to look for. Absolutely, we're not catching everything an inspector would, but we know enough of what we're looking for to guide our purchase decisions, then we have our team come in and determine what needs fixed before a tenant moves in.

We did look at a duplex once that was an older building (maybe around 80 years old). It was nicely renovated, but some things were off kilter in the property. We went into the attic, for example, and we noticed odd signs of asymmetric settling in the house. We saw this in other places too. There was enough to raise some structural alarm bells, so we got an inspection, and we didn't like what we saw. The inspector found the same things we did and said that they would eventually need to be addressed. We backed out of the purchase. I didn't really think about the property much after that, but Rachel tracked it. Not too long after we backed out, it went under contract again, then went back on the market and sat for a while. Finally, someone purchased it. A while later, we saw that they were trying to rent it. One of our tenants, who could no longer afford our property, was looking at other options, and they found this one. While it looked nice, it had a very strong mildew smell, which turned them off. The inspection saved us here, as it would have been much more than we wanted to deal with.

One more point on inspections, asbestos is a real issue in older houses. If you end up with an asbestos problem, it can be very expensive to fix. This is where an inspection can be helpful. Not all asbestos is a problem, however. We were selling a house we flipped, and the buyers had an inspection done. The inspector thought the tape on the HVAC ductwork in the basement may have been asbestos-based. Asbestos isn't necessarily an issue if it's undisturbed and left alone. However, if it starts to degrade (like asbestos ceiling tiles that have started to fray or chip off), it releases microscopic particles into the air that we breathe in. If you put asbestos under a microscope, it has little hooks in it, and it latches onto lung tissue and doesn't release. Get enough of this in your lungs, and you're in trouble. If you're dealing with a ceiling tile issue, you probably want professional abatement. However, if you have tape on the ducts, there is a sealant paint that you can use to cover the tape and keep parts of it from flaking off. We bought another property that might have had asbestos floor tiles. Instead of trying to rip it up (and thus putting a lot of particles into the air), we just covered it with new floor. That protects it from getting disturbed and keeps it from being an issue.

Mold is similar to this. You want to know if mold is going to be a problem, because certain types can cause health issues, sometimes chronic, if the people have been exposed to it long enough. And mold isn't always easy to detect, particularly when there is a moldy foundation wall that was covered up with a new wall, so people wouldn't know there was a mold issue. We heard about this from someone's personal experience. Mold is most often found in basements, so if you don't have one, that's one less thing to worry about. However, mold can also form anywhere water might be getting to, like leaky pipes, so pay attention to your plumbing. Lastly, mold can also form in chronically humid climates, like Florida. Believe it or not, if you leave your house in Florida to spend the summer someplace cooler and less humid, and you shut off your air conditioning while you're gone, you will likely come back to a house with mold in it. It's that humid in Florida.

If you're new to real estate investing, you really should be using reputable inspectors. They are worth their weight in gold and can save you from nightmare scenarios. They can be valuable consultants for you in deciding if the house is worth buying, how problematic the finds are, a rough estimate of how much certain issues might cost, and perhaps even have recommendations for contractors who can address the issues that have been found. Having an inspector can also flush out some unethical sellers or Realtors. In one of Inspector Preston's videos on Facebook, he talks about a seller who wouldn't allow the potential buyer to do an inspection. The buyer brought Preston along to the 'walk through', and it was a disaster. No wonder they wouldn't allow an inspection. Another seller, once they found out Preston was doing the inspection, drastically shortened the inspection window in the hopes he wouldn't have time to complete it before the deadline. He made sure he fit it in, and the house had lots of problems. It's sad to say, but the way a seller responds to an inspection (with the exception of choosing a strong offer that has waived the inspection clause) may indicate the need to walk away.

While inspections may be the most obvious way to de-risk how you choose properties, there are other things you can do to further help yourself. One of them is to choose properties in good areas. We know people who bought houses because they were affordable but weren't in great parts of town. They got tired of dealing with the renovations and tenants and decided to sell.You won't get much of a return on investment, even if you did fix up the properties. In addition, these areas take longer to sell, unless they're bargain priced. The old adage of the three most important words in real estate absolutely comes into play here: location, location, location. Location not only helps you get more rent and better tenants, but if you decide to sell, you're likely to get a better return on investment and a faster sale. All this makes the property less risky. It's also important to know that even within the same school district, not all locations are created equal. We looked at a reasonably priced single-family home that was fairly nice inside. However, the property next door to the east was industrial and not very attractive. We passed on the property. Speaking of location, there are certain parts of the country where it is getting difficult to affordably insure a property. I'm looking at you Florida and California. Due to hurricanes and wildfires, some insurers are pulling out of the state or drastically increasing the cost of insurance. That makes these areas a fair bit riskier in my book.

Getting the right insurance

This is a huge thing you need to get right. There are all sorts of ways that you can mess up your insurance coverage. It might save you some money on premiums to cover depreciated assets than paying for full replacement of assets, but you're going to wish you did otherwise when you need to use the insurance. For example, if you're not paying for full replacement cost with your insurance and you need to replace your roof, the insurance company will only pay out to you the value of what is left in the life of your roof. So, if it costs $12,000 to replace your roof, and the old roof was 15 years old, you may find that the insurance company is cutting you a check for $5000, and you have to cover the rest. That's because you're only paying for coverage on the depreciated (or remaining) value of a roof that's 15 years old. A 15-year-old roof might only be worth $5000, so that's what you're getting from your insurance company. We've had to replace two roofs on rentals, and the whole cost was covered, because we got the right insurance.

There's a lot of fine print on insurance that will be tough to navigate yourself. That's why having a trusted agent that you work with can be helpful, as they can be a good consultant for you. But it's not just about getting full replacement value when something breaks. It's about being adequately covered if you get sued by a tenant (or someone else who gets hurt on the property). Again, it can be tempting to get lesser coverage to save on premiums, but you want to make sure you're being adequately covered. Once you have a good number of properties in your portfolio, you may want to consider an umbrella insurance policy. These policies extend your coverage to higher dollar amounts for additional protection, often spanning across multiple properties. That's why these are better than just increasing your coverage on your primary policy. You'd have to increase your coverage on every single property, which can get expensive. The umbrella policy covers all the properties and adds further protection.

Deciding on your business entity

Many landlords who only own one or two properties just have them in their own name. This can be for several reasons, one of which is that putting properties in your own name allows you to get conventional loans. This allows you to amortize the property over 30 years if you want, versus 20-25 with commercial loans. This means that your monthly payment is lower, pushing up your cash flow. It also gives you access to lower interest rates, thus also increasing your cash flow. You'll find, however, that more seasoned investors will have their properties in an LLC or multiple LLCs. LLC stands for Limited Liability Company. The main benefit of an LLC is that it can provide protection of your personal assets against a lawsuit.

Let's say that you bought a rental under your personal name and have $500,000 in liability coverage. Someone gets hurt on your property in a way that you could have prevented, and you lose a lawsuit, making you liable for $1,000,000. Your insurance will pay half of that, then you have to come up with the other half. You may be forced to sell the rental house for $300,000. Once the debt is paid off, you have $150,000 left from the sale to apply toward that total. You still owe $350,000. In this situation, they could come after your personal assets (savings, house, etc.) to cover the rest of the judgment against you. The idea of an LLC, in the same scenario, is that they're only allowed to go after the assets within the LLC. If that's the only house in the business, you may be forced to sell, but they can't come after your primary house or savings to cover the rest. If you have other properties in the LLC, they can go after those, but that's the purpose of umbrella insurance. One note on an LLC – you have to do it the right way for it to provide that protection.You must strictly keep personal and business expenses unmixed. You can't use your business credit card to buy groceries for yourself and have the rent payments go into your personal account. The business financials have to be kept separate, or else the LLC can't protect you, because you're not treating it like a separate entity.

Underwriting

I've mentioned underwriting above, but now is the time to give it the full treatment, so you know exactly what I'm talking about. Prior to getting into real estate, I had only heard of underwriting in terms of insurance or getting loans. Essentially, underwriting is the process of determining risk. When an insurance company does underwriting on you, they are deciding whether you're too risky to cover, and if they can cover you, what risk level you represent (and therefore what price level they should charge). When a bank underwrites your loan, they're also determining your risk level, based on the information you have provided to them. In the same way, when you underwrite a property that you're considering buying, you are looking at the property through a financial risk lens. We'll look here at what that all entails.

- **Gather important property data** – In this step, you're looking to see what you can find out about the property and how it's currently being used. If the property is empty, then you'll want to figure out how old the house is, what condition it's in, and more about the neighborhood and general area. Is the neighborhood trending in the right direction or is crime rising nearby? If it's currently being used as a rental, you'll want to know how much is being collected in rent, what the operating expenses are (things like insurance costs, maintenance, taxes, utilities, etc.), as well as current lease terms and some information about the renters. The current lease terms are really important, because legally you don't just inherit the renters, you inherit the lease as well. So, if a tenant just signed a year lease two months ago, you have to honor that lease for the next 10 months before you can make adjustments to it.

- **Calculate Net Operating Income (NOI) or Cash Flow** – This is more important for commercial properties (both large multi-family and those used for commercial purposes) than for small residential (four units or less in a building). NOI is important in commercial settings, because it's used (or should be) to help calculate the sales price. If a commercial property is listed correctly, they'll have a pro forma, which is telling you what they are projecting the income and expenses to be going forward, sometimes even giving you a spreadsheet with a five-year prediction. My experience is that you never trust a pro forma. They are almost always predicting best-case scenarios that will never occur. That being said, the current NOI should be an accurate calculation.

Just a reminder that NOI is calculated by taking all the forms of income from the property and subtracting all the costs associated with operating it. What you don't subtract out is debt payments, taxes, and capital expenditures (also known as CapEx). If you're buying a smaller residential property, you won't calculate NOI, as such. You'll be calculating cash flow, which is done a little differently. Many people, when they underwrite for cash flow, will include lots of intangibles that go beyond the operation of the property. They'll include the mortgage payments. They'll estimate how much CapEx will cost each year, as well as basic maintenance costs. They'll even bake in projected vacancy into the cash flow calculation. During underwriting, vacancy is treated like an expense, although it's actually a reduction in income. Personally, I like cash flow underwriting better than calculating NOI, because it's a more comprehensive and accurate number. See below for what a cash flow projection might look like.

Let's analyze this for a moment before moving on. It can be very tempting to underwrite just based on the fixed costs (PITI – principal, interest, taxes, and insurance) and leave out the unplanned costs (CapEX, maintenance, and vacancy). This is a mistake. Leaving out this last group makes it look like you're going to cash flow $180 per month. Maybe that's good enough for you, and you buy the property. After several years, you can't figure out why you're not profiting on a property you thought should be cash flowing. You weren't planning on the $375 monthly cash flow difference that CapEx, maintenance costs, and vacancy caused in real life. Good underwriting goes beyond just the fixed costs.

Cash Flow Underwriting Analysis

Item	Amount	Notes
Rent	$1500	Start with this amount and subtract everything else from it
Mortgage	$750	This will usually be your biggest expense
Insurance	$170	Varies widely by location and type of property
Taxes	$400	Varies widely by location
CapEx	$150	Most suggest 5-15% of gross rent; I went with 10%
Maintenance	$150	5-10% of gross rent, depending on age of property
Vacancy	$75	5-8% of gross rent; I went with 5%
Total Cash Flow	-$195	

- **Find comps in the market** – Again, if you're looking at commercial property, this matters less, because prices are calculated by dividing the NOI by the cap rate. One bowling alley won't cost the same as another, very similar, bowling alley if one is more profitable than the other. That's why NOI and cap rate matter for commercial properties. They allow for the success of the business (not just the real property itself) to impact the sale cost, which is as it should be. However, with residential real estate, you determine a reasonable sale price based on what similar properties are selling for in the area. I go on Zillow and find homes that have sold within the past six months that are similar in size and quality and within the same school district. This gives me a good sense of what my property might be able to sell for. However, I'm not just looking for sale prices. I'm also looking for rent prices and how long rentals are sitting unoccupied. You can also find this rental data on Zillow, where you can search for rental properties, see what they're asking for rent, and how long some of them have been sitting.

- **Evaluate Debt Service Coverage Ratio (DSCR)** – This number is really important to banks. And this is one place where knowing NOI comes in handy. Banks want to know whether the income you're collecting is enough to cover your debt. Let's say your NOI is $1500 each month (rent minus non-debt expenses), and your mortgage is $1300. You just divide $1500 by $1300. That's it! In this case, you'll have a 1.15 ratio. That means your income more than covers your debt service, but it's pretty close. Banks like to see 1.25 or higher, because they know you'll have taxes and CapEx coming your way from time to time. Essentially, the bigger the number, the safer a bet it is for the banks.

- **Run more than one scenario** – Don't just plug ideal numbers into your calculations and decide from there. What I mean is this – if you assume 100% occupancy all the time, your numbers will be off, because there will be times when your property is empty. Let's say a long-term tenant leaves, and you need to fix some things before the next person comes in. That could take three days, or it could take three weeks, depending on the problems. Sure, run the numbers in a best-case scenario, but also calculate how you'd do if the property had to be empty for two months a year. That will give you a sense of how much cushion the property is really giving you. Some things you might want to shift in your scenario testing are vacancy rates, increased maintenance and CapEx costs, and rent decreases.

- **Assess the physical property itself** – This could involve getting an inspection, for example. However, let's say that you're looking at buying raw land. It would do you no good to hire a building inspector then. But you may want to bring someone out to see how close the utilities are to the property. Maybe there is electricity you can tie into, but the closest connection is 200 yards away. You'll likely have to pay to bring the power from that connection to your property. Maybe there's no sewer connection around, so you must use septic. Has a perk test been done for septic? Is there bedrock just underneath the soil that would make this expensive? Is the property in a flood plain that makes building too risky (you should check this out when you're buying buildings too)? Are there physical roads that can take you to your property? If so, who does the maintenance on them? Would they be open year-round or blocked in the winter? There are lots of things to consider and assess, even with raw land. One thing you should probably inspect if there are buildings on the property – see if there are trees near where your wastewater stack leaves the building to go into a septic tank or out to the sewer line. If those lines are blocked, even partially, you're going to have big issues on your hands eventually. Trees have a funny way of growing roots into those pipes, and the last thing you want is to have a bunch of wastewater backing up into your house.

- **Legal and compliance issues** – Make sure you know any zoning restrictions. We bought a duplex once that was commercial downstairs and residential upstairs. We called the township to see if we could convert the downstairs back into residential. We were told no and that the whole building was zoned commercial, so no part should be used as residential. When I mentioned that the upstairs unit had been used residentially before we bought it, we were informed that a residential part can be grandfathered in if it had been used that way within the last three years. Sometimes there are environmental restrictions on a property, based on how it has been used before. There may be title or ownership issues with a property, which is where title companies earn their keep. They should be clearing these up for you.

An example of what you'd want to be looking for here is one of the reasons why we don't invest in Canton city itself. We live in a surrounding township, so we aren't affected by what I'm about to describe. Canton city charges a fee to landlords annually for each property that you're renting. They also require inspections periodically to ensure that the property is being taken care of. I guess this makes sense, to a certain degree, because they're trying to protect renters against slumlords. However, if you're like us, who are high-end landlords, it just becomes a costly bureaucratic hurdle that I'd rather not deal with. Lastly, they also charge a 2.5% tax on the net profits of the property. I avoid all that by investing in the township.

Also, remember that the usage of your property matters. If you don't want headaches, don't do short-term rentals in Denver. And don't try to mislead them to get one of the coveted licenses for short-term usage - it could end with a felony conviction on your record. I also discovered that in Prescott, AZ, the city will tax you on your revenue in certain situations. You need to do your research to uncover as many of these data points as possible.

- **Consider trends that impact future value** – I have heard a real estate podcaster say that they follow the 'Chick fil-A rule'. Essentially, wherever a new Chick fil-A restaurant is going in, he wants to buy properties nearby. It's not that this restaurant increases property values so much. It's that Chick fil-A is really good at vetting locations. If that area is good enough for Chick fil-A, it's good enough for you. Look at market trends in the area. Are prices rising or falling? Are people moving to the area or moving out? What does the unemployment rate look like? Are new neighborhoods being built in the area? That's a good indicator that people are moving in and there's housing demand.

- **Have an exit strategy** – An exit strategy is essentially what you're going to do with the property if the reason why you're buying it doesn't work out. Essentially, what's your plan B? The term exit strategy can be a little confusing, because it doesn't necessarily mean you're exiting the property altogether. It just means that you're exiting your initial plan. As I said before, if you buy a property in a D class neighborhood, just because it's cheap, and you get sick of dealing with it, then you'll need to implement your exit strategy, which is probably selling. However, you're not likely to realize much benefit from this exit strategy. You're not going to get a great return on your investment, and it may sit for a while with little interest, forcing you to keep dropping the price until a bargain hunter is willing to jump on it. The idea here is that you want to have at least one viable exit strategy. So, if I buy a house that I want to use as a mid-term rental, I need to run the numbers to make sure it works as a long-term rental as well. If it doesn't, then that's not a viable exit strategy. With the house we just bought for mid-term rental use, one of our possible exit strategies would be to flip it. So, if it's sitting vacant, and we're not getting renters, we could decide to treat it like a flip and make some money on it that way. We could also open it up to long-term renters. So, we have at least two exit strategies on this property. That means it looks like a pretty safe bet.

Before I move on to other aspects of de-risking your investment, I'd like to do a brief case study-type scenario to show what underwriting looks like. In scenario 1, I found a single-family, 4-bed, 2.5-bath home on the open market for $350,000, and it looks to be in pretty good shape. It's in a B+ neighborhood (good part of town), and economic indicators of the area look solid. I go to the open house and look around. The house appears to have solid bones but would need some updating before a renter goes in.

Let's say I estimate about $20,000 worth of work for the updating. Rental values are strong in this area, and I think I could get $2500 a month with a long-term renter. I have $100,000 in cash that I plan on putting down on the house. I find out that property taxes are 1% per year ($3500), and insurance would be about $200 per month. An interest rate of 6.48% over 30 years would make my monthly PITI payment $2068.55. This number includes $291.67 of property tax and $200 for insurance. This leaves a principal and interest payment of $1576.88. If I take my $2500 rent and divide it by $1576.88, I can calculate my DSCR, which is 1.59. I'll have no problem with the bank with this ratio.

Because I want long-term tenants there, I won't be paying for utilities. It's also a relatively new house, with $20,000 in updates going in, so I won't estimate lots of maintenance and CapEx at this point. Many sources say 10-20% of revenue should be held back for these expenses. I'm going to go with 10%, because I think the property is sound. Also, with long-term rentals, vacancy should be low, because the tenants plan on staying at least a year. Let's say we lose three weeks' vacancy every other year when a tenant moves out. That means I'm getting about 10 days' vacancy per year that I'm baking into the calculations. This 'costs' me about $800 per year, or about $66.67 per month. Let's total the numbers now. PITI is $2068.55. I'm adding $250 to cover maintenance and CapEx, and $66.67 to cover vacancy. That means my expenses are $2385.22 per month, giving me $114.36 per month cash flow. Over the course of the year, then, I can expect about $1377.36 in total cash flow.

In the grand scheme of things, that's not great. Making that much per year, it will take me a long time to recover the costs of purchasing the house. That doesn't mean that I should walk away, though. There are more things to consider than just cash flow. Remember, it's a nice house in a B+ neighborhood in a strong economic area. That means I can expect good appreciation on the property. Properties appreciated at a 5.4% rate in 2024, and if I expect that to stay steady, due to the strong economics of my area, this house will be worth $700,000 in 13 years. In addition, I'm receiving tax benefits all the way along. If you're looking for cash flow, this isn't a strong investment (although this will climb over time as you raise rents). If you're looking for total return over time, this could be a great investment.

Given that it's a 4-bed house, I would expect a lot more vacancy as a mid-term rental, so I might not want that exit plan. This house is in an area that isn't a strong tourist destination, and local regulations are restricting short-term rentals. I'm not in a flip scenario with this house. However, I did put a large down payment on the property, so the solid equity I have in the property means a sale scenario would be possible without being upside down on the mortgage if property values dropped. In addition, if the values went up, I'd stand to make a good profit from the sale. So, this is a viable exit strategy if I decide at some point that the long-term renting isn't for me anymore.

While I wouldn't call this a slam dunk, it seems to do well enough to pull the trigger if it matches my strategy. As I said earlier, you shouldn't run just one scenario. Adjust some of the numbers, like assuming 15% CapEx and maintenance costs and see what it does to my underwriting. This adds $125 to my monthly expenses, which means my cash flow is -$10.64 per month. If I have good cash reserves, and I'm banking on selling the house after 10 years, I might still go for it. If I'm banking on the cash flow to replace income, I'll likely pass on this property.

Due diligence, particularly on syndications

Due diligence is part and parcel to investing in real estate. If you are going to be a landlord, you need to do your due diligence on the property you're buying. You need to do your due diligence on your tenants. If you're going to use a property manager, you need to do your due diligence on property management companies. If you're going to be doing something like arbitrage, you'll be doing due diligence on the properties and landlord, to ensure they will work with you the way you need them to. If you're going to be investing in notes, you'll need to do your due diligence to ensure that the platform on which you buy and the notes that you're buying fit your goals and are ones that won't put you in a bad financial position. So, there's lots of due diligence in real estate investing.

What I want to focus on here is what your due diligence looks like when you are giving money to someone else to invest in real estate, where you don't own the asset yourself, and someone else is managing the investment in a way that isn't always transparent for you. This is where you can lose a lot of money if you're not careful. Sometimes your due diligence has largely been done for you, like if you invest in a Real Estate Investment Trust (REIT). They are regulated by the SEC and must meet certain criteria to be offered publicly. That doesn't guarantee that you'll make money or that you'll meet your investment goals with them, but they've largely been vetted and have a fiduciary responsibility to their investors. But what if you're approached by someone who is putting together funding for a syndication. Will they use your money like they should? Are they actually buying properties, or are they scamming you out of your money? What if you're looking for a partner to invest with on a project that's bigger than you could afford alone? What if they bail and take funding with them before the property is purchased?

There's a lot that could go wrong if you're not making sure your investment is a sound one. So, let's look at some ways to protect yourself if you're giving your money to someone else to invest and manage.

- **Review their track record** – See if this person or organization has done this sort of thing before and how successful they have been. Ask for data and reports and examine how they handled problems when they came up. While a syndication is less regulated than a REIT they do have to make SEC filings. If someone is claiming to have run a syndication before, you should be able to locate those filings. Check their online reputation in forums and social media. See if you can locate lawsuits or complaints. Ask for references and do a deep dive with them. Look into the depth of their team, to make sure they have things well covered, as far as property managers, asset managers, CPAs, legal counsel, etc.

- **Review the deal** – They should have something like a prospectus or private placement memorandum. Review this thoroughly, and make sure they have a thorough discussion of risks. Review the operating agreement to ensure it protects your rights as an investor. Have a lawyer review these documents to look for any red flags. Underwrite the financials and pro forma. Determine what kind of legal entity it is and make sure you'd be listed as a member or limited partner. As a rule of thumb here, if it looks too good to be true, it is.

- **Review the properties** – I have invested in several REITs previously, and they always provide detailed information on the properties that they're investing in, to include the location, purchase price, occupancy rates, planned CapEx financial investments, etc. If you're investing in a syndication, you should be getting this same type of information. If you're being recruited by a potential partner for an investment, you may want to discover this information for yourself. You probably won't fly to London and San Francisco to investigate the office buildings that your REIT is investing in, but you can visit the 50-unit apartment building that you're being asked to invest in through the syndication. You should be able to see inspection reports, CapEx plans, cash reserves, exit plan, fundamentals in the market locally, and the terms of the debt being taken on. Don't be afraid to ask questions and demand answers when you're not getting them. Lack of clarity is a major red flag.

- **Fraud prevention** – As I said above, too good to be true is almost always a big red flag. Unclear answers, avoidance of answers, or emotional reactions to pressure for answers is another major red flag. Also, make sure that the funds are going to a reputable third party (escrow). You should not be giving your money directly to an individual. That's extremely risky. To the degree that you ignore these things, you are opening yourself up to a lot of heartache.

Unfortunately, it's so much easier to just ignore risk and hope nothing happens along the way. Don't put yourself in this position, especially when you're just getting started. You don't want to build risk into your business.

16

De-risking Your Operations

Now that we've talked through some ways to manage risk at the beginning of your real estate venture, I'd like to go over some areas where you can protect yourself as you grow the operations of your business.

Choosing tenants

If you're investing in real estate in such a way that will have you dealing with tenants, these people can make or break your investing experience. If you have a great group of tenants, which we currently do in our long-term properties, you can sleep well at night and have very little to worry about. However, if you get the wrong tenant, it can be a bit of a nightmare. Here are some things to screen for to ensure you're getting the kind of tenants you want:

- **Income and employment** – There are three things you should be looking for here:1) Are they currently employed? Verify this with pay stubs or W-2s or bank statements, if they're self-employed. 2) How long have they been employed? You want to make sure they have stability with their employment. 3) How much are they getting paid? You want to make sure that their income is three times as much (or more) as the rent you'll be charging. So, if you're looking for $1500 in rent, they should be making $4500 per month or more. Less than this, and you're starting to be at risk for their budget being too tight to consistently afford the rent. Don't be afraid to call the employer to get confirmation of employment, even if the applicant is producing documents that look correct.

· **Credit score** – A lot of landlords like scores of 620 or higher. This doesn't have to be a hard and fast rule, depending on other factors. For example, if it's a young adult looking for their first rental, they may not have enough credit history to get a 620 score. If parents are willing to co-sign, then your tenant's credit score isn't as important as their parent's score (which you should be checking). Sometimes you'll run into a situation where a stay-at-home mom goes through a divorce, and her ex-husband paid all the bills. This means she had very little opportunity to build credit. Just because her score is lower doesn't mean she's not creditworthy. Look for non-payment, late payments, or things going to collections. If she has a sparse credit history, but everything's clean, you can be flexible. You want to be very cautious about people who have had bankruptcies and evictions. That's not to say that they wouldn't be good tenants, but you want to see a lot of good recent history over several years if you're going to take the risk.

· **Rental history** – Make sure you're collecting information on where they've lived before and who the landlord was. You'll want to talk to the previous landlord(s) to see how the tenant operated.Unfortunately, it's not terribly uncommon for people to fake previous landlords by putting a relative down, instead of their real former landlord. We've run into this sort of thing ourselves. While you can't prevent it, you can be savvy by doing the following: 1) Ask for a complete list of previous landlords and call all of them. Not only is it harder to fake multiple landlords, but talking to multiple fake landlords will increase the odds that you'll catch on to something not quite right. 2) Put a release of information in your application where the applicant gives permission for previous landlords to release part of the lease that proves tenancy. They probably won't release the whole lease if there's private information on there (like emails, phone numbers, addresses, etc.). 3) Check the county auditor website to see if the owner of the property matches the name that the applicant gave you. A mismatch is a sign of a problem. A match isn't proof, however, because they might put their mom down and their mom's address – which will be a match on the auditor but false information. 4) Probably my favorite tactic is to ask a question that you know is false and see if the person on the other end of the line corrects the information. For example, if you know the applicant claims that they lived at the former landlord's property for the past two years, you can ask the following, "I understand from the applicant that she moved to your property nine months ago, is that correct?" In most fake landlord cases, they've simply been coached to give a good reference by saying that they were good tenants, paid on time, etc. They're often not coached to answer specifics. That's why leading them to believe the applicant said they'd been living there for 9 months when the applicant said two years on the application, often leads them to agree with you. That's a dead giveaway for a fake reference. If the person on the line says something like, "That doesn't sound right to me. While I don't have the lease right in front of me, I think it was more something like 18 months to two years," you can have more confidence that you're talking to the right person.

- **Criminal background** – If you're doing the application process correctly, you'll be using a platform that does the credit check and background check. If you're into mid-term rentals, Furnished Finder has a process to help with this. Zillow also does this through their rental manager platform. What's nuts to me is that some municipalities have tried to limit the use or even not allow the use of background checks while evaluating potential tenants. Fortunately, this isn't the case in most places. Personally, I want to know if people have a drug arrest history, because I'd rather not have a meth lab in the basement burn down my house. As a landlord, I don't just have a responsibility to my tenants but to the neighborhood and the surrounding community as well. I don't want to expose neighbors to illegal activity. These people care about their neighborhood, and I do as well. Can you imagine a situation where you're looking to hire someone, and you're not allowed to see their resume? Can you imagine entering the dating world and not being able to ask about someone's relationship history? I'll stop grinding my axe about this now, but if you're allowed – make sure you're checking their criminal history. That said, a reckless driving conviction six years ago probably shouldn't be causing you to sweat much.

- **Financial stability** – While some people might have steady income and pass the 3x rule for income versus rent, that doesn't mean that they have any financial cushion. You are allowed to ask for bank statements (although they should be redacting the account numbers, if they're present in full on the documents). This helps you see what kind of financial cushion they have if they were to lose their job or have to get $3000 in car repairs. You don't want those repairs to lock them up financially and keep them from paying you rent.

- **Pets and household size** – You are legally allowed to only rent to people with no pets, and if that's you, then you should be screening for animals. Even if you do rent to folks with pets, you'll want to know how many they have and what types. It's possible that your insurance won't cover you if they have certain exotic pets or dogs that are considered risky. You'll also want to ask about household size, because municipalities often have rules for how many people can live in houses of a certain size. For example, some rules say that the maximum is two people per bedroom. So, if you have a 3-bedroom property, and there are 10 people looking to move in, that isn't going to work.

- **Applicant behavior** – Some applicants really don't present themselves well. We had an open house at one of our properties, and a woman pulled in and people piled out like it was a clown car. Smoke poured out of the car when they got out.One of the kids was running around the house, kicking walls, and climbing on a half wall dangerously. The family didn't look all that clean either. So, what in my description could a landlord use to reject a potential tenant? Believe it or not, not much. I can't reject her because she smokes (although I can demand that she not smoke on the property). I can't reject her if she has more kids than I would want in the house (as long as they're not over the housing guidelines for residents in a property), and I can't reject her because she doesn't have good control of her children or that they don't seem very clean. However, I could reject them because I believed that they were being destructive inside the house, which one of the children was being.

So, what behavior can you use to reject a tenant? 1) Respect – if they're rude or hostile, you can reject them. 2) Cleanliness/care – This isn't how clean you think they are. This is about them tracking mud through the house when you show the property or having a sign asking people to remove shoes and they don't. Maybe they leave empty drink containers on the counter without throwing them away. Perhaps they're not taking care of the property during the showing (like was the case above). 3) Timeliness – If they're not respecting your time by showing up on time, then you can reject them. 4) Attentiveness – If you have certain rules or requests that you're asking them to follow, and they ignore them during the process, then you don't have to accept them as tenants. 5) Follow-through – Maybe you set up a date to show them the property and they don't show up, then they do it again – you can move on. Maybe you have certain deadlines, and they don't meet them, or they don't give you the bank statements you're requesting, you can move on to someone else.

The important thing, as is true in all areas of tenant screening, is that you're being consistent with your criteria. It's fine if you reject a tenant who shows up late. It's not fine if you accept white tenants who show up late but reject black tenants who do the same, all else being equal. Document well why you moved on from someone, and be consistent. If you accept women with credit scores of 550 or above but require men to have above 600, then you'll get yourself into trouble. Be consistent and don't discriminate or you could be violating Fair Housing laws. Federally, you can't discriminate based on sex, color, race, religion, national origin, disability, or familial status (having children or being pregnant). There are some states or municipalities that also add sexual orientation, marital status, source of income (Section 8, for example), age, military status, among others. If you want to de-risk yourself, know the laws surrounding fair housing in your area.

Taking care of your property

No matter how good your inspector is (if you used one), there are going to be issues with the properties you buy. We recognize how significant these financial investments are, and we also recognize that one of the best ways to protect that investment is to take great care of your properties. This is best done three ways:

- **Fix what hasn't been done right** – We had our plumber look at a property we had just bought, and he discovered that one of the sections of pipe that led wastewater to the stack out of the house wasn't even secured to the section it was inserted into. He literally just pulled it out. We recommend trusted plumbers and electricians look at properties that you purchase and fix what's wrong. It's absolutely true that an ounce of prevention is worth a pound of cure. I'd rather pay my plumber $3000 now to address an issue than to pay them $8000 later to fix something that has gotten worse and caused damage.

By the way, unless the house is new construction, you're likely going to run into situations where a previous owner tried to DIY something, and they just didn't do it right. We've run into situations like this a good number of times. Even if we could possibly get away with sub-standard or not-to-code work, we always fix it. I once said to a therapy client of mine who complained that life was always kicking her when she was down (even though she was really just running into the consequences of her bad choices), "You can't expect your future to be free of negative consequences until your present is free of poor choices." We absolutely follow that motto with our rentals. We don't want a poor choice now (like ignoring a potential problem that we inherited) to create negative consequences for us later.

- **Don't defer maintenance** – If you have a slight leak in your roof, and a little bit of water is getting into the attic, don't put it off. It's easier to fix a small leak than to address an out-of-control mold issue. Most people defer maintenance, because they don't have the time or the money. If you think fixing a minor maintenance issue takes time and money, then wait until you have to deal with the fallout of not fixing it. Then you'll really be spending time and money. Also, it's these known issues (both things that weren't done right and regular maintenance issues) that leave you more open to lawsuits. Let's say some winter weather over time has caused part of your sidewalk to heave up a bit right in front of the main entrance. Let's say that there's a glass storm door in front of the main door. Let's say your tenant is coming home from grocery shopping one day and trips on the heaved sidewalk lip and falls forward, throwing their arms out to brace themselves. They fall through the glass storm door, which then cuts their arms wide open, leaving scarring and nerve damage. I'd rather pay to grind the heaved surface down a bit or to raise the adjacent part of the sidewalk to reduce the tripping hazard than to deal with the scenario I just described.

- **Use contractors who know what they're doing** – Lots of people use a handyman to do all sorts of projects, like plumbing and minor electricity. While they may know generally what they're doing, they're more likely to make a mistake than a licensed professional in those areas. We only use licensed people to do our specialized work. That makes it more expensive, but we can sleep well at night knowing the work has been done the right way. We have also learned the difference between price and cost. We might be paying a higher price for a licensed professional, but the overall cost can be lower when we're not bringing people in to undo and redo something that wasn't done right or to fix the damage that resulted from poor work. Also, just because someone is licensed and knows what they're doing doesn't mean they're always ethical. They may be 'fixing' things that don't need to be fixed, just to take more money from you. That's why finding good, trusted members of your team is so important and why I wrote a whole chapter on that.

1099 your contractors

This is a controversial topic amongst landlords. Legally, if you pay your contractors more than a certain amount, this is something you need to do. As of this writing in 2025, if you've paid a contractor more than $600, you should issue a 1099 to them. 1099s are tax documents that show how much you've paid your contractors. If you get audited and can't prove that you paid that money, then you can't count those expenses, and you'll have to pay more tax. If you can prove that you paid them, but you didn't issue a 1099 when you should have, then you can get fined for that oversight. This whole process is designed to prevent under-the-table payments to contractors that the IRS then can't collect taxes on. This is a controversial topic, because many landlords don't issue 1099s. Maybe it's because they don't know the rule, they don't understand how to do it right, or they want to save money on contractor fees. We were told a story one time of a landlord who talked to their contractor about issuing them a 1099. The contractor said he didn't want one and if he was given one, he would charge something like 25% more for the project to cover his increased tax costs. The landlord just gave in and didn't issue the 1099. One thing to be clear about here – the $600 amount doesn't include the cost for materials; it's the contractor's labor costs that count here.

Pay attention to scams

I'm not just repeating here what I just said about fraud prevention. That has to do with due diligence. What I'm going to talk about here is something pretty scary. People have gotten ingenious at stealing your money, which is different than needing to do better with due diligence. The first thing I'll discuss here is wire scams. Anytime you buy property, you need to wire money to the title company, who will then disperse the funds to close the deal. Title companies will give you instructions that you take to your bank that tell them where to wire the money. Scammers will email you fake wiring instructions, so when you take the instructions to your bank, instead of sending the $350,000 needed to close on the property to the title company, it will go into the scammer's own bank account. And your money is gone, mostly irretrievably. I can't imagine going through something like that. Title companies have gotten better telling you what to look for, but it's never a bad idea to call the title company to confirm you've received the correct instructions if you don't recognize the sender's email address or if something doesn't seem to match up with what you expected. I'm extremely grateful that this is rare, but it is increasing. Don't let yourself be a victim.

The second scam that we're starting to see is just as scary. Scammers will focus more on rental properties or vacation properties, where the owner is likely to take longer to figure out that something fishy is going on. These unethical actors will forge a quitclaim deed, often making it look officially notarized, and they'll file the deed with the county recorder's office. This means that the county thinks the scammers are now the owners of the property. Yes, that's right – the deed with your name on it, proving that you own the property, is now replaced with a fraudulent deed. This frees the scammers up to sell the property to someone else, put liens against the property, or even use it as collateral against other properties. I heard about a situation where someone put their house up for sale and was even under contract, only to find out that the sale couldn't go through, because the title company 'discovered' that someone else was now the deeded owner of the property. Imagine finding out that someone literally stole your property right out from under you. What about minding your own business with a vacation property that you own outright, only to get a foreclosure notification, because you've made no payments on a home equity loan that you never took out? These are nightmare situations that often can only be fixed through an expensive legal process. Some counties offer deed alert services, so sign up for that, notifying you of any changes to the deeds. Go onto your county auditor's web page occasionally and look up your properties. Are you still showing up as the owner? Protect your sensitive documents, and check what protections you have with title insurance. While these are scary, they are still rare, and the savvier you are, the more protection you have against them.

Beware of condos and HOAs

Even though condos and HOAs aren't bad in and of themselves (although some of you may beg to differ with me about HOAs, based on your personal experiences), they do create certain risks for investors. While these entities are a little different from each other, the problems they cause are similar. I'll cover two of them to watch out for here.

- **Restrictions** – Condos and HOAs can restrict how you use your properties. It would be uncommon for them to say you can't put a long-term renter into a property, but they may restrict usage against mid- and short-term renters. You don't want to sink a bunch of money into a property, having underwritten it with the revenue a short-term rental would produce, only to find out that you can only do long-term renting -and now the numbers don't work anymore. Not only can they restrict how you use a property, but they (particularly HOAs), restrict your personal expression with your property.You can't paint your front door just any color. You can't park your car on the street. You can't build a retaining wall without your plans being approved. You can't even plant a second tree in the front yard. Are your tenants following those rules? If not, you may find that there are financial consequences for you.

- **Fees** – HOAs always have fees. You may find that you're paying $75 monthly to support the HOA. While that's not a big deal, you can't control when that amount climbs. You might find that the HOA decides to put a pool in the neighborhood, and now your HOA jumps to $150. Condos are even worse. Not only are their fees much more expensive, because they're often paying for your building's maintenance and CapEx so you don't have to, but condos have become especially risky over the past few years. In 2021, the Surfside condo in Florida collapsed, killing 98 people. It exposed a problem with a lot of aging condos, in that some major structural upkeep wasn't always happening. Laws were passed that required condos to do special assessments to determine how much they needed to spend to address any issues. Sometimes these mandatory repairs cost millions of dollars, and who pays for these repairs? The condo owners, as part of their HOA fees. But since the HOA fees were no way close to covering those unexpected costs, the condos needed to issue massive special assessments, sometimes passing on bills of $30,000 or more per unit to the owners. So, if you owned two rental units in the building, you could be getting a $60,000 bill. Many people couldn't afford the special assessments and were forced to sell. Some people put their condo on the market, but it didn't sell, because none of the buyers wanted to take on the cost of the special assessment. Can you imagine owning a condo, getting served with a massive bill you can't afford, forcing you to list a property for sale that no one wants to touch? I'm hoping the condo situation has settled down a bit and has been de-risked, but for my money, I'm avoiding HOAs and condos. They're not always the wrong answer, but make sure you have a compelling reason to buy into these, and do your level best to de-risk the property for yourself.

Litigation

There may be times when you're confronted with a lawsuit, where either current or former tenants are suing you. In most cases, to protect yourself from a landlord liability lawsuit, you need to pay attention to two things. First, the tenant needs to be able to demonstrate that you knew or should have known that there was an issue. Second, they need to be able to demonstrate that you didn't do anything about it or didn't respond in a timely manner or in a way that would reasonably attempt to fix the problem. So, if a tenant brings an issue to your attention, and you don't move on it, you're increasing the likelihood of risk. If you already knew of an issue, and you don't do anything, you're increasing the likelihood of risk. For example, new tenants recently alerted me to a ground-based yellow jacket nest on one of our properties. Unfortunately, I've emptied several cans of spray into the nest, and it hasn't fixed the issue. It looks like a certain powder is my next move. The key here is that I'm taking steps to fix the problem. Now, what if my tenant never let me know that the nest was there? Does that protect me? Not always. In this case, I mow the lawn over there, so it's possible to argue that I should have known or caught the issue at some point while I mowed. Now, if no one gets stung and dies of an allergic reaction, then I don't have much to worry about. It's just not in my business model (or my ethics) to take that kind of a chance. So, your best protection against liability like this is to know your property's problems, fix them, and respond quickly to issues brought to your attention by your tenants.

Permitting

This is another one that is somewhat controversial. Some areas go way overboard on permitting. There are places where even switching out your toilet (particularly to water saving models) may require documentation and inspections – just changing out a toilet! Putting in a new water heater can require permits in some areas. It can be really over-regulated, in my opinion. You can see why some people just ignore the permitting process. Just understand that if you don't permit something, you may be running into challenges. While you're not likely to run into many problems getting nailed replacing a water heater, there are times when not getting permits can create problems down the road. This is particularly true when you're building an addition or renovating in a way that changes the plumbing footprint. For example, if you renovate your basement and add a bathroom, you'll likely need a permit.

If you do what we did in our first mid-term rental and upgrade the terrible bathroom that was already down there, you may not need the permit. We recently closed on the house that will be our second mid-term rental. The previous owners made changes to the physical structure of the property, and I could see on the auditor's page that the additions were permitted, because the changes were shown on the floor plan drawings. If you do major unpermitted work, this can be discovered when you go to sell the house, and it can cause a problem with the sale and/or the inspections. If it is discovered that you did unpermitted work, then you can be fined. Again, some people just don't want to mess with the headache and oversight, so they don't get permits, but this is a chapter about de-risking your investments. It's always less risky to go through the permit process.

Okay, so those were two long chapters on how to reduce risk in real estate investing. My hope is that all that information won't scare you away from jumping in. It's just much better to jump in with your eyes wide open and create processes that protect you, rather than expose you. The good news is that once these processes are set up, you're not reinventing the wheel with each new investment or tenant. It's also a bit like running – it's hardest at first and gets easier as you go along.

17

What's Your Strategy?

Strategy can sound like a complicated term. Businesses have strategies that they will pursue to help them become successful. These strategies can be complicated and multi-faceted. The good news is that your strategy doesn't have to be super complicated. As I spelled out before, our strategy is to own properties in our school district, be a high-end landlord, and operate in the long-term and mid-term rental spaces. We want to buy properties under market value that don't need a lot of fixing up, because we want to get people in the properties quickly. We want to capitalize both on property appreciation and cash flow.

Your strategy will guide your decisions. I mentioned above about a property we looked at that was next door to some heavier industrial properties. That doesn't match our strategy of being high-end landlords. That's why we passed on the property. Because we don't want much expense before getting long-term renters in, we passed on a duplex that looked like it had some structural issues. A good strategy makes your decisions for you. With that in mind, let's look at a few strategies people have used along the way. By the way, there's almost an infinite number of strategy combinations, so I'll just cover a few here.

Work with what you've got

It gets expensive to buy and maintain properties. Scaling your business is hard sometimes, particularly when cash is limited or you don't have access to much debt. When this happens, it can be a reasonable strategy to take what you have and make the most of it. There are a few ways people can do this:

- **ADUs** – These are accessory dwelling units. These essentially are extra living units on a single-family property. Not all areas will let you do this, so make sure you're checking with zoning officials and getting appropriate permits for the work that you're doing. These usually take several forms. First, where I used to live in California, a popular method was to turn garage space into separate living space. Second, some people close off a wing in their house to create a separate unit. Third, people will build additions, like a mother-in-law unit to the house. Another method people use is to convert existing structures, like standalone garages or barns, into a rental unit. Some people will build them from the ground up, but that's obviously more expensive than converting a structure. Technically, if you're adding or converting something that's not attached to the main building, it's considered a DADU, or detached accessory dwelling unit. To count as an ADU, it has to be fully self-contained, meaning it needs a bed, a bathroom, and at least a kitchenette.

- **In-home renting** – I'm more of an introvert, and I like my space, but some people don't close off a wing of their house – they just rent the extra bedroom and allow the renter access to the kitchen and living space. While this is the cheapest way to make rental money off your property, it just feels a bit too awkward for me. Some do it and really like it, and it is a great way to turn your extra bedrooms into additional income – if you're okay with someone else in your space.

- **Garage rentals** – We looked at a duplex once that had a huge, detached garage. Some people make this part of their rental strategy. They'll buy properties with additional storage space and rent that out to generate extra income. A space as big as this garage (and it was heated and had power), you could perhaps get $750 a month in storage rent for it, depending on what people need it for. Even an extra $500 monthly is a great addition to the rents you're collecting.

The point of this strategy is to take what you've got and make the most of it. This generates additional income, while capping how much it costs you to generate it.

Short-term vs. mid-term vs. long-term

If you're buying real estate to hold, you'll have to figure out what mix of this you want. With short-term rentals, the stays for the tenants are short, and it's pretty taxing on the landlord, as you have a lot of turnover, perhaps 'turning over' the house (meaning getting it ready for the next renter) once a week or more. That's an awful lot of work, but the payoff is the biggest here, as the daily rates are highest with short-term rentals. Mid-term rentals have less turnover than short-term and more than long-term. With our established mid-term rental, we've turned it over about twice per year. You might not turn over a long-term rental for several years, but they're the least lucrative. So, you have to decide what your strategy will be. Do you want more work and more money or less work and less money. You've already seen what we decided. We don't like the amount of work required with a lot of turnover, so we've stayed away from short-term rentals. With mid-term, we believe that the amount of work is more like long-term than short-term, and the pay is more like short-term than long-term. That's why we're shifting our strategy slightly in the direction of mid-term. We won't go in this direction with all our properties, because I'm not sure we could keep them all filled as much as we'd like. We're still in the 'feeling out the market phase' with mid-terms.

Buying and holding, then selling vs. buying and holding

The opposite of buying and holding is house flipping, where you own it a short period of time, fix it up, then make a good profit on it when you sell it. So, if you're not a flipper, you're a buy-and-hold investor. However, there's more than one way to do this. Some buy and hold and keep, like forever. That's been our strategy so far. Others are buy and hold then sell. That means they are a landlord, maybe for five years, maybe for seven, but the goal isn't to keep all their properties. Many will buy single family homes and run them profitably until they can build up cash reserves. Then they'll sell their portfolio and 1031 exchange it into a commercial multi-family unit, like a 25-unit apartment building. These investors didn't intend to keep their houses forever. Instead, they want to build their business, then leverage it to jump into something new or bigger or perhaps just more profitable.

Sometimes people decide to sell to focus more on appreciation, rather than cash flow. This often happens when someone doesn't have enough money to get into the nice area of town, so they buy several properties in a rougher area. Remember that these properties tend to generate good cash flow, because they can be purchased cheaply. However, the plan isn't to stay there. They generate enough cash from the rentals to sell and upgrade into single family homes in a nicer part of town. While they might be losing out on some cash by upgrading location, they've put themselves into properties that are going to appreciate much better over time, which tends to be where most of the long-term wealth is generated in real estate. My point here is that just because you're a buy-and-hold investor, it doesn't mean there's never a good strategic reason to sell some of your properties.

BRRRR method

This acronym means Buy, Renovate, Rent, Refinance, Repeat. This strategy works better with cash buyers, and it looks like this. You plop $225,000 on a house that needs a fair amount of work, and you invest $60,000 to get it really nice. Although you now have $285,000 in it, the house might be worth $375,000 once the work is complete, if you bought well initially (remember how I said that your money is made at the purchase?). Because you're not flipping it, you find a renter and begin to generate revenue that way. However, you have almost $300,000 of your money sitting in the house. So, you do what's called a cash-out refinance, and this is often for 80% of the appraised value of the house. The house appraises for $375,000, and 80% of that is

$300,000. The bank puts a $300,000 mortgage on the property, and they give you $300,000. I realize that there are closing costs and insurance and property taxes along the way that impact the numbers, but we'll just go with the basics to show the idea. When the cash-out refinance is done, you have $15,000 more in your pocket than what you started with. You then take this $300,000 and buy the next property with it and do the same thing again, which is the repeat part.

The beauty of the BRRRR method is that you're not spending $285,000 x 4 to buy and renovate four properties this way. If that was the case, then your total investment stuck in those properties would be $1.14 million. That's a lot of money out of pocket to buy those properties. With this strategy, you'll be spending the same $285,000 four times, because you get it back in between. Now it's true that you'll have mortgages on each of those properties now, which reduces your cash flow dramatically, but it allows you to grow without needing limitless capital. The key to using this method successfully is to buy a property cheaply enough that your forced appreciation makes it worth a lot more than you paid. Otherwise, you won't get back the money you put into it when you refinance. In other words, if I put $285,000 into it, and it appraised for $300,000, I'm only getting $240,000 back at the refinance, and I've just stuck $45,000 of my money in the property. Ideally, you want to get back at least what you put in each time, and any extra is a bonus. If you don't do this well, you'll eventually lock up that money across different properties and not have any to carry forward.

Non-deeded investing

I've talked a lot about real estate investing from the perspective of you actually owning the properties. But I haven't forgotten about those who are arbitraging or investing in syndications. As part of your strategy, you need to evaluate your tolerance for risk, how much time you have to invest in the process, and how passive you want things to be, as well as how much money you have laying around to invest with. If you have time but not money and are willing to tolerate some risk, then arbitrage might be a great way to go. If you have money but little time and assume that syndications are going to be better at evaluating and mitigating risk, then this is where you might want to put your money, particularly if your goal is to be as passive as possible with investing. There's nothing wrong with investing in ways that don't involve putting your name on a deed. In fact, as I just described, there can be situations where it's the best fit for your strategy. So, don't overlook these non-deeded ways to invest in real estate. You might even want to pursue some of these while you are doing things like flipping properties and owning rentals. That's the beauty of strategy – you can be pulling more than one lever at once!

Affordable housing

One thing that I haven't spent much time on, that some people love as part of their strategy, is offering affordable housing, otherwise known as Section 8 housing. Admittedly (perhaps unfairly) this type of housing has a bad rap. People think of welfare recipients trashing their place and selling drugs on the property. While it's true that these things are less likely when someone pays for their own rent in a nicer area, it doesn't completely eliminate the risk. Likewise, while this may be more likely simply because the area in which you're offering Section 8 housing isn't as nice, it doesn't follow that most of these folks will treat your property poorly. The main attraction for landlords with this strategy is that payment comes directly from the government each month. You are much less likely to have to go through a non-payment eviction process and lose lots of rent in the meantime. This is steady, guaranteed money, and the rent prices you can collect are usually fair. You do have to be approved as a landlord to collect Section 8 rent, so there is a bit of a bureaucratic process, but if steady, predictable income is part of your strategy, you may want to consider this. In addition, there are often long waiting lists for Section 8 housing, so this also eliminates the risk of a lot of vacancy in your property, which is also an attractive benefit of this strategy.

Remember that strategy is simply the roadmap you're using to accomplish your goals. As such, your strategy may change over time. So, if you are just looking to have a property or two to supplement your retirement income, your strategy will be necessarily simple and may not change much at all as you execute it. If you're like me, and you want to grow and scale, your strategy will be more complicated and shift over time. For example, we started off paying cash for our first property through our HELOC with a slow growth strategy in long-term rentals. However, my goal was to replace my income, and I realized this approach wasn't going to cut it. So, we accelerated our growth by using more debt. That was helping us grow, but it was limiting our cash flow on the properties. So, we pivoted to mid-term rentals to generate more cash flow. While Rachel and I don't necessarily have the same vision of growth (I want to grow more than she does), part of our goal is to be more business owners than property managers. This will require the execution of our strategy to shift a bit. In the beginning, you might be trading your time for profits. Eventually, you want your strategy to be trading efficiency for money.

Let me spell out what I mean through a metaphor that I heard one time. It's a metaphor of a fisherman, who excelled at his trade. He was one of the best at catching fish. Once he brought his haul in, he had to clean the fish and take it to market. That was fine in the beginning. However, the money he made at market allowed him to buy better equipment and a boat, which led to greater catches of fish. The problem he found was that he didn't have enough time to clean all the fish he caught and still have enough time to get to market and sell what he caught. He wanted to spend more time catching fish, but he couldn't afford to, because he'd be spending less time selling. And he couldn't sell more fish to grow his business, because the time he spent cleaning and selling limited how much he could catch. He felt stuck, until he realized that fishing was what he was really good at. Anyone, with a little training, could clean the fish and sell them at the market. That didn't require any specialized skill. So, he hired people to do that work, and he could spend most of his time fishing. His enjoyment of his work improved and so did his income.

So, what do we learn from this little parable? If all you want is a tiny fishing operation, feel free to fish, clean, and sell. If all you want is a rental or two to supplement income, feel free to property manage and be the handyman.

Because I want to scale, I want to eventually run a business, rather than manage properties. Part of our strategy now, as you can tell from previous chapters, is to get a great team around us. If I don't have to clean and sell the fish, I don't want to. Sure, we still do some of that, but if you're like me, you have to adopt a strategy that will require you to grow out of doing everything yourself. You'll have to let go of the littler things to get better at the bigger things. And, as our wealth grows, our goal is to spend more time doing what we love and delegating what we dread. We're obviously not there yet, so the strategy we're using now may not be the one we use forever. In fact, I'm excited to see how it changes.

Much of what I discussed in previous chapters laid down the foundation of how you can think about your strategy – finding your why, choosing your entry point into real estate, managing your finances strategically, creating alignment with your key person (if you have one) around your strategy, developing a strategy to guide your first property purchase and how you'll finance it, the strategy behind the creation of your team, your negotiation strategy, determining how much risk tolerance your strategy allows for, etc. This whole book is ultimately about strategy.

But let me touch on one more strategic topic before I provide a case study. Let's talk about your day job. Many people have the goal of replacing their income and being able to go to work part time or retire early. It can be very tempting to quit your job at the earliest possible moment when you think you have enough income coming in. I would strongly advise you to rethink that strategy. Let's say I make $100,000 a year with my day job. My stated goal is to replace my income, so I don't have to work anymore. But remember one of my 'why's is to spend more time with my kids when they've moved away from home. Let's say that I can't afford to do much travel with my current salary, other than a vacation or two a year. If I jump ship ASAP, I don't have to work anymore, but I'm still making $100,000 and don't have quite enough cushion to travel like I wanted to. I essentially find myself in the exact same financial situation, just without the work. My goal isn't simply to avoid the work, it's to be able to afford a more flexible life than I have right now. So, let's say that I replace my income. Instead of quitting, I work for two more years. During those two years, I bring in $200,000 each year ($100k each from work and real estate), the last $100,000 being pure profit (minus taxes, etc.) That second $100k really opens things up financially. Maybe I use the additional money each year to further pay down property debt, so my property income rises to $115,000 per year. Maybe I use that money to buy another property, also increasing my cash flow. Maybe I put it into my IRA, to add to my financial flexibility once I hit my sixties. See how just two more years changed my financial picture? Your day job is often one of the most powerful parts of your strategy and its impact shouldn't be overlooked regarding your ability to achieve your real estate goals.

Case Study

In this case study, I'm going to show a potential strategy of a young adult with little money to get started, both to demonstrate how it can be done and how strategies can shift over time. Let's call our person Anna. She's 23 years old and has been renting her apartment for six months. She has her first professional job post-college and makes $45,000 annually before taxes. That's enough for her to support herself, as she is single with no kids. She has a car loan and college debt, so she hasn't had a lot of time to build up her savings, although she does have $6000 in her bank for an emergency fund. She pays her bills on time and is a responsible tenant for her landlord. She has a dream of getting into real estate investing but doesn't know how. She has no experience with it and isn't handy at all. Her dream feels so far away, because she has so little money to her name. Her family isn't wealthy and doesn't have a lot of resources to tap into if she wanted financial help to make investments. However, she is determined and willing to do what it takes to move in the direction of her dreams.

She finds a podcast called the Landlord Diaries, which focuses on mid-term rentals. She decided to listen to it, because she had never heard of this type of investing. One of the very first episodes she listens to describes the arbitrage method of real estate investing. But it all sounds so complicated. It feels intimidating to walk up to an owner of an apartment building and just rent out apartments, while furnishing them and finding renters. One evening, she is stewing on this idea, trying to find out how she can make arbitrage work for her. It's attractive, because she doesn't have to own the property. She's just not sure how to get started. Then lightning strikes. She has a flash of inspiration, and she thinks she's figured out a way.

She doesn't have to approach some random landlord somewhere and try to convince them that she's worth taking a risk on. She's not sure how well she would sell the arbitrage idea to a stranger or if they would even view her as credible. Her flash of inspiration is that she already knows a landlord and has a track record with him – her own landlord. She starts to devise a plan. Her apartment is already furnished, and rather tastefully, if simply, done. The more she thinks about it, the more she realizes that her own apartment would be a great arbitrage unit. She could approach the landlord with her idea, which would involve her renting a second apartment (she knows there's usually a vacancy in the building somewhere at any given time). Instead of incurring the cost of fully furnishing an apartment, she can just bare bones the new one, where she will live. Because she is a responsible tenant, who takes care of the property and pays on time, she won't have to convince a stranger that she's reliable.

She approaches the landlord, who she has good rapport with, and floats the idea. He's a bit unsure at first, as he hasn't heard of the idea before, but she explains how these will often be traveling professionals or displaced families. He likes the idea of better occupancy in those units, not having to find new tenants, and the fact that Anna will be cleaning the units regularly, each time the mid-term tenants leave. She likes the fact that she knows the landlord and understands how responsive he is to maintenance issues, which she won't have to mess with. The landlord thinks about it for a day or two, then agrees. He gives Anna several weeks before signing a lease on a new apartment, which gives her time to advertise her unit on Furnished Finder.

Her lease costs her $1000 per month, and her research indicates that she could charge $2000 per month for her unit as a mid-term arbitrage. Two weeks after her listing, she finds a tenant through Furnished Finder, does the background check, gets a lease signed, then collects $3000 at signing ($2000 for the first month's rent, and $1000 security deposit). As an aside, mid-term rentals often collect a smaller security deposit than long-term rentals. She signs the lease with her landlord for her new apartment, handing over $2000 ($1000 in rent and $1000 security deposit). She spends another $2000 frugally outfitting her new unit.

Keep in mind that each month she owes her landlord $2000, $1000 for each of the units she is renting. But she is now collecting $2000 each month. Think about what this has done for Anna. Her original $1000 rent used to come straight out of her pocket. Now it's being covered by the renter. She's living for free, and she has freed up $1000 per month from her paycheck. That means it only takes her two months to recover the $2000 she spent on furnishing her apartment. She takes the $4000 she saves over the next four months (because she's not covering rent herself anymore) and uses that money to set up her new apartment nicely – just like she might want it to look like to arbitrage it again.

So, she approaches her landlord and proposes doing the same thing with her new apartment. It's working well for him so far, so he allows her to sign a lease on a third unit once she locates a tenant for the one she is currently occupying. Now she owes the landlord $3000 in rent each month, but she's bringing in $4000 from the arbitraging. That's not counting the fact that she is still saving $1000 more each month from her paycheck, because she doesn't pay for her rent out of that anymore. She's one year into this experiment, and she's now making $2000 per month more than she used to, between cash flow and not paying her own rent. Like before, she spends $6000 over a six-month period of time, slowly outfitting her current apartment into arbitrage condition. Then she approaches the landlord again. He kind of chuckles but agrees, as he has another vacancy. Anna now arbitrages three apartments and lives in a fourth. She owes $4000 in rent monthly, but she's collecting $6000 in rent and still has an extra $1000 from her salary that is freed up. She does this two more times over the next year, until she has five arbitrage units and the one she is living in. Looking at her financials, she owes the landlord $6000 in rent each month, but she's bringing in $10,000 plus the extra $1000 from her paycheck she isn't spending on rent.

She approaches her landlord again, but this time there aren't any more vacancies, and he's reluctant to tie up too many with Anna. She decides that the arbitrage method is lucrative for her, but she doesn't want to keep apartment hopping for the rest of her life. She has a dream of owning her own property. Up to this point, she has managed to save $40,000 from her income and the arbitrage arrangement, and she is currently netting $5000 per month through real estate. She decides to stop her arbitrage growth strategy and stabilize what she's doing, so she can focus on saving. Anna decides that she doesn't want to start over with arbitraging in a new apartment complex with someone she doesn't know. She likes her current arrangement. Therefore, she adopts a sit-tight policy, and saves $100,000 over the next two years, on top of the $40,000 that she had saved. At this point, she decides to change strategies. She has listened to a lot of podcasts and read a lot of books (perhaps this one?) and decides to buy a duplex. She takes this approach, because she has decided to house hack the duplex. This will free up her apartment to arbitrage, she'll live in one side of the duplex, then rent the other. She takes her cash and puts 50% down on the duplex. She does this because it will lower the mortgage enough to allow her to live for free on her side, with the renter on the other side covering the cost of the mortgage.

She doesn't want to saturate the market with mid-term rentals, so she decides to have a long-term renter with her in the duplex. Keep in mind that the duplex has a net zero impact on her financials. It's not making her money, and it's not costing her money – but it did free up her apartment to arbitrage. She has six arbitrage units now, costing her $6000 per month but bringing in $12,000, plus the $1000 extra from her paycheck, because she's not paying rent anymore. Now Anna is looking at $7000 per month in cash flow, or $84,000 per year. She goes into a sit-tight strategy again for two years and saves $150,000. She uses this money to buy a single-family home and fund some necessary renovations, which are done after five months. She gets a long-term renter in place and does a cash-out finance. This puts a mortgage on the property, which allows her to draw $180,000 in cash. So, she not only got her original investment back, but she has an additional $30,000. She uses this money to buy another rental and repeats consistently, purchasing three more homes over the next two years.

Let's say Anna is 30 now. What does she have to show for her efforts? She keeps $12,000 per year from her income, because she's not paying for her own housing anymore. She profits $60,000 each year from her arbitrage units. She owns a duplex, with a net zero impact on her cash flow. She also owns four single-family homes that cash flow $300 per month each. That's $1200 per month total, making $14,400 per year. Let's add that up: $12,000+$60,000+$14,400= $86,400 annually. Keep in mind, that's not her rental income – that's the profit she's walking away with. That's not even counting the equity she has in her properties and the market appreciation that she is gaining. Anna is still working her full-time job, where she is now making $75,000 annually. She is 30 years old and has more than replaced her income.

Admittedly, doing a case study like this involves round numbers and some glossing over challenges. For example, it assumes 100% occupancy in her arbitrage units, which isn't likely. However, this is designed to show how someone with no experience and little money can begin their real estate journey. Interestingly, she started by doing what I call arbitrage hacking. As far as I know, this strategy has never been described before. House hacking is well known (which is a strategy that Anna utilizes in her duplex). Arbitraging is well known, but she puts a unique spin on it that combines house hacking and arbitrage, where she consistently arbitrages the apartment unit where she lives, then moves on to a new one, then does it again. It's a very reasonable strategy for someone like her. She already had a relationship with her landlord, which de-risked her proposition and made it feel less 'salesy' when she approached him. Although idealistic, this case study is in no way unrealistic for a smart, motivated investor, who deploys their strategy well.

I want to make one final point in this chapter, with the help of the case study. I want to make sure you understand the difference between a goal, a strategy, and a tactic. Anna's goal was to get into real estate – but that's too general. She ultimately shifted her goal to replacing her income. Strategy supports your goal. Tactics are the levers that you're pulling to execute on your strategy. Think of your goal as the destination, strategy as the road you travel on to get to your goal, and tactics as things like the speed you're traveling, how many stops you take along the way, etc. Notice that Anna did change strategies along the way, but they all supported her goal. She went from arbitrage hacking to house hacking to long-term rentals. So, her first strategy was to create cash flow through low-cost means. She then shifted strategy to acquiring properties that cost her more money (and generated less cash flow) but would allow her to benefit from appreciation. Her tactics also shifted. Sometimes she was actively investing, and sometimes she stopped to save money.

What I think is important to say here is that your tactics can shift more than your strategy does, and your strategy can shift more than your goal does. So, if your goal shifts a lot, then you probably haven't thought it through much. If your strategy is shifting a lot, then it's probably undermining your ability to reach your goal effectively. It's most acceptable to shift your tactics. I've already explained how Rachel and I have done this, where we've gone from engaging in growth tactics to shifting to paying debt down. Both tactics have been used to support the strategy of generating cash flow, which is used to achieve my goal of replacing my income. So, hopefully you can see how switching tactics can still support the strategy. However, switching strategy a lot can undermine your goal.

If I have a cash flow strategy (to achieve my goal of replacing my income), but I see an opportunity for a great appreciation property that doesn't cash flow, I've tied up money in the property and perhaps stopped my ability to get more cash flow properties. This new purchase doesn't support my goal and may actually work against it. That's not to say you can't switch strategies. In the case study, Anna switched from a non-deeded strategy that generated a lot of cash flow (but no appreciation) to a deeded strategy that generated some cash flow (but a lot more appreciation). As she approached her goal of replacing her income, she could shift her strategy without undermining her goal.

Does that mean that your goal can never shift? No, remember those investors I mentioned above who just want a property or two to supplement their retirement income? Maybe they realize they love doing it and want to do more of it.Instead of a goal of income supplementation, they set a new goal of building real, generational wealth they can pass down to their kids. But your goals should be shifting the least. As I said above, goals that shift frequently are goals that haven't been thought through. Goals that haven't been thought through are goals that don't have much energy behind them. So, please remember the difference between a tactic, a strategy, and a goal. Tactics can shift to support strategies, and some shifts here and there are normal.Strategies are the tracks you ride on to get to your goal. These can shift too, but they shouldn't shift often, and they should all align with your goals. Goals should shift the least often and should have a lot of thought and meaning behind what you're chasing – because they're driven by your 'Why's.

18

Finding Tenants

I could have ended the book with the strategy chapter, but I didn't like finishing on something abstract. I want my last two chapters to be more action-oriented, to inspire ideas and perhaps generate movement. So, let's jump in to the ever-interesting task of finding tenants. This is an important chapter, because acquiring a property is only half the battle.Without tenants, the carrying costs will bleed you dry. This isn't going to be a rehash of what we talked about before regarding screening applicants. It will be a practical, hands-on discussion about the nuts and bolts of where you can find them, because they're out there.

Craigslist

I've never used Craigslist, for reasons I'll get to shortly, but it remains a place where people will list their rentals. They do this for the following reasons: 1) it's free to list the rental, 2) it's fairly easy to make adjustments to your listing, 3) there is still relatively heavy traffic to Craigslist, giving listings good visibility, and 4) you can directly communicate with tenant leads. So, why don't we list anything on Craigslist? First, it is the least regulated, so scammers come out in full force (both on the listing side and applicant side). If you're up for competing against fake listings and people pretending to be interested tenants to phish, have at it. Second, Craigslist doesn't have any built-in vetting tools, so you'll need your own system for background and credit checks. This leads to the third problem. It's the lower quality potential tenants who flock to Craigslist in the hopes that you'll be lax in checking up on them. Fourth, have you ever heard of the Zillow murders? Neither have I. But I have heard of the Craigslist murders. There are just more bad actors on this platform, and I'd rather not deal with it – or put Rachel in the position to deal with it.Lastly, because of how many shenanigans take place on Craigslist, it can be a big time drain trying to figure out what is a good, legit lead and what is not.

Facebook Marketplace

We have used this platform to find renters, but we often regret it, so it's now moved into backup status. This can be an attractive platform, because of how many people are on it. If Craigslist has a large user base, Facebook puts it to shame. Again, it's free to use and allows for easy communication. Marketplace tends to be safer than Craigslist, because you can often view the profile of the person who has reached out. This helps you see if you have mutual friends and get some insight into what type of person they are. Marketplace also allows for posting in groups. Let's say that you've joined a local Facebook group for real estate investors, you can post your listing there and see if it gets focused traction. Lastly, you can run ads on Facebook to increase your visibility. Those are big enough pros that we've used this platform before.

The cons of Facebook Marketplace are very similar to Craigslist, in that it can attract lower quality applicants, doesn't have any vetting tools, scammers are attracted to the large audience and can potentially learn something about you from your profile, and you may spend more time than you want trying to sift the good from the bad. The primary problem with Facebook Marketplace, however, and the major reason why we don't like using this platform if we don't have to is the idiotic hate from people who just don't have the strength of character to scroll by something that has nothing to do with them.

Imagine that you have spent a lot of time fixing your rental up, doing your research to make sure you're in the ballpark of market rent, and you list your property right before you go to bed, full of hope that you're going to find a good tenant. When you wake up in the morning, you're almost guaranteed to find comments like the following in the feed of your post: "What!$1300 for that piece of crap rental? I hate landlords like you, just looking to take advantage of people who have nowhere else to live," or "It's selfish, terrible people like you who make this world such a bad place. How can you sleep at night?" or "The place I'm renting is bigger than the one you're offering, and I only pay $800 per month." It's clear that these people have never been landlords and are absolutely ignorant of the economics and time investment behind it. It's clear they can't tell the difference between someone who just bought a house at market prices and spent money to fix it up and the person who pays $800 rent and lives in a place where the owner paid $53,000 for it 36 years ago. If you paid market prices for the house, you have to charge market rent to make it worthwhile. If you're a glutton for punishment, want to expose yourself to completely unnecessary negativity, and lose all faith in humanity, feel free to use Facebook Marketplace.

Facebook

You might be asking, "Wait, didn't you just cover Facebook?" That's a great question, but I'm not talking about Marketplace here. I'm talking about using your own network. We do this with just about every rental. Rachel will typically post to her page, because she's more active and has a bigger network on the platform. People will often share her post to their pages, increasing visibility. It's not unusual for us to get several leads this way, and they tend to be higher quality leads, even if they don't end up working out. This is because we're getting leads directly from people we know.It's also much harder for scammers to get at this post, because it's not posted publicly in a forum where lots of people you don't know can see it.

There is an added benefit, in that the postings have let enough people know over time that we're landlords. So, people will reach out to us unprompted on occasion to see if we have any openings, as they know someone who needs a place. This is a great place to lay the groundwork for direct leads from people you know. While it's free and allows for easy communication and data gathering on leads (both from the person who passes the lead along and from viewing the lead's profile), it has a few drawbacks. These are primarily that the audience who sees your post is limited, so it's probably not the only way you want to recruit potential tenants. Also, there are no built-in ways to vet the interested parties, so you'll need to use this in conjunction with another platform (like what you'd need to do with Craigslist and Marketplace). So, we absolutely use Facebook as a regular part of our strategy for finding tenants.

Zillow

I'm sure there are many platforms out there to post your rental property, but the one we use is Zillow Rental Manager. One of the main reasons we use this is simply the name recognition of Zillow. It's one of the most popular real estate sites, which means it's going to drive traffic. It's free to use, allows for easy communication, and has a robust platform for putting lots of details and information about your property. The nice thing about Zillow Rental Manager is that it's designed specifically for landlords. This means that it's less susceptible to scammers, completely cuts out the nonsense of hecklers, and has good capabilities to help vet your applicants. They will pay a fee to apply, and this will give you a background check and credit history, as well as all the other information in their application, like how many in the family, salary information, as well as the opportunity for them to upload pay stubs, rental history information, employer information, etc. If you want, you can manage more of your tenant actions there as well, like uploading your leases, but we don't use it for that functionality. We get leads straight from our Zillow listing, and if we get leads from our Facebook posts, we'll get their email address, which we enter into Zillow, and it sends them an invite to apply. No matter what platform you use, make sure it gets adequate traffic and allows you to manage your applications through it.

One last comment here – something Rachel and I have wrestled with is if we require an application before letting an interested party see the property. Since applications cost money and some good potential tenants are reluctant to spend money before knowing if the property is a good fit, we'll set up an open house day/time and invite anyone with interest to view the property before they apply. We've also done individual showings as well. Once you get a tenant, make sure you take the listing down, as you'll get random people applying without even seeing it. I would hate for someone to waste an application fee on a property that's no longer available.

Furnished Finder

If you're using your property as a mid-term rental (or arbitraging a property), I highly recommend using Furnished Finder. This is a website that was originally set up to help traveling medical professionals find temporary housing, but it's become much bigger than that. You can use it to research the potential demand in your area, as well as how much competition you have. They have educational information for landlords, as well as a high-quality podcast. It's really a website that is designed to help property owners be successful. In addition, they don't charge booking fees, like Airbnb and Vrbo. So, you keep all the rent you collect. You just pay a very reasonable per-property annual fee for each of your listings. It's currently less than $200 yearly to list a property there.

They also have features that allow you to do the credit and background check, collect rent, get insurance coverage, and even create an editable lease that is specific to your state laws. In addition to that, there are two other things I like about the website. The first is that you get notified of any unmatched leads. So, if someone is looking for housing in the area, and their needs don't quite match an available property, you get notified, which allows you to reach out and see if you can make something work. The second thing I like is that companies that find housing for people who are displaced, due to insurance claims, look on this website. I believe we've been contacted three times like this.Unfortunately, we didn't have any availability the first two times, and the third time led to one of our mid-term rental tenants.

Vrbo/Airbnb

Most everyone knows these platforms, and I'm sure there's a good chance you've used one of them. We all know that they are places to go if you want to stay in a vacation rental. So, if you own a vacation rental, these are the places to have your listing. While the brand recognition is huge on these platforms, which can help drive traffic, they have become pretty saturated. For example, if I type Destin, FL into Airbnb, it says, "Over 1000 homes within map area."I don't want to compete with that. In addition, people are having to add loads of amenities to their properties to get noticed. For example, properties with a hot tub get rented more often than those without. You're also at the whim of the ratings of your renters, which opens you up to scammers. They'll do things like shut off the AC and threaten to give a bad review for non-functioning AC if you don't give them half off, even though the AC actually works just fine.

There are a few other issues with the platform itself. You don't know who your tenant is until they book, making it difficult to communicate with them on your own terms and/or decide if they're a renter you want in your property. In addition, they charge booking fees, which can be expensive. While Vrbo is currently a touch under 10%, Airbnb can be over 15%. This can be a lot of money. We initially listed our first mid-term rental on Airbnb (which isn't that uncommon) for $3000 monthly. Fortunately, we found a tenant off the platform, and we've never used it again. Those tenants stayed 10 months with us. We grossed $30,000 in those 10 months and would have had to fork at least $4500 of that over to Airbnb if the whole stay had been managed through them. I think most landlords who do mid-term rentals through these platforms only sign a month lease with the tenants, then sign a new lease directly with the tenant for the rest of the stay, to avoid paying the big fees. One last point on these platforms – because they are so expensive, some short-term landlords with a strong reputation, repeat clientele, and great properties will set up their own direct booking website and use things like email lists, online advertising, and search engine optimization to drive traffic to their site, keeping much more of the money they collect.

Your Personal Network

One of the rules of thumb of real estate is 'Always talk about real estate'. You never know who you might run into and what type of outcome it might bring you. We own a triplex now because I was talking about real estate with someone at a networking event. You can make great connections, learn a few things, perhaps locate a few off-market properties, and maybe find a renter. You just never know when someone in your network can create a connection between you and a renter. This is similar to using your Facebook connections to make known that you're looking for a tenant – you're just doing this offline.

Signs in the Front Yard

I know this is old school, but people still put 'For Rent' signs in the front yards of their rentals.Honestly, I don't know how much traction people get with this, but the fact that they're still doing it says that people may get some hits from it. There are only two things I'll say about this method: 1) I would think this works better if your property is on a main thoroughfare. If not, you probably won't see much action from the sign. 2) This method would seem to put you in direct contact with someone without having any chance to vet them first. If you get a lead on Facebook, you can look at their profile before any further contact. If you get a lead on Zillow, you might have their application, background check, and credit history before you have any meaningful contact. Here, you're jumping right in, typically with a phone call before you have any information. This is the old school way of doing it. It's very possible you have a phone call to screen their interest, and if it looks like a good fit, get their email, and send them a link to the application.

Property Managers

Maybe you don't want to mess with finding tenants. If not, then using property managers to find them is a viable option. You pass along your tenant criteria, and they'll try to match that to an applicant. They'll cover the lease signature, collecting rent and security deposit, etc. It's relatively hands-off for you. However, there are some significant reasons why we don't go this route. The first is the cost. Property managers often charge you one month's rent to find a tenant. Cash flow is too important to our strategy to give this up. Second, it's never taken us longer than a week to get a long-term tenant into a property. We've heard stories of property managers taking more than a month to find someone for a landlord. They're just not as urgent as you to find someone for your unit. Lastly, we like to pick our people. Not only do we think we can do a better job of it than property managers, but we don't like to be the anonymous landlords who want nothing to do with their tenants. I doubt that we'll ever go this route.

19

Property Management

Now we come to the last, and certainly not least, chapter. If you've followed the progress of the book, you've gone from the absolute basics of preparing yourself to get into real estate investing, like figuring out if it's for you and determining if your finances are in the right place, to more advanced topics, like developing your strategy and figuring out how to find tenants. This last chapter, then, is the culmination of the content, in that we'll be discussing some tips on how you can actually manage the property once you own it and have people in it. In many ways, this is the real work of being a landlord, and it can make or break your enjoyment of investing and how successful you'll become, not to mention the community reputation you're developing as a landlord.

Speaking of reputation, one that you don't want is that of a slum lord. I've mentioned some stories above that applicants have told us about how bad previous landlords have been. We knew going into investing that this was not our ethic and never would be.We want to be high-end landlords, not by purchasing luxury houses, but by taking care of our properties and treating our tenants well. Part of this decision was understanding the difference between being cheap and frugal. I've always been frugal, a trait I picked up from my parents. However, when I was a broke graduate student, I was also cheap. We had a very limited budget and needed to stay within it. I was pretty strict with it (which created some tension early in the marriage), but we needed to be as careful as possible. However, once you get into the 'cheap' mindset, it can be a challenge to get out of it. Fortunately, while money is important to me, I've always been clear on the role money plays in my life. First, it's not an end in and of itself – it's a tool. Second, that tool is not more important than people. That mindset helped me get back into being frugal without being cheap.

This was a very important transition for me to make. When we put carpet into a rental, for example, we could buy builder-grade carpet with the cheap padding. But we don't. We know we want to be frugal, but we also want to be high-end landlords. So, we buy mid-grade carpet (ideally on sale) with high-end padding. Sure, we spend a bit more than if we were being cheap, but the carpet lasts longer, and our tenants have a better experience. The problem with being cheap is that money is viewed as more valuable than the more important things, which ends up undermining your success. I've heard of landlords not fixing real issues in their property, because they're cheap. I know this isn't news for most of you, but letting house-related problems sit only makes them worse. Once this happens, it either costs more for you to fix it than it would have initially or it begins to pull down the value of your investment and/or the amount you can charge for rent. Being cheap always extracts a cost, and it's often a big one.

This brings me to a related point. I also needed to learn the difference between price and cost. When being cheap, I save on the price, but I'm often paying a higher cost. Here's what I mean. Let's say I buy cheap, builder-grade carpet that costs me $3000. It shows wear and dirt very quickly, and I end up needing to replace it every three years. I also bought the cheap carpet padding for $750, and it quickly starts to degrade because of liquid spills on the carpet, etc. So, every three years I 'm spending $3750 to replace the cheap product, not counting the $500 in labor to put the carpet down, which puts me at $4250. If I were to buy mid-grade carpet with high-end padding (which is often waterproof), I may be paying $4500 initially for carpet, plus $1500 for padding, plus $500 for installation. That's $6500. This carpet will wear better, clean up better, and the padding often lasts longer than the carpet. That means I might replace the carpet every seven years and replace the padding every other carpet replacement. After six years of owning this rental, I will have paid $8500 for the cheap carpet and its replacement and $6500 for the nicer stuff. What Rachel and I have decided to do is actually not carpet most of our rentals, except stairs for safety reasons. We use LVP (luxury vinyl planking), because it lasts a long time.It's more expensive up front (both in materials and labor), but it lasts a lot longer and looks much nicer. Higher price but less cost over time.

As another example, you can buy the lowest end hot water heater for $750 and have it last for 5 years or buy a higher-end one for $1500 and have it last for 15. In the cheap scenario you'll end up spending $2250 over that 15-year span (not counting installation costs), rather than $1500 for the nicer water heater. And the nicer water heater is less likely to rust out the bottom and dump water all into your basement, which will cost you even more money. The price is how much you actually pay for the item or service, while the cost is how much that decision is going to cost you in the long run. That's why we use licensed professionals to manage our plumbing and electric work. We don't want to pay someone to come undo and then redo what someone messed up who didn't really know what they were doing. Learning the difference between cheap and frugal and price and cost is a major component of you being a good property manager and successful investor.

Next, let's talk about systems. If you're going to manage your property effectively, you'll need good systems. However, you won't need them all up front. If you listen to some real estate podcasts, you'll hear guests come on the shows who are real estate systems gurus. They have apps that automate this. They have systems and procedures that automate that. They have QR codes to automate tenant experiences. They have virtual assistants that take care of the tasks they don't like doing. It can all be overwhelming and make you feel like you're failing if your business isn't running as slickly as these investors run theirs. Quite frankly, you do need good systems to succeed, but you don't need them right from the start. For example, you could literally drive around to your tenants picking up rent checks each month. That's perfectly fine, but it doesn't scale well. The more properties you get, the more time you're spending driving around. Plus, you'll be doing a lot of texting back and forth to ensure they'll be home, so you're not wasting your time driving to the property. It's not a big deal if you own one unit. It becomes a big time drain if you own 20. Just a quick reminder here – the farther away your properties are, the more important it is that you have good systems and processes in place. Since you're geographically removed from the property, you'll need to have a tighter ship with these, because you can't drive around collecting rent in Arizona if you live in Florida.

So, let's look at a quick example of how property management can start off pretty basic and grow as your business grows. Let's say you buy your first property, and you want to maximize cash flow. This means you're probably doing a lot of things yourself, rather than turning it over to a property manager or hiring contractors to do the work. So, a tenant calls you with a leaky toilet, and you go over and fix it. The tenant may be communicating with you via email, text, or phone call at any given time. You're figuring out ways to collect rent, perhaps by check or something like Venmo, and when they're late, you're communicating with them. You're trying to remember to record your vehicle mileage related to your investment, and you're either writing out your income and expenses by hand or using a spreadsheet to track them. You meet with tenants individually to go over the leases and have them hand-sign with you. That's the way a lot of us start out.

Let's fast forward to you having 10 units. You might still meet with tenants to sign leases, communicate over email or text, and use a spreadsheet to track expenses, but by this time, you're beginning to realize that doing 10 units like you did one is a tall order. Maybe you've adjusted some of how you operate to accommodate this. Perhaps you've found an online platform that sends automatic rent reminders to your tenants, so you have fewer late payments and a big reduction in the number of reminders you have to send yourself. You might have downloaded an app that tracks your drives, so you can stop tracking this yourself. You might have a strict Venmo or Zelle policy for rent collection, so you don't have to worry about picking up checks or being around for the tenant to drop them off, let alone worry about them bouncing. Perhaps you have good relationships with some contractors, so you don't have to spend so much of your time working 'in' the business.

Now, we'll look at a scenario where you own 25 units. You may have hired a virtual assistant (or more than one) to manage communication with the tenants and coordinate with contractors to fix issues. You may have the virtual assistant be the one who connects the utilities when you buy a new property. You may be operating through an online property management platform that allows you to send electronic leases and get electronic signatures. If you've got some mid-term or short-term rentals, you might have QR codes around the house that the tenants can scan to help them problem-solve or know important information. Your online platform may even be where rent is paid, so you're not even worried about Venmo anymore. Your virtual assistant is entering receipts that you've scanned (as well as revenue) into QuickBooks, so much of your financial data is entered either automatically or by someone other than you. This platform can also prepare reports for you and make tax preparation much easier – and you're probably using an accountant now, so you don't need to do the taxes yourself.

See how your processes mature and morph over time to match the maturity of your business? It wouldn't make much sense to hire a virtual assistant, pay for the online property management platform, use QuickBooks, etc. all with your first property. That would be a bit overkill and probably be too expensive. The idea here is to just get the tasks done, then as you grow, figure out which tasks bother you the most. The pain points are the ones where you want to intervene first. If you're using a spreadsheet to track your finances, you know that it needs to get done, you're nine months behind, and it just seems so overwhelming, then you need to do it differently. Hire someone to do your books for you or find some way to leverage QuickBooks to make it less painful. Then, once you've reduced that pain point, move on to the next one. As long as you're doing things correctly, do it however you want until you dread it, then systematize it. And remember, the bigger your business, the more important your systems become, because you are one person and can't be involved in everything as you grow. And don't ever start from scratch with your systems. Go on ChatGPT or another AI platform and ask it how to do certain tasks as an investor. Do online searches for what systems other people use. There might be some websites that have their systems readily available for free or at a nominal price. It's worth it not to have to recreate every wheel yourself.

Take a moment and think through what I just said. If the journey to becoming less involved in every task of your real estate business as you grow rubs you the wrong way, you have some soul searching to do. If your goal as a real estate investor is to stay hands-on, frugal, and over-involved as a property manager, stay small. It will just generate too much stress, and you'll enjoy it less as you go along if you're doing this and growing. It's just too hard. However, if your goal is to essentially be the CEO of your growing business, you are free to scale as much as you can. In this case, go big with your systems and processes. Invest in them as you grow and make them robust, so that you can spend more time working 'on' your business than you do working 'in' your business. Figure out what type of property manager you want to be. As I've said before, I got into real estate to run a business, not to be a property manager, so we definitely want to create systems that will take the property management load off us over time.

That being said, there are essentially three approaches to property management. They are the DIYer, the Coordinator, and the Hands-off approaches.Let's look at each of them briefly.

DIYer

This pathway is often taken by new investors who need to keep costs low to generate cash flow. It's also used by people who are handy and know exactly (or mostly) what they're doing when it comes to fixing things. If you're a DIYer for the first reason, you'll probably grow into a Coordinator eventually. If you're handy, you might resist growing into a Coordinator.Perhaps you take a lot of pride in doing the work yourself. Maybe you don't trust that other people would do it as well as you. It's perfectly fine to stay a DIYer, but remember my caution above – don't expect to grow much if this is your lane. But if you're investing because you're 60 and finally have enough money to pull it off and want to cap yourself at two units to supplement your retirement income, then have at it and DIY to your heart's content.

Coordinator

This is where we are currently. While we still are being relatively hands-on, we (and especially Rachel) are acting more like project managers than the contractors. When an issue arises, the tenants contact us, and we coordinate with the tenants and contractors to get the work done. We'll be on-site and do some work alongside the contractors, but we don't bear the weight of doing the lion's share anymore. While this is less work than the DIYer, we are still heavily involved in day-to-day property management. The nice part of being on this pathway is that we still have clear lines of sight with what's going on, which allows for good decision-making.It also limits our time-based involvement. There are weeks where we spend less than two hours total managing our properties. There are also weeks where we're more involved, but being coordinators, we put a cap on how much time we're spending. For example, we're doing some renovations on our new property that we're turning into a mid-term rental. We've had contractors in the property for the better part of the last month. Rachel probably spent about 10-12 hours over there one week, and I spent around 5-6, in between work travel and my work-from-home schedule. If we were doing it all ourselves, we could easily have spent 50-60 hours that week at the house between the two of us. The downside of being a Coordinator is that it is more expensive, because we're paying other people to do the work. In our situation, it's worth it, because we aren't experts at renovation, and it's not the best use of our time. Even if we don't grow beyond our current 10 units, I'd like to eventually move more toward the Hands-off approach. I don't want to be a property manager forever.

Hands-off

This is the dream of many landlords, where your operations run smoothly without your frequent, direct involvement, and you can spend more time pursuing your interests that your real estate is supporting financially. It's important to understand, however, that if you jump to this too quickly, you may be operating inefficiently, and your lack of involvement may mean that decisions are being made that ultimately aren't good for the business. If you're going to eventually pursue this, it's important either to be doing it by having great systems and processes or by handing this off to property managers.

Two things quickly if you're goal is to be a hands-off landlord. The first is that you have to communicate effectively. My dad once told me that effective communication is 'the meeting of meanings'. This means that knowing what you *intended* to communicate or knowing what you *meant* by what you said isn't good enough. It's vital that the other side knows what you intend to communicate – at the same level that you intended to communicate. You don't need to worry about this as much if you're a DIYer, as others aren't very involved. However, if you're a Coordinator, you need to communicate what you want and oversee the project, without doing it yourself. If you're hands-off, it requires even more clarity of communication, because you might not even be doing the overseeing – just the communicating.

Let me share an example of what I mean: Let's say that you hire a virtual assistant to call the utility companies every time you buy a property. You obviously can't just tell them to hook up the utilities and leave it at that. They probably have no idea how to do it. So, you have to communicate the task to them at a deeper level. Currently, I call the utility companies myself, and I have a step-by-step process for each utility, so I know how to do it without wondering how I did it last time and needing to reinvent the wheel. However, this process wouldn't be good enough if I handed it off to a virtual assistant, because some of the steps assume certain knowledge in the user. I have that knowledge, because I've done it for every property. I would need to see the task through new eyes and create a process that doesn't leave anything out. What I mean is this – I might have on my process, "Click on the New Account tab, and enter the data that it asks for." In my process for a VA, I would need to spell out where the user can find the New Account tab, so they're not missing it. My point is ultimately this – hands-off landlords need to be expert communicators, so that whoever is doing whatever task has clarity on what they're supposed to be doing. Anything less means they're pestering you with calls and texts to get clarity (which makes you more like a Coordinator) or you'll find out later that something was done incorrectly.

The second thing you'll need to be good at is contracting effectively. When you're a hands-off landlord, you'll be contracting with your virtual assistant, you'll be contracting with your contractors, you'll be contracting with your property management company, etc. If you want people to carry out your wishes who are executing part of your business without you being directly involved, then the contract must be clear, both on the scope of work and the compensation for that work. Looking at a virtual assistant example again, let's say that you contract with them for 10 hours per week.Maybe it's been a busy week for them, and they hit 10 hours on Thursday and don't check emails again until Sunday. Because of that, they miss an emergency email from a tenant on Friday, and nothing gets done until Monday, because they can't get a contractor out on Sunday. Should you be upset about this? These kinds of issues are a result of problematic contracting. Maybe your virtual assistant is in your time zone and works from 9-5 (although not all of those hours are dedicated to you). Perhaps a rental springs a leak at 10pm, and the tenant sends an email that isn't seen until 9am the next day. Should you be mad at the assistant for not checking their email before going to bed? This is a result of problematic contracting.

Expectations need to be spelled out and contingencies planned for. If your virtual assistant stops work at 5pm, you need to figure out what to do in the evening hours and overnight. If you're a hands-off landlord, you won't want to be taking these duties on yourself. Many hands-off landlords will hire a virtual assistant in the Philippines or somewhere like that, so that they are 'on duty' during your off hours. Effective contracting is about making sure the person you're paying is doing what you want them to do, not simply because you've told them you want it done, but because it's in the contract, and it's a shared expectation. Life is so much easier if you get good at contracting.

One more thing on property management before discussing the pros and cons of turning things over to property management companies. Whether you're a DIYer, Coordinator, or Hands-off landlord, don't forget about landscaping. We often think about landlording as being about fixing leaks, unclogging toilets, and cleaning up between tenants. We tend to think of the things inside the house that need to be taken care of.

Landscaping is extremely important to keeping your property attractive and retaining value. While long-term tenants are often responsible for lawn care maintenance, they're often not regularly weeding flowerbeds, trimming hedges, or replacing dead plants. The need to pay attention to this goes up if you find yourself with a property in an HOA. The last thing you want is to get notifications and fines from them because your tenant isn't keeping up with the yard work. For those of you who are thinking about mid- and short-term rentals, it's not typical to expect tenants to do this type of work. While I spoke at some length about the reasons why I might avoid condos, they are attractive for hands-off landlords, because much of the maintenance and landscaping is part of what you're paying for in the HOA fees. So, don't forget about the outside of the house, no matter which property management approach you take.

I have one last topic to cover here and of special interest to those who would like to eventually be hands-off landlords and perhaps aren't super excited about developing and managing their own processes. Historically, the goal of many landlords was to hand off operations to a property management company. This is what they've been building for. They've toiled for years managing their properties on their own and can't wait to relax and enjoy the fruits of their labor. The answer for many is obvious – they just need to do a little research and find a property management company that meets their needs. Doesn't sound too hard, right? Not so fast. There's a reason why many of today's more sophisticated landlords are relying on systems and processes and not third-party property managers. We all know the advertised benefits of these organizations (they take most of the work from you – which is a BIG benefit), so let's spend some time instead looking at why many are moving away from them now.

They're expensive

This is a major reason why I would have a hard time imagining ever using one. They often charge 10% of your monthly rent to manage the property, and a month's rent to find a tenant. Currently, we gross about $15,000 monthly from our properties, and I'd have a hard time handing over $1500 each month. What makes this feel even more expensive is that in an average month, we don't hear from most of our renters to address any issues. And if we do hear from them, maybe the toilet is running, we call our plumber, and it's fixed. Do we want to pay the property management company $150 over the course of that month (10% of the rent) to simply call our plumber? Plus, there's no part of me that wants to give up a month's rent to find a tenant. First, that's really expensive. Second, I'm not convinced they can do it any more effectively than I can.

They don't care as much as you do

This is another big one for us. As I've said before, we view ourselves as high-end landlords, where we work hard to make living in one of our properties a great experience for our tenants. Property management companies are a business, and they are in business to make money. Sometimes they make money by providing a sub-optimal experience for tenants.They may not respond as quickly to issues as you would. They may not communicate as effectively as you would. While you might contact a tenant if they are late for a payment, property managers might just wait two days and slap a 3-day notice on the door (which means the tenants have 3 days to pay up or leave). I've seen situations where tenants in someone else's property run into a situation and don't know who to contact. If they do have contact information, they may call or email and not get a response (or at least not consistently). This leads to massive amounts of frustration. With our tenants, they reach out to us, and we fix the issue, often in less than 24 hours. With the property management arrangement, we've seen issues linger for weeks without resolution. If property managers are an extension of your ethic and values as a landlord, they may reflect poorly on you.

They won't necessarily make the same decisions as you

You might inspect your own property after a tenant moves out and decide to replace the carpet and fix the two burners on the stove top that don't work. A property management company might decide to just do a half-hearted carpet cleaning and do nothing with the burners, because two of them still work. Many times, they'll make decisions on fixes that are less than a certain dollar amount, without needing to get your approval ahead of time. Maybe they just decide to ignore those little fixes. Maybe they'll do too many, and that cost gets passed along to you, cutting into your cash flow. Maybe their cleaning thoroughness is different than yours between tenants, and now you're not quality controlling it anymore, because you're not actively managing it. Over time, you might notice a decline in the appearance of your property because of these decisions that are all minor in the moment but cumulative over time.

They don't always communicate with you about their decisions

Sometimes property management companies will post a 3-day notice of eviction, and you don't know about it. Sometimes your tenant will be 6 weeks late paying rent and eviction proceedings are initiated, and you had no idea that anything was off with your tenant. Remember that property management companies get paid if you have a tenant in place. If there aren't good candidates, they might drop some selection standards without notifying you, and the next thing you know, you've got problematic tenants in place (although you often still have the final say in the selection). In other words, you're at risk of being surprised with something you hadn't expected, or the property may be managed in a way that you don't approve of but don't know about.

You can't control the add-on fees for tenants or their additional rules

I've seen situations where the property management companies charge double or triple the fees to applicants to apply through them. I've seen situations where they only take payment on their platform, which comes with a $25 fee each time payment is made on that platform. I've seen them charge $250 just to add them to the mandatory platform. Sometimes they charge an additional administrative fee to the tenant each time a lease is signed. So, they're not just making money off you, they may also be targeting tenants in a way that I think is predatory. They can also look for reasons or loopholes not to do the things they should be doing. These rules are outside of the lease and can impact the experience of the tenants in ways that you may never know about.

They can take a long time to get things done

If you want efficiency, property management companies aren't the way to go. Rachel has done some work finding tenants for other landlords, because she's pretty good at it. We've seen situations where it was consistently taking the property management company a month to find new tenants. Rachel then gets asked to find a tenant. She advertises it, holds an open house, and hands over several good leads to the landlord. Within a week and a half they've got a tenant. Also, if you remember from the chapter above about de-risking your investments, knowing about an issue and not doing something about it in a timely manner opens you up to liability. While it's true that property management companies open themselves up to liability by taking a while to fix an issue, the liability doesn't stop with them.Because they're acting on your behalf, and you chose them, they become an extension of your business. So, if they're being sued for an issue, be sure that you're going to be sued as well. Even if they're slow on things that won't cause a liability issue, they can be causing unnecessary inconveniences for your tenants or causing property issues for you by not addressing problems quickly. For example, the leak under the sink that they didn't address in a timely manner may begin to cause damage to the bottom of the cabinet that didn't need to happen.

They're quality controlling the work, not you

We have high-quality contractors who we trust. Remember, however, that property management companies are a business and sometimes they may be making money by using low-end contractors. Remember the discussion above about the difference between price and cost? They may be using people with a low price, who may be working in a way that increases your overall cost. Remember the wet dog smell after carpet cleaning? This is a classic example of them doing the task without following up to make sure the outcome was right. As I mentioned above, perhaps their cleaners don't have the same standards you do between tenants, and the property is getting turned over to new tenants in a way that you wouldn't approve of if you knew about it.

They may not be doing what you've asked them to do

It would be extremely frustrating if I was using a property management company and I found out they weren't doing things like I asked them to. Unfortunately, this is one of the most common complaints of landlords. For example, you might have told them to contact you before returning a departing tenant's security deposit. Next thing you know, the entire deposit has been returned, and there are issues the deposit was supposed to cover. Maybe you tell them to let you know when people are paying late, so you can be involved in determining when to start eviction proceedings, but they start without your approval. You may tell them to increase rent every other year, but they keep renewing the lease at the same rate. There's plenty of opportunity for them to 'forget' what you've asked them to do, drop the ball communicating within the property management company, or simply just passively, or accidentally, ignore what they're supposed to be doing.

I'm sure there are more issues you could run into with property management companies, but this will serve as an adequate sample. Do your own research. Talk to landlords you meet and ask them about their experiences with these companies. To be sure, this doesn't mean that they're all bad. It just means that they're not likely to be as good as you. Many times, landlords are willing to go with a company that's a little less diligent than they are for the benefit of not having to actively manage their properties. But you often don't find out until it's too late that the property management company is way off from your standards. So, if you choose to go this route, get references and rely on the reports of people you know from their own experiences. And don't just go with the first one. Do your research. See what their online reputation is. If you see a property management sign outside of a building, talk to some of the residents and see what their experience has been with that company.

So, what is a landlord to do who wants to be hands-off but doesn't trust a property management company? One option that tends to be for the more advanced landlord (meaning it's not likely this will be your entry point), is that you directly hire your own property manager. This wouldn't be some company that ends up not representing you well. This would be an employee of yours who you trust and choose yourself. Again, this is an advanced move, so you're probably not starting here.However, you can start with someone part-time, so the cost isn't as significant. If you want to be a hands-off landlord, we've now covered the three most common options: 1) create advanced systems and processes to automate as much as you can and hire someone like a virtual assistant to manage as much as they can, 2) hire a property management company to run things for you, and 3) hire your own property manager.

Property management is something that is part of the job description for any landlord. The good news is that it doesn't have to be complicated at first, and your approach can change over time. Your skills and systems can grow with your portfolio. Just make sure you're covering your bases and don't put too much pressure on yourself to have everything figured out from the beginning.

20

Conclusion

If I did my job, then you've been exposed to a lot of information in this book. Maybe you feel like the amount of information is a bit overwhelming. Don't worry – it doesn't have to be. The chapters are somewhat independent, so you can review the chapters that have the most to do with your part of the journey and come back to the other ones later. I also understand that part of what's driving the amount of information is my promise to you in the introduction that this wasn't going to be a book of generalities. It's true that a book could be written on each chapter that I've included here, so I've tried to find the right amount of detail without getting too bogged down. Time will tell if I got that balance right. However, what I hope does show through is my passion for real estate. It's a dream that has been a long time coming.It might be a long time coming for you, and I hope you're feeling in some way inspired that you can get there too.

After reading this book, you may realize that you're still a ways off from getting started. If that's you, I hope you have an idea what you need to work on to move yourself toward your dream. Maybe you realized that you're closer than you think. Use this book to focus your efforts on taking that first step. Perhaps you've already started and feel a bit stuck. Find a suggestion or two that could help you move forward into your next step. That's my ultimate goal here – that you'll find a few things from this book that will help you become directional.

Let me take a moment and talk about directionality. Being directional means that, no matter where you are on your journey, you're doing something that moves you in a direction that's consistent with your goals. When I was reading books and interviewing people who were investors, I was being directional. When I met with a Realtor in Prescott, I was being directional. When I began to sketch out some potential chapters for this book, I was being directional. Even if you don't currently have the levers in your hand that you need to pull to become an investor, you can be doing things that are eventually preparing you to pull those levers. So, don't be discouraged – be directional. Find something, even if it's small and seemingly insignificant, and move on it. As a friend of mine says, "Shavings make a pile." If you've never heard that saying before, a small shaving doesn't make much of a difference, but a lot of them add up. If you take a lot of small steps, then you'll find that you've made good progress.

There's one topic I'd like to address here quickly. Some of you may have read the book and thought something like, "Yeah, all this is great, but the prices you're talking about aren't even close to what I'm dealing with where I live." I recognize that this may be true. For me to write the most authentic book, I had to write from the lens of my experience.With that said, it doesn't change most of the tactics written about in this book. You de-risk high priced properties in much the same way as you do lower priced properties. The same advice applies for screening tenants. You find your team in many of the same ways no matter where you live. So, don't dismiss the book because the economics of buying is different where you are compared to me. What changes is your strategy. For example, you may not use a HELOC to get started with investing and leverage your properties at 100%. However, you may use partners more than I did. You may do more driving for doors and poring over tax delinquency lists to find cheaper, off-market properties. You may decide to work a second job to save more money for a down payment. You might start off with arbitrage or house-hacking. You might decide that long-distance investing is your ticket in, because it's just too expensive nearby. Please hear what I'm saying on this – the economics of your area doesn't invalidate anything about this book; it just requires different strategies for different areas.

I'll be the first to admit that this book doesn't have all the answers – no book does. But I hope that it provides some inspiration and gets the gears turning. Perhaps you had some ideas as you read through the different chapters. Maybe it got you thinking about how you would run a certain part of your business and helped you get some clarity. If any of that happened, then I consider this book a success. But reading the best advice in the world isn't going to get you anywhere.Progress (and ultimately success) is a result of doing. The end result may feel far off, but figure out what the smallest step is that will move you forward and take that step. Here are a few ideas for what that small step might be:

- Begin to talk about your interest in real estate investment as often as you can. You might be surprised what doors open if you do.

- Take the smallest debt you have and get laser-focused on paying it off. It will be energizing to have that in your past and to free up personal cash flow that you can use to pay down more debt or increase your savings.

- Join an online real estate forum and learn from the people in that group. It's a great place to ask questions and learn from people who are in different locations than you.

- Talk to your network and get some recommendations for a good investor-friendly Realtor. These people are great resources for information and learning about the local market. You may be reluctant to reach out to a Realtor if you're not ready to pull the trigger and buy, but that would be a mistake. They're often willing to have conversations with you, because getting to know you now could lead to business down the road. In addition, they will likely have a lot of connections with investors and perhaps be willing to connect you with one to learn from them.

- Have regular conversations with your significant other, if you have one. These shouldn't be pressure-based conversations to get them on board. These should be exploratory, 'let's dream together' sort of conversations. It allows you to think out loud about how real estate could shape your future into something that both of you would look forward to.

- Go back and reread some chapters and begin to sketch out what your processes might look like if you had a property. This will make the work a bit easier when you get your first one.

- Take another look at chapters 4 and 5 and think through the different ways to invest in real estate. Do some research on each one and see which of them appeal to you. Depending on what you find, you may be able to invest in real estate sooner than you think, if you decide to purchase debt notes, for example.

- If you're at all considering long-distance investing, go to a website like Realtor.com or zillow.com and begin to research the area. See what properties are going for. Take notes on where the good schools are. Take a look to see how expensive property taxes are. Go to a website like areavibes.com and see what crime and jobs look like in the area. If you're anything like me, this type of research can be a lot of fun.

- Set small goals for yourself. Set a goal for debt paydown. Set a savings goal. Set a networking goal, like attending two real estate networking events per month.You're much more likely to succeed if you've set a goal than if you leave something as just a desire.

- Begin to underwrite properties on websites like zillow.com and realtor.com. Get practiced at figuring out what's a good deal and what isn't, what will cash flow and what won't. If you get good at this, once you're ready to buy, you can move with confidence.

- This is a fun one – visit open houses. This will not only help you figure out where the nicer areas of town are (if you don't know already), but it will also help you see what's on the market and what it's going for. Keep in mind that what it's being listed for isn't necessarily the same as the final sale price. This is also a great way to network with Realtors.

These suggestions should give you some things to think about regarding moving forward. It's nice to have some actions you can take, but remember to be patient. It can take a while to lay down a strong financial foundation and have enough knowledge to make your first investment a responsible step.

One last comment – remember that no one becomes successful alone. One of the best moves you can make is to find a good mentor or coach. A mentor is someone who will, in a relatively unstructured way, take you under their wing and help you out a bit over time, perhaps by giving some sound advice here or helping you make a connection there. These can be very valuable people. However, they often aren't taking much personal responsibility for your success. That's one of the things that differentiates a mentor from a coach. A coach provides a much more structured relationship that focuses on goals and progress, with the stated purpose of bringing you closer to your version of success. Good coaches can be hard to find, and they can be very expensive. That's because many real estate coaches make their business around working with people who have already started and are looking to make a big leap forward. The assumption is that you're already having some success and are willing to make a significant financial investment to get yourself to the next level.

I've been a coach for a long time. I was a therapist for years, which is essentially a highly educated, highly credentialed coach in the mental health arena. I've been an organizational consultant for years, and I've coached CEOs and executives all over the country from organizations of all sizes. I've enjoyed my real estate investment journey so far and have learned so much over the past few years that I'm excited to begin coaching people who are looking to start their journey. If this book has sparked your interest and generated as many questions as it's answered, then you may be a good candidate for coaching. This book can't answer all your questions or deal with the nitty-gritty details of your particular situation, but a coach can be extremely helpful with just that. If you'd like to chat about real estate or learn if coaching is a good next step for you, please feel free to reach out to me at Jared@TheOutsiderMethod.com. I'm looking forward to hearing from you!

About the Author

Jared Detter is an author, organizational consultant, and active real estate investor with a portfolio of single-family and multi-family homes with both long-term and mid-term renters, as well as flipping several houses. He is a former military psychologist, police psychologist, and has been trained as a hostage negotiator with the San Antonio Police Department. He currently lives in Canton, OH with his wife, Rachel, and three sons.

Also by Jared Detter

The Other Side of the Door

It's the beginning of summer, and Luke Detter can't wait to spend those carefree days with his friends. However, he suddenly finds that his family will be soon moving to the UK, as a result of his father's new job.

Meanwhile, he is plagued by a recurring dream about a mysterious house with rooms that seem to be from different places and times. Once he gets settled in his new home across the ocean, he meets a mysterious stranger who points him in the direction of an abandoned building nearby that happens to look just like the house from his dreams.

His adventures start when he begins to sneak out at night and explore the building, each room taking him to a different time in history and bringing him in contact with danger and adventure beyond his wildest imagination.

Dreams and Curses

After meeting and falling in love, Justus and Anna have gotten married and moved into their new home. The first night in their new residence, Justus explores the unique library inside the home that is filled with old and rare books, where he finds and begins to read a mysterious book with a dragon emblazoned on the cover.

Much to his amazement, Justus finds himself on a horse with a knight charging at him. He is quickly knocked off his horse, forced to yield, and taken to the stronghold of a local noble. He is thrown together with a knight named Logan, who befriends him and teaches him the skills of a medieval warrior.

Each night that Justus reads in this book, he is transported in his waking dreams to this medieval landscape that sweeps him up in the drama of battles, political intrigue, and betrayal. He is forced to fight for his life and for a king he has never met, making alliances and becoming a leader, finding himself outnumbered and facing the biggest threat the land has ever seen.

Back in his everyday life, Anna falls ill and inexplicably worsens quickly, until she lingers on the brink of death. Justus discovers the corpse of an ancient woman in a nearby cave and must discover how the woman, the book, and his waking dreams are all related, and it's a race against time to uncover the connection between them and his wife's mysterious illness.